Trumpet

FOR

DUMMIES®

Trumpet
FOR
DUMMIES®

by Jeffrey Reynolds

John Wiley & Sons Canada, Ltd.

Trumpet For Dummies®

Published by
John Wiley & Sons Canada, Ltd.
6045 Freemont Blvd.
Mississauga, ON L5R 4J3
www.wiley.com

Copyright © 2011 by John Wiley & Sons Canada, Ltd.

Published by John Wiley & Sons Canada, Ltd.

For general information on John Wiley & Sons Canada, Ltd., including all books published by Wiley Publishing,
Inc., please call our distribution centre at 1-800-567-4797. For reseller information, including discounts and
premium sales, please call our sales department at 416-646-7992. For press review copies, author interviews, or
other publicity information, please contact our publicity department, Tel. 416-646-4582, Fax 416-236-4448.

For technical support, please visit www.wiley.com/techsupport.

Wiley also publishes its books in a variety of electronic formats. Some content that appears in print may
not be available in electronic books.

Library and Archives Canada Cataloguing in Publication Data
Reynolds, Jeff, 1946-
 Trumpet for dummies / Jeffrey Reynolds.
(–For dummies)
To be accompanied by compact disc of audio samples. Includes index.
Issued also in electronic formats.
ISBN 978-0-470-67937-1
 1. Trumpet–Methods–Self-instruction. 2. Music theory–Elementary works. I. Title. II. Series: –For dummies
MT448.R463 2011   788.9'2193   C2010-907507-2

ISBNs: 978-0-470-96348-7 (ePDF), 978-0-470-96350-0 (eMobi), 978-0-470-96349-4 (ePub)

Printed in the United States

1 2 3 4 5 RRD 15 14 13 12 11

WILEY

About the Author

Jeff Reynolds has been a trumpeter for almost 50 years, since the first day of band class, when the trumpet seemed to be a magical gift, possessed of supernatural powers. Since then, he has performed all manner of engagements, from funerals to weddings, from jazz gigs and dances to orchestra concerts. He has toured North America with ballet companies, played fanfares for Shakespeare plays, played onstage in tights for a pantomime and in tails for the great symphonies of Beethoven and Mahler, and entertained the folks at country-and-western bars. He once popped out of a (fake) cake to play "Happy Birthday" for the president of a corporation. In spite of, or because of, all these various engagements, he retains a great pleasure in playing the trumpet and has an insight into the whole spectrum of music making available to the modern trumpeter.

As long as he has performed, Jeff has taught, from the Grade 8 beginners he started with (when Jeff was a whole grade more advanced) to doctoral students at the University of Toronto, where he has taught for 30 years. Explaining, analyzing, encouraging, and cajoling hundreds of students over the years has given him another kind of insight: the understanding of how to communicate trumpet playing to others. Teaching has always been as important to Jeff as playing, always as challenging and rewarding. Many of his former students are professional players and teachers.

Dedication

This book is dedicated to all my students who have taught me so much of what I know, and how to teach it, and to all my teachers, for all the rest. In particular, the late Vincent Cichowicz was a model of humanity, musicality, and communication whose influence is always with me.

Author's Acknowledgments

Special thanks to: Katharine Rapoport, for recommending me as a potential author for *Trumpet For Dummies;* Robert Hickey, who helped me shape the book and gave me the chance to write it; Elizabeth Kuball, my editor, whose firm and patient shepherding of me toward the completion of the project were invaluable; Gillian MacKay, who in addition to acting as the book's technical editor, gave generous assistance in the form of suggestions, advice, and much appreciated encouragement; Geoffrey Tiller, Jamie Reynolds, Ryan Cameron, Gillian MacKay, and Robert Hickey, who were great partners in the recording session; Gary Honess, our brilliant sound engineer; Robert Hickey, Lisa Hartl, and Nathan Saliwonchyk, who facilitated a smooth photo shoot; and my family, for their support and encouragement throughout the project.

Publisher's Acknowledgments

We're proud of this book; please send us your comments at http://dummies.custhelp.com. For other comments, please contact our Customer Care Department within the U.S. at 877-762-2974, outside the U.S. at 317-572-3993 or fax 317-572-4002.

Some of the people who helped bring this book to market include the following:

Acquisitions, Editorial, and Media Development

Project Editor: Elizabeth Kuball

Acquiring Editor: Robert Hickey

Copy Editor: Elizabeth Kuball

Technical Editor: Gillian MacKay

Production Editor: Pamela Vokey

Editorial Assistant: Katie Wolsley

Cover Photo: iStock #4347825 © Claudia Dewald

Cartoons: Rich Tennant (www.the5thwave.com)

Composition Services

Project Coordinator: Kristie Rees

Layout and Graphics: Laura Westhuis

Interior Photos: Nathan Saliwonchyk

Proofreader: Lisa Young Stiers

Indexer: Claudia Bourbeau

John Wiley & Sons Canada, Ltd.

> **Deborah Barton,** Vice President and Director of Operations
>
> **Jennifer Smith,** Publisher, Professional & Trade Division
>
> **Alison Maclean,** Managing Editor, Professional & Trade Division
>
> **Karen Bryan,** Vice-President, Publishing Services

Publishing and Editorial for Consumer Dummies

> **Diane Graves Steele,** Vice President and Publisher, Consumer Dummies
>
> **Kristin Ferguson-Wagstaffe,** Product Development Director, Consumer Dummies
>
> **Ensley Eikenburg,** Associate Publisher, Travel
>
> **Kelly Regan,** Editorial Director, Travel

Composition Services

> **Debbie Stailey,** Director of Composition Services

Contents at a Glance

Table of Contents

Introduction

· ·

*A*liens visiting Earth after human life has disappeared might be confused by many of the random objects lying around: tape cassettes (there's a whole generation of humans already confused by them), eyeglasses, and even trumpets. But I believe they would soon discover — assuming that they have lips and lungs or facsimiles thereof — that trumpets are for making sound, and a whole new culture of trumpet playing would eventually emerge. People — and I'm betting aliens, too — love to make sounds with their mouths and the trumpet has always been endlessly fascinating. A trumpet instantly commands attention. The legendary New Orleans trumpeter Buddy Bolden's brazen sound attracted people in throngs, as did the music of Louis Armstrong in Chicago. Trumpets have been called the "voice of God." They've led armies and crumbled mythological walls. So, of course, you want to try playing the trumpet. Why *wouldn't* you?

I was attracted to the trumpet in high school, and I found it compelling from the very first day. The combination of its clear, strong voice; its beautiful look; and the way I felt holding one in my hands was hard to resist. My first trumpet was a $35 pawn-shop special — and it was the best Christmas present I ever received. I couldn't *wait* to play it. Not only did I play my new trumpet every chance I got, but my whole family wanted to try it, too.

The thrill of simply making that initial sound has never worn off, and the skills and technique, the musical inspiration, and, for me, the professional career, became added layers of a rewarding experience. This book is an introduction to many aspects of the trumpet — from how trumpets are made and how sound is produced, to what to look for when shopping for an instrument of your own, to starting to play and developing your technique, to continuing your trumpet journey as your skills advance. I hope that you feel the same excitement about playing the trumpet that I do, and that you retain that excitement throughout your life.

About This Book

This book is a reference, which means that you don't have to read it from beginning to end. You can dive in wherever you want and find the information you need. You also don't have to memorize this book — it isn't a textbook, and there won't be a pop quiz.

I provide all kinds of examples — both on and off the accompanying CD — to guide you in your own trumpet playing. And I give you tried-and-true strategies from my years of experience both as a trumpet player and a teacher. This book has all the information you need to get started as a trumpeter and take your trumpet playing to the next level.

Conventions Used in This Book

I don't use many conventions in this book, but there are a few you should be aware of:

- ✔ When I introduce a term, I put the term in *italics* and define it shortly thereafter (often in parentheses).

- ✔ The action parts of numbered steps are in **bold,** so you easily can find what you're supposed to do.

- ✔ Web addresses are in monofont, to make them stand out from the surrounding text. *Note:* When this book was printed, some Web addresses may have needed to break across two lines of text. If that happened, rest assured that we haven't put in any extra characters (such as hyphens) to indicate the break. So, when using one of these Web addresses, just type exactly what you see in this book, pretending as though the line break doesn't exist.

- ✔ The track numbers of items on the CD appear above the paragraph where the item is mentioned or, if a corresponding piece of music appears in the book, at the top of the exercise or before the song title.

What You're Not To Read

What you read or don't read is, of course, entirely up to you, but not everything in this book is critical to your understanding of the subject. The Technical Stuff icon marks information that expands on a topic or gives technical detail that you may prefer to skip (see "Icons Used in This Book," later in this introduction for more on this icon). Sidebars (the text in gray boxes) are asides — they're interesting but not essential, so if you're short on time, you can safely skip them.

Foolish Assumptions

As I was writing this book, I made a few assumptions about you:

- ✔ **You're interested in music and attracted to the trumpet.** Even though you may not have any previous experience, you have a more-than-passing desire to learn more about music and, specifically, how the trumpet fits into the musical world.

> ✔ **You have a trumpet and you're interested in trying to play one.** If you don't own a trumpet of your own, I assume that you're willing to borrow, rent, or buy an instrument, a mouthpiece, and all the equipment, such as maintenance products and a music stand.

> ✔ **You may not read music, but you're open to the possibility of learning to do so.** You're eager for new experience, and the prospect of learning a whole new language is exciting and stimulating for you.

> ✔ **You have a place to practice.** You need somewhere to play where you won't constantly be told to stop or go away. If you don't have a place to play your trumpet, you're willing to find one (whether that's in a music studio or an abandoned coal mine).

> ✔ **You have a stereo or a computer with good speakers.** The CD that comes with this book adds a very helpful dimension to your understanding of the trumpet. Because you'll be given the opportunity to play along with the CD, it's important to have speakers that are good enough that you can hear the CD while you're playing.

> ✔ **You're serious about learning about the trumpet, but not too serious.** Throughout this book, I give you tunes to play that are fun and entertaining, and tell amusing anecdotes about trumpet playing and trumpeters. I have fun playing the trumpet, and I hope you will, too!

How This Book Is Organized

The chapters in this book are divided into five parts. Here's what each part covers.

Part 1: Ta-Da! A Prelude to Trumpet Playing

Part I is your introduction to the brass family. I fill you in on the role of the trumpet in culture and in people's imaginations. I describe the mouthpiece and its importance. I tell you how the valves work, and then I introduce you to the first steps that you take as a trumpeter. I cover the anatomy of the trumpet and the *natural overtone series,* nature's good vibrations that make trumpet playing possible.

Part I also provides information on choosing the best trumpet and mouthpiece for you, including renting versus buying, used versus new, and the type of finish. I even recommend specific models you may want to consider.

Finally, Part I introduces you to reading music. I explain the language of music and show you the way to begin using the written language to help you further your trumpet knowledge and skill.

Part II: The Noble Sound of the Trumpet

Can buzzing be beautiful? That question and many others are answered in Part II, where I escort you through the process of making a beautiful sound on the trumpet. I describe respiration for trumpet playing, offering advice on posture, exercises to increase your lung capacity, and ways to keep your breathing relaxed.

I also introduce you to mouthpiece buzzing — that weird thing that only brass players do. I fill you in on the ways in which you can sound beautiful — yes, beautiful — on the mouthpiece alone, and give you ideas for your solo repertoire for lips and brass.

Making the best sound possible on the trumpet is covered in this part. I give instruction on standing and seated posture, how to hold the trumpet, and the best note for your grand entrance to the trumpet world. I introduce the relationship of good tone and accurate intonation and tell you how to start notes.

In this part, you add more notes and play them with a smooth connection. You discover the importance of scales — they're important building blocks in developing technical skill and fluency. Finally, I explain why warming up leads to greater success.

Part III: Developing Your Technique

In this part, I cover lower-register skills and the development of the high register, every trumpeter's holy grail. I tell you how air speed can help you with the extremes of range and how to maintain a consistently clear and beautiful sound in all parts of the trumpet.

Here, you add more scales to your repertoire and try your hand at arpeggios. Because you're playing more notes in more formulations, I discuss the development of strength and endurance. I reinforce the importance of a strong breathing habit — you need it to play well for longer periods of time.

More notes and greater endurance enable you to play a much greater variety of repertoire. Part III contains advice and exercises on becoming more conversant in the language of music, using more advanced and varied articulation.

Finally, in Part III, I introduce you to the different styles of music, or the different characters of the trumpet, that your developing technique allows you to explore.

Part IV: The Complete Trumpeter: Knowledge and Skills for the Advancing Player

Part IV offers a practice approach that will give you the best odds for a successful trumpet experience. I offer different articulations and combinations thereof, etudes for technical development and endurance, and solo repertoire for you to play, so you can enjoy the fruits of your labors.

I broach the subject of playing by ear, without reading music, and outline the benefits of learning music aurally. I explain what improvisation is and tell you why it's a direction that you want to consider.

A whole barnyard full of strange sounds is presented in Part IV — I describe all the tricks and techniques that the trumpet is capable of producing. In a more serious vein, I fill you in on the art of vibrato, as well as the advantage of becoming a good sight-reader and ways to achieve that goal.

Taking care of your trumpet is an important topic, and I cover it in Part IV. I also give you a guide to the various accessories that can make your trumpet playing more interesting and rewarding.

In this part, I discuss the advantages of studying with a good teacher and strategies for finding the right one for you. You can be an equal partner in a productive relationship with your teacher, and I describe some ways to do that.

The joys of playing music with other people is the final topic in Part IV. I tell you about the different kinds of ensembles and how you can join them in making music. Included are three duets specially written for *Trumpet For Dummies* that I hope you'll enjoy playing either with the CD or with a duet partner.

Part V: The Part of Tens

We all need role models, people to look up to. Included in this part are brief introductions to ten inspirational trumpeters. I hope that learning a little about some of the players who have created and are continuing the tradition of wonderful music making on the trumpet will enhance the enjoyment of your own playing.

In this part, I also fill you in on ten bad habits you want to avoid — habits that trumpeters who've gone before you have had to work hard to overcome. I've been a perpetrator of many of these ten bad habits myself, so don't worry: I don't preach to you in a holier-than-thou voice. Just consider this chapter a warning of pitfalls you want to sidestep on your journey.

Finally, I end this part with ten ways you can be the best possible trumpet player. This chapter is sort of the flip side to the one that comes before, full of hope and optimism and encouraging words.

Icons Used In This Book

Throughout this book, you see icons in the margin. Each one designates a special kind of message, one that I feel is deserving of extra attention. Here's a key to the icons:

Whenever you see the Tip icon, you're sure to find a bit of helpful advice that can save you time or help you do something better.

The Remember icon alerts you to something so important that I want to make sure you never forget it.

The Warning icon alerts you to information that can save you from a whole lot of trouble.

When you see the Technical Stuff icon, you can choose to read it and explore the topic at hand a little deeper, or you can move right on by, knowing that the information, although interesting, is not vital to your progress as a trumpeter. You can always return to it later, or ignore it completely! It's up to you.

The On the CD icon appears next to recordings on the CD.

Where to Go from Here

This book is designed to be read in many different ways. You can be traditional and start at the beginning. Or you can dip into the book wherever you see fit, using the table of contents and index as your guides.

If you're a beginner, starting with Chapter 1 may be the best approach. If you've been playing for a while and feel like you need some new practice material, Chapter 16 may be a good spot to jump in. If you're looking for a new warm-up, Chapter 9 is a good place to start.

Think of this book as a travel guide. Wherever you start will offer a rewarding vista of an interesting part of the trumpet world. Bon voyage!

Part I
Ta-Da! A Prelude to Trumpet Playing

The 5th Wave   By Rich Tennant

THE EARLY YEARS OF ELEVATOR MUSIC

In this part . . .

An aspiring trumpeter needs to know a lot about trumpets and how sound is produced, about music in general, and about how to prepare for taking on this wonderful musical instrument.

In Chapter 1, I give you some background on the brass family and lip-reed instruments and about the parts of the trumpet. I also introduce you to making a sound on the instrument and offer some tips on how to practice.

If you like to know how things work (and many trumpet players do), head to Chapter 2, where I explain how the instrument is constructed, the materials used, and how the trumpet uses the vibration of your lips to produce its glorious sound.

Chapter 3 gives you practical advice on choosing an instrument that will help you achieve success.

Because you also need to know about how music is constructed, Chapter 4 is an introduction to music theory — a step-by-step guide to understanding all those strange shapes on the page.

Chapter 1

The Instrument of Royalty

Kings and queens have used the authority of the trumpet sound as part of their pageantry since the Egyptian pharaohs. That tradition continues: The wedding of Prince Charles and Lady Diana was accompanied by a brilliant trumpet solo, and modern-day royalty and other dignitaries are invariably announced by trumpet fanfares.

More than any other instrument, the trumpet has always had a mystique about it. Nothing against the clarinet or the flute, but neither of those instruments blew down the walls of Jericho or announced the end of all things, as in Handel's *Messiah*. By learning to play the trumpet, you've decided to be part of a wonderful tradition.

All in the Family — The Brass Family, That Is

The trumpet is a member of the brass family, which shares a rich history and development. All members of the brass family have one thing in common, besides being made mostly of brass: They're all sounded by the buzzing of the lips. (That makes them part of an even larger family, the lip-reed instrument group.)

Every brass instrument has a mouthpiece, usually detachable from the instrument, against which the lips buzz. It, too, is made of a brass alloy. The mouthpiece consists of a rim on which the lips rest, a cup into which the air is blown, and a throat, which is a narrow opening that streams the air into the instrument. The mouthpiece channels the buzz created by the lips and helps create the standing sound wave that gives the instrument tone. (Turn to Chapter 2 for information on how mouthpieces are constructed and Chapter 5 for instructions on how to produce a beautiful tone on the mouthpiece.)

Every brass instrument also has a length of brass tubing that culminates in a widening of the *bore* (the inner measurement of the tube), called a *bell*. The bell serves to project the sound, in the same way that your hands cupped around your mouth help you to be heard at a distance. And all the modern brass orchestral instruments have a method of changing the length of the vibrating column of air to produce many pitches.

But the members of the brass family all look different from one another, and they vary widely in size. In this section, I introduce you to the main members of the modern brass family.

The trumpet

The trumpet is the highest voice in the brass family, and it has an important role in orchestral, band, jazz, and popular music. As the top part, it is heard the most clearly and has a strong melodic role. The trumpet has a generally straight tube, with one or two bends to create an oblong shape, making it easier to hold.

The trumpet was primarily a signaling device in ancient Egypt, Europe, and China. In the Medieval Era (from the 5th to the 15th centuries), the trumpet became more of a musical instrument, helped by the high status that it held in its military role. In the Baroque Era (from about 1600 to 1750), an early version of the trumpet called the natural trumpet or baroque trumpet attained prominent status. This simple instrument was a long narrow tube with two bends and a bell section. Unlike the modern instrument you might be used to seeing, the baroque trumpet (shown in Figure 1-1) had no valves. It was used by composers as a melodic instrument and required trumpeters to play in the extreme high register; only a few lower notes could be sounded. Handel and Bach wrote extensively for the natural trumpet, as did many other composers.

Very few players were able to play this demanding instrument. Guilds were formed, with strict initiation and apprenticeship conditions in order to maintain the highest possible skill level and to strictly define the trumpeter's role in society. These organizations were similar to modern-day trade unions, only far more secretive and exclusive. After Bach and Handel, the guilds fell into disarray and the art of high trumpet playing was temporarily lost. It probably didn't increase morale when Gottfried Reiche, the trumpeter who performed the incredibly high and difficult parts in the works of Bach, collapsed and died of a stroke the day after playing a particularly demanding concert.

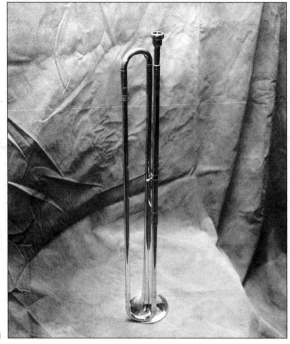

Figure 1-1:
The baroque
or natural
trumpet,
a melodic
instrument
without
valves,
played in
the music
of Bach
and Handel.

In the late 18th century, a trumpet was developed that was able to play the normal diatonic scale (the doh-re-mi-fa-so-la-ti-doh one you grew up listening to Julie Andrews sing) in the lower range of the trumpet. Since this fluency in the lower register was not possible on the natural trumpet, the new instrument was an exciting development. Haydn's famous *Concerto in E Flat* and Hummel's *Concerto in E* were both written for this new version of the trumpet, called the keyed trumpet (shown in Figure 1-2). The fact that two of the most famous composers of the day wrote for this new instrument showed just how important the trumpet was and how significant it was that trumpets could now play fluently in all registers.

The modern trumpet — the one you're learning to play (see Figure 1-3) — emerged in the 19th century, along with the invention of the valves. (For more on valves, see the nearby sidebar, "The value of valves.") Berlioz wrote for the valved trumpet. Later, Wagner, Mahler, and Strauss expanded the role of the orchestral trumpet. Military bands also used trumpets and their cousins, the cornets, extensively, and in the late 19th century, bands like the Sousa Band created a huge following for the cornet and trumpet soloists. In the 20th century, the trumpet became dominant in Dixieland jazz, big band swing, and modern jazz, as well as in symphonic music.

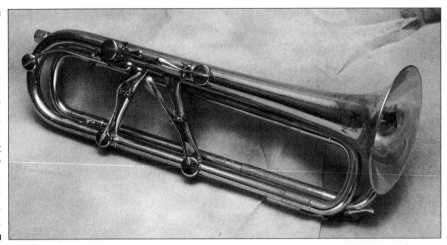

Figure 1-2: The keyed trumpet. Five keys could be opened or closed, allowing the trumpet to play scales in the lower, more accessible, range.

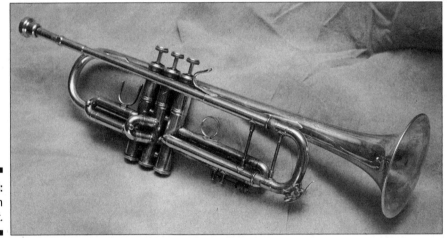

Figure 1-3: The modern trumpet.

But the traditional roles still apply: To this day, if a fanfare is required to announce a new building or a presentation of any kind, the trumpet gets the call and the trumpet (or bugle) still plays at ceremonies honoring fallen soldiers.

The value of valves

Valves are historically very important to the development of the modern trumpet. If it weren't for valves, we'd still be clinging to the backs of horses or the sides of stage coaches, trying desperately to squeak out the right signals without falling off or bashing our teeth in, getting shot at as we try to organize the troops on the battlefield, or playing just a few low notes in classical symphonies. So, if you get frustrated when you practice your trumpet fingerings, just imagine the alternative — it could be a lot worse.

What the valves do is quickly and temporarily change the length of the standing sound wave, by blocking or opening different sections of tubing. If the length of the tubing and sound wave change, so does the pitch of the sound, which allows you to play different notes. If the tube is lengthened, the note is lowered; if the tube is shortened, you hear a higher pitch. These notes are like words in a musical language, giving you the ability to communicate musically.

In North America, the valves are usually cylinders that go up and down; these are called *piston valves.* In much of Europe, the changing of the tubing is effected by *rotary valves,* which rotate, as the name implies, opening up the different lengths of tubes, called *crooks* or *slides.* (See below for a photograph of piston and rotary valves. The pistons are on the top and are the most common type of valve in North America.)

The fingers of the right hand must move these valves with quickness and accuracy. So, we practice. That's not *all* we practice, but agility on the valves is an important part of the trumpeter's daily regimen, and you have to put in the time to develop your agility. In Chapters 7 and 8, I offer exercises you can do to increase your skill with the valves.

The horn

The horn is a close relative to the trumpet, sharing much of the same historical signaling role. It's descended from the hunting horn and, before that, from hollowed-out animal horns (see Figure 1-4). The earliest horns were used for signaling, because they produced a sound that's louder than the human voice, with greater projection.

Figure 1-4:
The animal horn (left) and the hunting horn (right) were predecessors of today's horn.

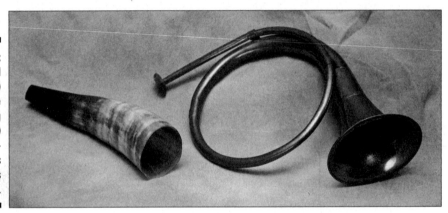

Hunting horns (refer to Figure 1-4) helped early hunters organize the chase of the next meal. Much later, the brass version marshaled the ladies and gentlemen for the fox hunt — although how anybody can play a brass instrument while riding a horse is beyond me. ***Disclaimer:*** Nothing in this book will prepare you to play while clinging to a galloping horse.

The *post horn* was another brass copy of the original animal horn. By changing the lips or the wind, different signals were created: "Here comes the mail — letters for all!" or "Help, highwaymen!" The post horn's shape imitated the curve of the animal horn, making it more compact and easier to hold than a long, straight tube.

As horns became larger, with a richer sound, they began to be employed in musical situations, but they still often played passages based on the calls of the hunt. Horn players learned to change the pitch of the sound using the right hand cupped in the bell. By moving the hand in and out of the bell, notes could be raised and lowered, a practice that continued well into the 19th century.

The invention of valves (see the earlier sidebar, "The value of valves") enabled the horn to produce the complete musical scale. The horn (see Figure 1-5) has been an important instrument in the orchestra from the Baroque Era to the present, playing major roles in the works of composers such as Bach, Mozart (who wrote four concerti for the horn), Beethoven, Mahler, Strauss, and Stravinsky, to name just a few.

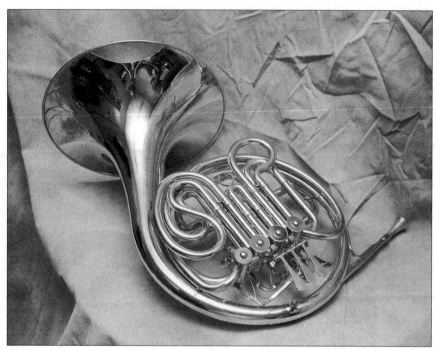

Figure 1-5:
The modern-
day horn.

The modern-day horn was at one time more commonly known as the *French horn,* for reasons that are unclear. Many French horn players now prefer to call the instrument simply "the horn."

The trombone

Trombone means "large trumpet" in Italian. The trombone had the strange name of *sackbut* in England during the Baroque Era. Like all brass instruments, the trombone can play the notes of the overtone series (see Chapter 2), but added to that is the use of a movable telescopic slide. The outer slide moves in and out on the inner slide, and because the length of the instrument can quickly and easily change, so can the pitch.

Trombones were used in churches throughout Europe, most famously in the Baroque Era, and often appeared in compositions with choirs. A style of music played by several choirs, including a brass choir, was developed in Italy, especially in Venice at St. Mark's Cathedral. The composer Giovanni Gabrieli wrote hundreds of pieces to be played at religious services, featuring trombones as a melodic voice. The bell of earlier trombones was much smaller and less flared than the modern trombone; otherwise, there has been very little change in appearance (see Figure 1-6).

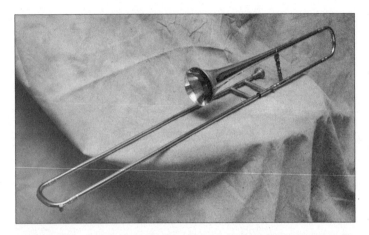

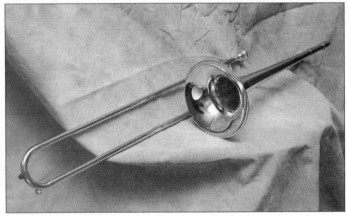

Figure 1-6:
The sackbut (top) and the modern trombone (bottom). Note the larger bell of the trombone.

The modern trombone has been an important member of the orchestra since Beethoven, whose *Symphony No. 5* was one of the first pieces written for non-religious use with parts for the trombone. Dixieland, big band swing, and modern jazz all include the trombone as an important voice. The "talking" trombone style of "Tricky Sam" Nanton used the sliding sound so annoying to band teachers everywhere (called *glissando,* or *gliss*) as well as a growl-tonguing and plunger technique to give a distinctive sound to the Duke Ellington Orchestra.

The euphonium

The euphonium (shown in Figure 1-7) is a recent addition to the brass family, coming along in the mid-19th century. It's a very mellow-sounding instrument. Because of its lyrical capabilities, the euphonium is sometimes called "the cello of the band" (usually by euphonium players).

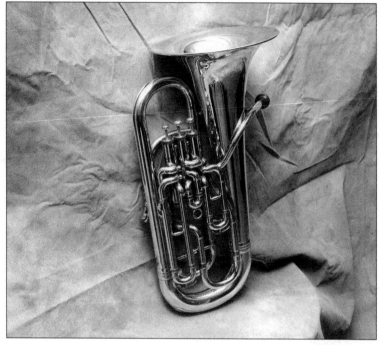

Figure 1-7:
The euphonium is a recent addition to the brass family.

The euphonium has a close cousin known as the *baritone horn,* which has a smaller bore. Arriving as late in the development of brass instruments as it did, and in some ways duplicating the trombone role, the euphonium has very few parts in orchestral music. However, in the brass band (brass and percussion instruments) and wind band (brass, percussion, and woodwind instruments) the euphonium has a distinctive role as a melodic specialist, which is very appropriate because the ancestor of the euphonium is a Renaissance instrument called the *serpent,* which often played melodic parts in mixed vocal and instrumental music.

The tuba

The tuba (shown in Figure 1-8) is another relative newcomer to the brass scene. Like the euphonium (see the preceding section), the tuba is descended from the serpent.

The invention of valves in the 1820s enabled the arrival of the tuba. Such a large instrument, with a length of tubing three times that of the trumpet, couldn't have played anything but a few harmonics.

If trumpets are the sopranos of the brass choir, and horns are the altos, then trombones are the tenors, and tubas are the basses.

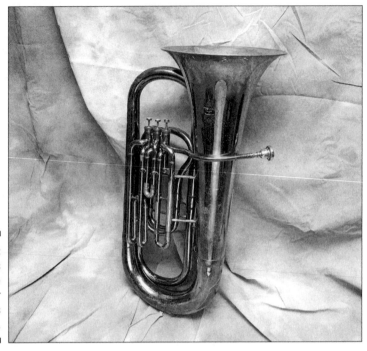

Figure 1-8:
The tuba is
a relative
newcomer
to the brass
scene.

Composers such as Berlioz and Wagner in the 19th century, and Strauss and Stravinsky in the 20th century, wrote important parts for the tuba. The brass and wind band repertoire relies on the tuba's strong, rich bass sound to anchor the sonority of the brass section.

Making a Start

As in most activities, getting off to a good start is helpful. Bad habits can be picked up easily and, as you probably already know, they're very hard to get rid of.

The first thing that you can do to start building your trumpet-playing foundation is listen to a lot of good trumpet players. Seek the best role models, the sounds that you love, the styles that interest you and thrill you. Listen a lot so that you absorb the details of sounds you hear.

The next step, as I describe in Chapter 5, is to practice taking deep, relaxed breaths, while standing or sitting with excellent posture. (Doing this while listening to great trumpet playing is a good habit to get into.) I describe some very helpful breathing exercises in Chapter 5, but the overriding principle guiding your approach to breathing should be very simple: Take a big breath and blow. Trumpeters (and other people) tend to complicate matters by thinking too hard.

Arnold Jacobs, the world-renowned tuba player with the Chicago Symphony Orchestra, and the greatest teacher I ever knew, told me (and everybody else), "Just be a dumb guy — don't think, just blow." Little did he know that I would one day write a book called *Trumpet For Dummies.*

Nurture an idea of the way you want to sound. That's why you listen. You learned to walk and talk by watching and listening to the people around you. Similarly, you'll learn to play trumpet by copying what others do well and what you admire.

Playing the trumpet is a physical as well as a musical art. In Chapter 6, I describe good seated and standing posture and holding the trumpet properly. The first note, that thrilling experience for all beginning players, is the other main topic of Chapter 6.

Because the modern trumpet is capable of producing many notes (with your help), in Chapter 7 I give you the information that you need to add to the first note that you make. And in Chapter 8 I show you how to connect those notes fluently.

Playing the trumpet is physically demanding and requires sensible playing habits. In Chapter 9, I outline a procedure to help you warm up for successful playing.

Reaching Upward and Onward

Playing high notes is only part of what trumpeters do, but it's definitely the most impressive part. Louis Armstrong was known for his high notes, and Maynard Ferguson developed the upper register to an almost unheard of degree. Actually, "almost unheard of" describes it well — Ferguson could play so high that he approached the frequencies that only dogs can hear.

Clearly, this interest (some would say obsession) with high notes goes back to the signaling role of the trumpet. The high notes carry farther, and, in a battlefield, this was useful.

But achieving success in the upper register, which I discuss in great detail in Chapter 11, is only part of the path of the aspiring trumpeter. You also move onward toward a pure, clear tone and the ability to flexibly move from note to note. Communicating exciting and beautiful music with your trumpet involves developing good valve technique (see Chapter 7), a strong and efficient *embouchure* (your lips and muscles around the mouth as you play), and, beyond all technical issues, the ability to play with fluency and artistry.

Playing more notes and more tunes

There are 12 different pitches, or notes, in most of the music that you'll play. Adding range means that those 12 notes are repeated in other octaves, so you have many notes to learn if you want to be able to play interesting and varied music. Arpeggios are part of the musical language and the technical development of a trumpeter, and I give you information and practice material on them in Chapter 12.

Music communicates feelings about human experience. The simplest songs — often children's play songs, like "Mary Had a Little Lamb" or "Twinkle, Twinkle, Little Star" — involve a limited range and very few notes. As people mature, their experiences get more complex, and so does the music that they play and hear. If you want to be part of the world as a trumpeter, you have to learn to play many notes in many different ways.

In Chapters 14 and 15, I explain how to add the variety that real music requires. A good word for this variety is *style.* Learning to play in different styles is interesting and enjoyable at the same time as it is challenging and sometimes difficult. But the reward is great — the range of expression and communicative power in music will repay you many times over for all the effort that you invest.

Developing flexibility and fluency

Flexibility is the term trumpeters use for the ability to move easily and with a consistent tone quality from register to register, from the easiest middle range down or up to the more extreme notes, and back again. Chapter 11 gives you pointers and exercises in developing flexibility, as does Chapter 13.

Fluency can be associated with flexibility, but it also includes rapid and smooth tonguing, fast finger action on the valves, and the ability to coordinate the fingers and the tongue. Chapter 14 has lots of information on both of these areas of trumpet playing.

Both flexibility and fluency rely on a smooth, consistent flow of wind. A trumpeter needs to blow a steady stream of wind, as if holding a long note, even when changing registers and tonguing rapid passages. I address this skill in Chapter 13.

You also need a firm embouchure. Blowing freely helps form the appropriate embouchure, because the muscles around the mouth firm up as you blow out. Try aiming a stream of wind out toward your hand and notice what happens to the embouchure muscles.

Regular repetition of mouthpiece and trumpet songs and exercises will develop strength in the embouchure muscles, as long as deep, relaxed breathing is reinforced daily. And the best guide to how well you're practicing is always your ear. Are you sounding the way you want to sound?

Taking It Up a Notch

Sure, it's great when you can play some music and impress yourself and your friends. But that's not all she wrote, is it? You can continue to develop your trumpet-playing skills your entire life.

Practice makes perfect

The good news is that practicing is fun — at least it *can* be if you do it properly. Slogging away on boring exercises may not be very enjoyable, so a good practice session needs variety and some beautiful tunes, as well as a certain amount of exercise.

In Chapter 16, I outline a practice routine that develops skills, maintains your embouchure and technique, and gives you musical pleasure in playing nice songs. I talk about becoming more versatile on the trumpet by playing without music in Chapter 17. In Chapter 17, I also address sight-reading, which enables you to play a wide range of music and much more of it.

Your guide to practicing is how you're feeling musically and physically. Any kind of tingling in the lips is a sure sign that you should stop and rest for a while. A sharp pain in the mouth area tells you clearly that you need to take a break. But more subtly, if you aren't focused on what you're doing, if your mind is wandering, then it's time to refresh mind and body.

You should rest as much as play in a practice session — that's an easy rule of thumb. Practicing — gradually approached with a good warm-up, relieved by frequent periods of rest, and varied with entertaining material — will make your trumpeting sessions a high point of your day — something you don't want to miss, rather than a daily duty.

Equipping yourself for success

Lots of cool stuff is associated with the trumpet — interesting and fun accessories to keep your trumpet in good condition and looking great. Chapter 18 gives you a guide to the care of your trumpet. Chapter 19 tells you about all the mutes that help you vary your sound and all the other accessories that can keep you entertained, and may even improve your trumpet playing.

Chapter 20 features advice on finding a good teacher, and getting the most out of your lessons. Getting involved with other people who are making music is very important, so in Chapter 21 I talk about the ways in which you can play in different ensembles and the benefits that that experience can offer.

Seeking the best role models

A very good way to stay focused and inspired while practicing is to include listening sessions throughout the day. Not only is listening to many trumpet players a lot of fun, but it's also a source of aural "nutrition." If you find that certain players thrill you, then get everything that they've recorded and flood your mind with their music. Go to concerts, because as wonderful as recording techniques and sound technology are, nothing can replace the excitement and musical thrill of a live performance. There is a visceral thrill, a physical and emotional response to live music, that will keep you inspired long after the concert is over.

Not only will the trumpet players that you listen to guide you by modeling style and sound, but they'll also inspire you to practice and energize you with the artistry of genuine mastery. All the ringing triumphant tone, the urgent quality of a call to arms, the persuasive, romantic subtlety of lyrical playing give the trumpet the aura of occasion and uniqueness — in a word, of royalty.

Chapter 2

How the Trumpet Works

*I*t has always seemed amazing to me that rocks in the ground can be turned into sophisticated metal creations, capable of producing beautiful sounds. Somehow, a combination of metals is shaped into a trumpet. Actually, we owe a debt to the medieval alchemists, who misguidedly thought that they could turn lead into gold, in the process discovering techniques for heating and shaping metals, and creating different combinations of metals, or alloys.

I start this chapter by giving you a look at how trumpets are made — covering everything from the metals used to how those metals are shaped into the beautiful instrument known as the trumpet. Then I move on to covering the mighty mouthpiece — that piece of metal that allows you to make the sounds you want to make. The whole point of playing a trumpet is to make sounds, and in this chapter I tell you how to do that. Finally, I end the chapter by covering the overtone series and open notes — the stepping stones to making music.

A Star Is Born: The Making of the Trumpet

At some remote moment in prehistoric times, somebody was walking along, minding his own business, and saw an animal horn lying on the ground, maybe beside what was left of the animal, maybe not. What possessed that person to pick up the horn and try to use it to make noise? Maybe it was just curiosity: "What can I do with this? Can I eat it? Ouch! No. But maybe I'll play a concerto on it . . . or at least call my friends." Staying in touch was just as important then as it is now and the communication value of a loud sound must've brought the horn into regular usage. And usage for humans leads to experimentation, which may be why the ability to play different notes developed: "Hey, Thorg, *my* dad can play *two* notes on *his* horn."

In this section, I introduce you to the materials that go into the making of the modern-day trumpet, and what those materials are used to make — the bell, leadpipe, and valves.

What trumpets are made of

Modern trumpets are made of an alloy of copper and zinc. Brass musical instruments need to resist splitting and be malleable enough to shape the bell and bend the tubing, so the proportion of copper and zinc in the alloy can vary. Sound quality is also said to be affected by the composition of the alloy.

There are four different finishes to choose from:

- **Raw, unfinished brass:** Raw, unfinished brass is believed by many players to have the most ringing tone. Brass polishes to a high luster, and was used for mirrors in ancient times, although it does tarnish and requires polishing.

- **Silver plating and gold plating:** Silver and gold plating impart acoustical changes and resist tarnish. Silver is less expensive than gold, but gold has a certain *je ne sais quoi* (although I don't know what it is).

- **Lacquered brass:** Most student instruments and many professional trumpets are finished by the application of lacquer to the brass. The tone quality loses some of the brightness and even resonance of unfinished or plated trumpets, but lacquered trumpets are very popular and have a rich tone of their own.

Even though I prefer silver-plated trumpets, my first instrument had a golden lacquered finish. I'll never forget how beautiful I thought it was when I opened the case for the first time, and I loved the sound it made.

The specific proportion of copper and zinc, and the various finishes are some of the variables in trumpet manufacture; others include the amount of taper in the leadpipe and bell section, the dimensions of the flare of the bell, and the type of fittings such as water keys, finger hooks, and slide rings. In Chapter 3, I cover how to choose the best trumpet for you.

The parts of the trumpet

Regardless of what a trumpet is made of or how it's finished, every trumpet has the same basic parts, including the bell, the leadpipe, and the valves.

The bell

The *bell* is the flare at the end of the trumpet. It helps project the tone outward, and its dimensions can affect intonation and tone quality. It also dents easily, because the metal is thinner, having been formed into the bell shape.

In the natural trumpet (see Chapter 1), a funnel-shaped fitting called a *garland* is attached to the end of the flare to strengthen it and give the maker thicker metal to decorate. The natural trumpet bells are things of beauty, with ornate designs in the brass.

Modern trumpets are made with either two-piece or one-piece bells:

- **The two-piece bell** is formed from a separate bell flare, spun by a lathe and shaped on a mandrel into the desired form. It's then soldered onto the other part of the bell section, using brass alloy or silver solder.

- **The one-piece bell** is made from a single sheet of brass, cut to a shape that includes the bell flare. Notches are cut along the edges of the metal. The sheet of brass is then folded together, shaped on a mandrel into a tube, connected by hammering the notches together, and finally soldered along the whole length of the bell. The final forming of the flare is done by hand shaping, using hammers.

Both types of bell are finished in the same way, with a wire made of brass (called the *bead*) folded into the very end of the bell to strengthen it. The final step is the bending of the bell section into a U-shape. To prevent the tube from buckling and collapsing as it's bent, the tube is filled with a combination of pitch and tar or sometimes with a frozen solution of water and soap. See Figure 2-1 for a finished bell section.

Different trumpets have different tone characteristics, intonation tendencies, and response features, such as the amount of vibration the player feels. All these variables can affect the sound, but there is little scientific testing of the relationship between physical characteristics and playing tendencies. Each player brings aural expectations and playing tendencies to the performance; the temperature and acoustic response of the performance venue and the size and enthusiasm of the audience add still more variability. Add to that the mood swings to which even trumpeters are susceptible, and it's no wonder that there are so many trumpet manufacturers, not to mention psychiatrists!

The bell does add projection and resonance to trumpet sound — of that there is no doubt. One-piece bells tend to have less extra vibration than two-piece bells do, and one-piece bells are preferred by a majority of professional players.

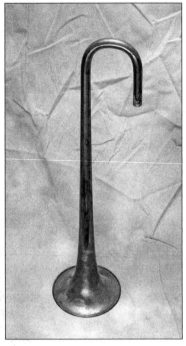

Figure 2-1:
A bell
section.

The leadpipe

The first section of tubing on a trumpet, called the *leadpipe* (pronounced *leed*-pipe), has a slightly flared section at each end (see Figure 2-2). The first flared section is called the *mouthpiece receiver,* because it's where the shank of the mouthpiece is inserted. At the other end is the *tuning slide receiver,* into which is inserted the movable tuning slide.

Some makers have begun to create a one-piece mouthpiece and leadpipe, reverting to the design of the ancient shell or animal horn.

The taper of the leadpipe affects intonation and response. With better-quality instruments, manufacturers take greater care with the taper of the leadpipe. The taper of the leadpipe influences whether the trumpet seems free-blowing or stuffy. The amount of vibration that the player feels in the pipe is thought to have an effect on resonance and tone projection.

The one thing that is beyond dispute is that the leadpipe has to be kept clean. Figure 2-2 shows a detached leadpipe. Chapter 18 tells you how to keep your trumpet in good playing condition.

Figure 2-2:
The lead-
pipe is the
first section
of tubing on
a trumpet.

The valves

The regular B♭ trumpet is about 4½ feet long. With just that length of tubing, many notes are available (see "Where the Notes Come From: The Natural Over-tone Series," later in this chapter) — but the valves give you many more notes.

The trumpet has three valves. The leadpipe is joined to the valves by the tuning slide, and the bell is connected to the valves on the other end. So, right in the middle is a mechanism called the *valve section* (shown in Figure 2-3). Three valves, side by side, have three lengths of tubing, called *slides* or *crooks*, connected to them. When a valve is pushed down, an opening is created so that the air goes into and around the tubing and back into the valve. These openings are called the *valve ports*.

The middle, or second, valve connects to the shortest of the three crooks. The length is determined by the amount of tubing required to lower the pitch by a semitone (see Chapter 4 for more on tones and semitones). The impor-tant thing is that this semitone is the smallest musical interval used. So, if you push down the second valve, the air rushes into the crook and returns to the main part of the trumpet, and the tone is lowered by a semitone. The first valve is the next longest, lowering the pitch by a whole tone, or two semitones, and the third valve is the length of the first and second combined, lowering the pitch by one and a half tones, or three semitones.

So, by lowering the valves singly or in combination, the large gaps between the notes of the overtone series can be filled in by semitones. An instrument that can play all the semitones in the musical scale is said to be *chromatic*, after the Greek word for "color." The trumpet is, therefore, a musically colorful, fully chromatic instrument.

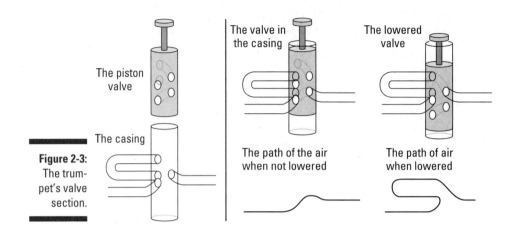

The piston valve

The valve in the casing

The lowered valve

The casing

The path of the air when not lowered

The path of air when lowered

Figure 2-3:
The trumpet's valve section.

Mouthing Off: The Mouthpiece

Where would trumpeters be without the mouthpiece? Well, very likely at the dentist or the plastic surgeon. The mouthpiece is a removable extra length of tubing with a wide opening and a flat rim where the lips touch. The flat rim adds a level of comfort to the playing of the trumpet, and the fact that you can take the mouthpiece out means that you can choose one that suits your lips and playing style (plus, you can clean it — a nice benefit).

How the mouthpiece is made

The mouthpiece is a widening at the start of the tube. The main parts of the mouthpiece are the rim (inner and outer), the cup, the throat, the back bore, and the shank (see Figure 2-4). Variables in each of these components have a significant effect on performance. In Chapter 3, I detail your mouthpiece options.

The purpose of the mouthpiece is to make contact with the lips more comfortable and the buzzing surface wider for more sound. Modern detachable mouthpieces are made from a solid piece of brass. Earlier designs involved a cast rim and cup soldered to a shank made of rolled sheet metal. The one-piece mouthpiece was a big improvement in comfort and tone quality. With modern techniques and computer design, mouthpieces are available now with detachable rims, cups, and shanks, all threaded securely in place, but most players prefer the solid models.

Mouthpieces are generally silver plated, but the presence of nickel in the silver can cause an allergic reaction, as can contact with raw brass. Gold plating is a rather expensive alternative, and plastic rims are often used in marching bands.

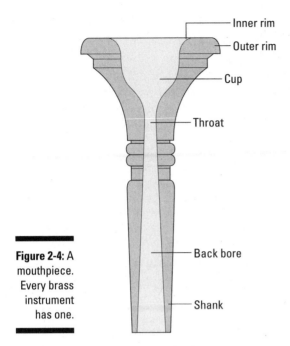

- Inner rim
- Outer rim
- Cup
- Throat
- Back bore
- Shank

Figure 2-4: A mouthpiece. Every brass instrument has one.

Two main variables: Different sizes for different styles

There is a lot of complexity in mouthpiece design, but at its simplest there are two variables: the depth of the cup and the diameter of the rim.

The depth of the cup

Trumpeters talk about tone in terms of dark and bright: A bright tone is associated with popular music and jazz; a dark tone, with orchestral players. Although there are many exceptions, a deeper cup will, in general, facilitate a darker sound, and a shallow cup will facilitate a brighter sound. See Figure 2-5 for a comparison of cup depth.

The Viennese trumpeter and engineer Vincent Bach came to New York in the early 20th century and began to standardize cup depth, using letters to designate depth. An A cup was very deep; an E cup, shallow.

Most trumpeters prefer medium depths, for more versatility.

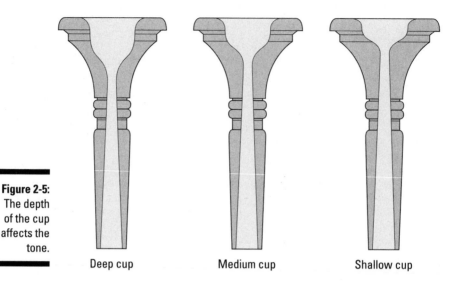

Figure 2-5:
The depth
of the cup
affects the
tone.

| Deep cup | Medium cup | Shallow cup |

The diameter of the rim

When it comes to rim diameter, the choices vary depending on the thickness of the player's lips and the style of music he's playing. A narrower diameter, labeled by Vincent Bach with larger numbers (10 is a narrow diameter; 1 is very wide), tends to suit commercial or jazz players who play longer engagements, and play higher and louder on average than their symphonic colleagues. A Bruckner or Mahler symphony has plenty of high and loud music, but a four-hour dance job on lead trumpet is physically demanding, and players have learned that the narrower rim facilitates it. Figure 2-6 shows how the different rims look.

As in most things in life, moderation is desirable, and except for specialists in a particular kind of playing, trumpeters choose medium-size mouthpieces.

Top view of a mouthpiece

Diameter
of inner
rim

Figure 2-6:
The diam-
eter of the
mouthpiece
rim can
change tone
quality and
comfort.

Wide diameter   Narrow diameter

Making a Sound

Trumpets are beautiful to look at and have been designed with great sophistication. But they're inert objects, totally silent. No sound comes out of a trumpet without a trumpeter. Your wind and your musical imagination are what create the beautiful tone of the trumpet. This concept may seem obvious, but you'll often hear trumpeters saying things like, "This trumpet doesn't sound good" or "I love the sound of this trumpet."

The instrument does have an influence on tone quality, but the *player* is, by far, the most important ingredient. The instrument houses the air in which a standing sound wave is set in motion by the buzzing of the player's lips, and helps project the sound outward. But the buzz is the thing.

Good vibrations

A clear, resonant buzz makes a better sound than a weak, breathy one. Trumpeters often forget how important the buzz is. They spend all kinds of time on mechanical aspects of the instrument instead of taking a big breath and buzzing a clear sound. In Chapter 5, I explain how to create a beautiful buzz, but the essence of it is the quality of the air that you blow through your lips. It's like the difference between high- and low-octane gas for your car: The better the fuel, the better the performance.

The way to produce high-octane fuel is to relax. Stand or sit with straight but not military posture, breathe deeply, and blow out freely, like a sigh. This action gets the lips buzzing in a consistent and efficient way.

The trouble is, trumpeters are ambitious — even competitive — and sometimes they get a bit tense when performing and practicing. Tension causes tight muscles, so they breathe with less freedom, actually restricting the amount that they can inhale. And they tend to push the air out, instead of letting it go naturally. So, the air passing between the lips is under pressure and inconsistent. The lips respond to the air going through them, and with low-quality air, they vibrate weakly.

The other variable is the way in which the lips form as the air passes through them. If the lips are too far apart, there will be extra air, which doesn't create a buzz. This sounds fuzzy and unclear on the mouthpiece and on the trumpet. The ideal setup, as I describe in detail in Chapter 5, is the shape your lips make when you say the word *dim*. This shape, strengthened by a healthy exhalation, is the perfect *embouchure* (the formation of the lips and muscles around the mouth while playing the trumpet).

Blowing, buzzing, playing

The sequence of first blowing, then buzzing, and finally playing is very direct, and it's very helpful to remember as you study the trumpet. People tend to forget the first steps, especially as their trumpet playing improves. No matter how good you are, you need to review the basics and strengthen the habits of good posture, breathing, and blowing.

Keep an eye out for sore lips, respiratory ailments, and bad moods. The healthier your playing habits are, the less such things will bother you. Happy trumpet playing with a clear musical result is the reward for your consistency.

Where the Notes Come From: The Natural Overtone Series

One of Mother Nature's gifts is the *overtone series,* also known as the *harmonic series of overtones.* Sound waves are organized in specific ratios, and the overtones above a fundamental pitch always occur in the same order. This phenomenon is parallel to that of light waves: White light has all the colors of the spectrum; various permeations of the light waves result in different hues.

Sound contains other sounds, in varying strengths. When you hear a strong note on a piano, and there is another pitch sounding as well, that other pitch is one of the overtones. Contained in every note are other pitches, which is why some sounds are richer, or more resonant, than others. The more overtones that are present, the richer the sound. A trumpeter, by blowing freely with a relaxed exhale, can make a more resonant sound than she can with a weak or inconsistent breath. But the overtones mean much more than good tone quality to a trumpeter. The ratios that produce the overtone series give trumpeters the notes that they play.

As shown in Figure 2-7, the second note in the series is an octave away from the lowest note, called the *fundamental.* In other words, the notes sound the same, except for the difference in register. (A soprano and a bass can sing the same song in their comfortable ranges, sounding an octave apart.) The next interval is a perfect fifth, then a perfect fourth, a major third, and a minor third. The intervals get proportionally smaller as the overtones ascend. The trumpeter, through air speed and lip adjustment, learns to choose which of these overtones to play. The military and hunting signals use the lower overtones in different order and varying rhythms, creating hundreds of calls, and natural trumpeters played beautiful melodies using the upper overtones. All the notes above the fundamental in a harmonic series are called *partials.*

Figure 2-7:
The over-
tone series

No Valves Necessary: The Open Notes

The trumpeter has to learn to hear the note that is called for and adjust wind speed and lip tension in order to produce it. It seems kind of miraculous, but army buglers have been doing it for centuries! Luckily, the extreme high notes — the partials of the overtone series — are not required by the bugler or the modern trumpeter, nor is the fundamental, which is also very difficult to play. Figure 2-8 shows the bugle notes, which are also those that a trumpeter plays without using the valves; these are called the *open notes*. Notice that the sixth note, high B♭, is written as a quarter note; this is a way of showing that the B♭ played open is a very out-of-tune note, too flat to be used by buglers or trumpeters.

Figure 2-8:
Bugle notes,
also called
the open
notes of
the modern
trumpet.

The higher the note, the faster the air must be blown and the firmer the embouchure must be. In Roman times, the trumpeters blew so hard that their cheeks puffed out and they couldn't control the sound. A trumpeter wore a leather strap, with a slit for the mouthpiece, around his head, to keep his cheeks in. In addition to learning to play softly, the baroque players controlled embouchure and wind speed to a high degree, enabling them to perform the beautiful and delicate music written for them. Modern players must also play softly with great delicacy, as well as loudly with control.

Buglers have a high degree of skill, in their somewhat limited role. The quick tonguing technique and control of wind and embouchure cultivated by the baroque and modern trumpeter are part of the skill set of the military bugler. Figure 2-9 shows examples of some popular bugle calls.

Figure 2-9:
Popular
bugle calls.

Chapter 3

Choosing Your Weapon

*I*n this day and age, there's no shortage of advice on how to select and purchase your trumpet and mouthpiece, and a plethora of choices await you. But you have to know who to believe — and that's where I come in. In this chapter, I give you some guidance on how to choose the best equipment for you, and how to acquire that equipment at a fair price.

Choosing the Best Trumpet for You

The increase in international trade and advances in technology have resulted in many different types of instrument becoming available to the budding trumpeter. But more doesn't necessarily mean better. There are trumpets for sale that are worth nothing, made from cheap material and haphazardly designed — and they're readily available from large retail stores at very low prices. I recently had to break it to a student that the new trumpet that his parents had bought at a large discount department store was not only worthless to him but could not be resold in good conscience. It could be used as part of a boat anchor, perhaps, but that's about all it was good for. On the other hand, there are highly sophisticated trumpets that are suitable for only a very few people — and they have the prices to prove it.

The good news is, you can find a high-quality trumpet for a reasonable price. You just need to do know what you're looking for. In this section, I cover some of the main decisions you need to make before you head out to a store with money burning a hole in your pocket.

New or used

You can find some very fine secondhand trumpets at music stores and pawn shops, through newspaper ads, or online. Trumpeters are notorious for wanting to find the instrument that will solve all their problems — the brass is always shinier on the other side — so they sell their old instruments and trade up to something new.

On the other hand, a new instrument has the security of the warranty in case of any problems. Although many older instruments are very good, technology has developed to the point where new trumpets are likely to be very well designed and built. Plus, they have that new-trumpet smell.

Previously loved

A used trumpet may have started as a bad instrument — sometimes they come out of the factory as poor quality. Or it may be a decent trumpet that's been abused or neglected. It may also be a very good trumpet that someone has decided to sell.

What you want is the third kind: a high-quality trumpet in good condition. The key is to inspect the trumpet carefully, or get a good player to check it out if you don't feel knowledgeable enough. Here are some things to look for:

✔ **Do the valves go up and down smoothly?** If they're sticking, they may just need valve oil . . . or they may be dented or the whole casing may be warped. If you feel any sticking at all, you need to find out the cause, and for this you should consult a brass technician, available at music retailers.

✔ **Is the trumpet leaking air?** To test this, remove each one of the valve slides in turn, checking each one by sealing the sleeve that comes out of the valve section with your finger. Hold down the valve, and then blow hard through the leadpipe. If you hear or feel air escaping, the valve has worn so much that it's leaking air and won't produce a clear tone.

✔ **Are there dents that could affect the flow of air?** A few dents in the bell won't cause much trouble and are easy to fix, but a large dent in the smaller tubing near the valves can be hard to repair and detrimental to the way the trumpet responds.

✔ **Are there obvious weak places in the tubing?** A condition called *red rot* eats away at the tubing from inside the trumpet and can wear right through. Acid in the perspiration on some players' hands will eat away at the metal from the outside. Red rot shows up as discolored spots on the outside of the tube and can be patched, which is worthwhile if the trumpet is otherwise very good.

✔ **Is the price reasonable?** Check the cost of a new model for comparison before you search for used ones. A trumpet older than 30 years selling for more than a couple hundred bucks is probably too much. To determine the age of the trumpet, you can check the serial numbers on the manufacturer's Web site, or on sites created by trumpet fanatics (like www.trumpetmaster.com or www.tpin.org).

Here are some of the better brands of used trumpets, instruments that age gracefully:

✔ **Olds Ambassador:** This trumpet was popular 30 to 50 years ago and isn't produced anymore, but many of them still survive, especially in junk stores and pawn shops. I once saw an Olds Ambassador bolted to the wall of a restaurant, with the mouthpiece still attached. I amazed everyone in the restaurant — well, okay, I was the only customer, and the staff politely averted their eyes — when I played the Haydn trumpet concerto on it while it was mounted to the wall. It sounded terrible, but it was kind of fun. Just one more reason for learning how to play the trumpet. Olds Ambassador trumpets were solidly built and made with precision and very good brass.

✔ **Getzen 300/400 Series:** Another oldie but goodie. These trumpets have an easy response, so they're very good for beginners. They're well built, and the valves are excellent.

✔ **Yamaha student model (YTR 2320):** These trumpets are newer, but they've been around for a while and have proven to be durable. They have good playing characteristics and are of consistently good quality.

Off the rack

Buying a new trumpet has many advantages, including that famous new-trumpet smell. Yes, that expression is usually used for cars, but it works just as well for trumpets, and it's especially poignant because trumpets lose that new aroma more quickly than cars do.

A new *anything* has a certain aura, a magical glow that some people value and will spend a lot of money on. But there are practical advantages, too — a new instrument of good quality will have a warranty and a guarantee, and it will feature up-to-date technology and materials. The retailer will have expert sales personnel who can give you good advice on care and maintenance. And in a store, there will be several instruments for you to try.

Have the salesperson give you at least three instruments to take into a studio and play. In addition to comparing the tone of the instruments, compare the valve action (after you've oiled the valves). Look for slides that move well and have a general feeling of solidity. If a trumpet is made well, of high-quality materials, it will feel solid with no rattles or extra vibrations when you play it.

Finally, see which instrument feels the best in your hand. Feel isn't a frivolous matter — after all, you'll be holding the trumpet for several hours a day and it should feel comfortable. How the trumpet feels will affect how you feel about playing it, directly influencing how successful you are. The balance should feel right for you — most players like an even balance, so the instrument doesn't feel like it'll tip forward or backward as you hold it up to play. The surface should feel good as well — lacquer is preferred by many players, but others like the feeling of silver or gold plating. (For more on finishes, turn to Chapter 2.)

It helps to have a friend along with you — if possible, someone who is knowledgeable about trumpets, or at least someone with a musical ear. The differences in tone and intonation are slight but recognizable.

Price isn't everything. There are some extremely pricey trumpets that are not as well made as less expensive ones are. Some people think that if an object costs more, it must be better, but this isn't necessarily the case with trumpets.

Professional or student models

I used to imagine that professionals in any field had equipment that was far better than anything a student or amateur could buy. But the very best trumpets are available to anyone who has the money. Custom instruments played by the top soloists are extremely costly, but anyone can order them. Many players have specialized adjustments made to their off-the-rack models; these are usually small tweaks and a skilled brass technician can do them.

Student trumpets are generally lighter and more responsive than pro models. They tend to lack depth of tone and the ability to produce a really strong sound, but they're designed with young, inexperienced players in mind. They respond easily — meaning that when you blow, the tone seems to speak easily. Student trumpets are considerably cheaper than professional models, but they're well made and carefully designed.

So-called "intermediate" trumpets are marketed to be for the advancing player, but I've never felt that these were any better than student models. The choice, in my opinion, is really between a top professional trumpet and a student model.

Starting small

A student trumpet made by one of the reputable manufacturers has many of the characteristics of the professional model. The materials may vary somewhat, but student trumpets can be very well made. Student models are usually lighter than pro models, so they're easier for younger hands and arms to hold. And student instruments are often one-third the price of the professional models.

Here are some student models you may want to consider:

- **Yamaha:** Yamaha student trumpets are the market leaders because of their high quality and consistency.

- **Conn-Selmer, Inc.:** Conn-Selmer owns the former Vincent Bach Corporation and makes a very good student model with characteristics of the Bach Stradivarius professional trumpet. Conn-Selmer also owns Benge Brass, makers of a very fine professional trumpet.

- **Getzen:** The Getzen Severinson professional trumpet has a little sibling that I mention earlier (see "Previously loved"), the Getzen 300/400 Series.

- **B&S Brass Instruments:** A German company, B&S makes a very nice student model.

- **Jupiter Band Instruments:** A Korean company, Jupiter produces good student trumpets.

All these instruments play well, with a quick response, meaning that they don't require as much air to make a sound. They're built correctly, so you can play them with good intonation; the valves work well; and they're solid enough that they don't dent easily. They also come equipped with tunable third- and often first-valve slides, which used to be a feature of professional trumpets only.

I don't recommend buying a trumpet that doesn't have movable slides with rings or triggers for adjusting intonation. Any trumpet without these necessary moving slides is unlikely to be of good quality.

Playing along with the pros

Professional trumpets are, not to put too fine a point on it, a lot better than student instruments. The valves work better; the slides slide better; and they're built to help the player produce a very strong, resonant sound. But they don't respond quite as easily as student models do, because they're built with heavier material and often have a larger bore size (the inner diameter of the tubing is larger). You have to work a bit harder to play most professional trumpets, but the result is more resonance and a stronger tone.

If you're blowing up a storm, having adopted the breathing habits advocated in this book, then you're probably ready for a professional trumpet, but most beginners do very well with a student model. The drastic difference in price makes the student model the first option you should consider.

Professional trumpets always have the tuning apparatus permanently fixed on the first and third slides. Whereas, in a student model, the rings are adjustable for growing hands, the pro trumpet has a finger ring or trigger soldered onto the slide. This soldered tuning ring or trigger can be adjusted by a technician, but adjustment is rarely necessary.

Triggers have the advantage of a spring, which returns the slide to the "in" position, but some players don't like the extra weight. Rings are less expensive than triggers and more readily available. Try both and choose whichever works best for you. Figure 3-1 shows the difference between a ring and a trigger.

Here are some of the better-known professional trumpets and the kind of response you can expect:

- **Vincent Bach Stradivarius:** This trumpet set the standard worldwide but especially in North America. The tone is rich and full, with unparalleled beauty, but this trumpet doesn't speak as quickly as some other trumpets do. It requires a good breath to get the best playing results, but those results have been the basis of comparison for all other trumpets for a century.

- **Yamaha YTR models:** Yamaha trumpets have wonderful projection, consistent intonation, and a quick response. They're very satisfying instruments to play and are quickly becoming the new standard.

- **Schilke:** Schilke makes only professional models. Schilke trumpets were designed as an alternative to the Bach concept, having a lighter tone and quicker response but, in the opinion of many, lacking the depth and resonance of tone. They're extremely well made and suit many players very well.

- **Benge X Series:** Benge trumpets have been around for many years. The Benge has long been a favorite of studio players, especially on the West Coast. The company is now owned by Conn-Selmer, Inc.

Conn was once a maker of top brass instruments, as was Selmer. That this company now owns Benge and Vincent Bach is strange, because they were once all fierce competitors for the trumpet market and each had quite a distinctive identity.

- **Monette:** This company is an example of the trend toward the idea of custom-designed and handmade instruments. David Monette is the founder/designer, and he reminds me of what Vincent Bach must have been like before his business was bought by a large company. Monettes are very expensive, and if you want a new one, you have to be willing to wait a long time. They play unlike any other trumpet, though. The most famous practitioner of Monette trumpets is Wynton Marsalis.

A beginner, no matter how wealthy, should wait a few years before trying a Monette.

Figure 3-1:
First and
third slide
triggers.

Choosing the Right Mouthpiece

If you think that selecting a trumpet is confusing, wait until you shop for mouthpieces. They're small and relatively inexpensive, but they have many variables and there are many more mouthpiece makers than trumpet manufacturers. In Chapter 2, I discuss the design of a mouthpiece. The mouthpiece may be much cheaper than the trumpet, but it's equally important, if not more so, to your success as a player.

Cup depth: Shallow versus deep

A mouthpiece can have a shallow or deep *cup* (the bowl-shaped end). The distance between the rim and the bottom of the bowl is the *depth.* The depth of the cup is indicated by a letter (from A through E, with A being the deepest and E the shallowest), in the system devised by Vincent Bach.

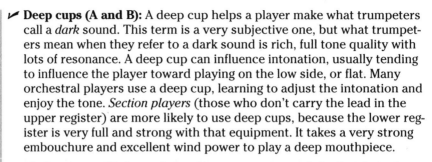

- ✔ **Deep cups (A and B):** A deep cup helps a player make what trumpeters call a *dark* sound. This term is a very subjective one, but what trumpeters mean when they refer to a dark sound is rich, full tone quality with lots of resonance. A deep cup can influence intonation, usually tending to influence the player toward playing on the low side, or flat. Many orchestral players use a deep cup, learning to adjust the intonation and enjoy the tone. *Section players* (those who don't carry the lead in the upper register) are more likely to use deep cups, because the lower register is very full and strong with that equipment. It takes a very strong embouchure and excellent wind power to play a deep mouthpiece.

- ✔ **Medium cups (C):** Specialists who are very accomplished seek the best equipment to facilitate the kind of playing that they do. But beginners, intermediate players, or experts who want to play in a variety of styles are well advised to find equipment in the middle of the spectrum. A medium-cupped mouthpiece, a C cup, is the most popular model by far, and it's the one that I strongly recommend for students.

- ✔ **Shallow cups (D and E):** Some players with very full lips find that their lips touch the bottom of the cup when they play, but players with lips of all shapes and sizes can adjust to different depths. It's the playing characteristic of a shallower cup that is more important in drawing players to it. A shallow-cupped mouthpiece facilitates a bright sound, with more edge and projection, and greater ease in the upper register. If they aren't careful, players who use shallow mouthpieces tend to play on the sharp side, sometimes with a thinner tone. As in the orchestral players with deeper cups, the commercial, jazz, and high-note specialists learn to adjust and find a way to play in tune. Some players seek shallow mouthpieces as an easy way to get high notes; these players usually aren't using enough air, so their high notes aren't very full or accurate. Successful equipment choices usually are made from a position of strength, by trumpeters who play well and want to find a way to advance a little bit farther, or play at the same level with less effort.

The inner rim: Wide versus narrow

The inner rim, where the flat part of the rim ends and the cup begins, is the other important variable for mouthpiece selection. The diameter of the inner rim is what matters most. A number 1 on a Bach mouthpiece indicates a wide diameter, a 7 is the medium size, and numbers such as 10 and 17 indicate mouthpieces with very narrow diameters.

There are other, more subtle, dimensions that more-advanced trumpeters investigate, including the flatness or roundness of the flat part of the rim, the part that your lips rest against. The shape of the inner rim as it joins the cup is also a factor for some players.

One of the factors in choosing rim width is the size and shape of your lips. If you have thicker, fuller lips, you may prefer a wider diameter. This isn't always the case though; many players with full lips like the feel and playing characteristics of a narrower rim and accommodate their embouchure to fit.

Generally, a wider rim helps a player attain a bigger sound; more lip area is vibrating, so the buzz is richer. A wider rim usually goes with a deeper cup, but not necessarily. The bottoming-out phenomenon, in which the lips touch the bottom of the cup, is very common with wide, shallow mouthpieces. A 1 diameter mouthpiece is most often used by symphonic players, especially those who play the lower parts.

A mouthpiece with a narrow diameter is preferred by high-note specialists, including jazz and commercial players and baroque trumpeters. The rim feels comfortable, and the fact that less lip surface is vibrating leads to less fatigue. If the rim is narrow, the cup can be, and usually is, on the shallow side, so the upper register is facilitated.

Younger players whose embouchures are still strengthening should use a middle-of-the-road rim size. The 7 rim in the Bach designation is ideal for most young players; in fact, it's a popular size for players of all ages and levels. With a 7 rim, there is sufficient lip vibrating for a good sound, yet it has a comfortable feel, helping with endurance.

An alternative is a mouthpiece on which the rim itself is very wide, as opposed to the inner diameter. With an extra-wide rim area, designated with a *W* by Bach, your lips contact more surface area, and greater comfort can be the result. As always, individual preference should be the guide.

The size of the throat opening was standardized by Bach to a #27 drill size for the stock mouthpieces. This can be enlarged by a technician, or by your Uncle Harry in his basement. Go for the technician. Many professionals use a #25 or #24 throat, but a #27 is the size recommended for young players.

Modular or solid

There are expensive modular pieces (trumpeters often call them their *piece*) designed to drive us crazy. ("Hmm . . . let's screw this #5 shank onto the B cup and try the #6 rim. That should help me play higher. Now, for the next passage I'll use the. . . .")

So, if you want to go crazy and bankrupt, modular pieces are a good option. Otherwise, a solid mouthpiece is probably for you. In fairness, modular mouthpieces can be useful for professional players in unique situations, but for beginning players, they aren't necessary.

Material: Silver versus gold

Mouthpieces are made of solid brass, and the plating can be silver or gold. Some people are allergic to the nickel in silver plating, so gold is the alternative. Many players prefer the feel of gold plating, but others find it harder to feel secure on a gold rim — the feel is more slippery than silver is. Silver has the advantage of being much cheaper and more readily available than gold. Of course, practicality is not the first priority of many trumpeters.

Marching-band players often use brass mouthpieces with plastic rims, or even solid plastic mouthpieces. Plastic mouthpieces have the wonderful advantage of not getting cold the way brass does for those joyful winter parades, but they aren't serious contenders for regular use.

Makes and models

Partly because the manufacturing equipment is smaller scale and the appetite for mouthpiece experimentation so ravenous, there are even more mouthpiece makers than trumpet makers (although all the trumpet manufacturers also make mouthpieces).

The standard and the system of calibration were set by Vincent Bach a century ago; even if a maker uses a different set of descriptions, they're always related to the Bach system.

The Vincent Bach 7C, a medium-size mouthpiece, is the first choice of a large majority of beginning players, teachers, and even some professional trumpeters. Here are some of the better-known mouthpieces, with the size corresponding to the Bach 7C:

- GR Mouthpieces 65
- Schilke 11
- Stork VAC 3 SM4
- Yamaha 13C4

Some other mouthpiece manufacturers are Dennis Wick, Greg Black, Jet-Tone, Reeves-Purviance, Warburton, and Zottola. Some manufacturers, like the Jet-Tone and Reeves-Purviance, are best known for shallow mouthpieces favored by high-note players, while others have a balanced offering. The latest in design innovation is offered by GR Mouthpieces and Stork, which use computer programs to create a desired balance of the variables like rim, cup, and throat size.

Beware the equipment bug

Trumpeters are notorious for being equipment fanatics. I suppose it's partly because most trumpeters are Type A perfectionist personalities. And they seem to have way too much time and money on their hands. If there's any way that a different mouthpiece, trumpet, leadpipe, tuning slide, water key, inner sleeve to remove the gap in the tuning slide receiver, specially designed screw-on shank to remove the gap in the mouthpiece receiver, extra-heavy caps for the bottoms of the valves, special plastic valve guide, adjustable bell, adjustable pitch finder to move the main tuning slide for each note, gold-brass or silver-brass or nickel-brass bell, adjustable-cup mouthpiece, removable lead-pipe, removable brace for the slide, adjustable weight for the bell or leadpipe, extra sleeve for the mouthpiece, multiple bells, pink trumpet, black trumpet, or red trumpet might possibly give a trumpeter an edge, then hey, why not?

But what about practicing, with a big breath and a clear idea of how you want to sound? What about not blaming equipment for real or imagined problems, and just playing for enjoyment and fulfillment? As my grandfather said, or somebody's grandfather said or should have said, "It's a poor workman who blames his tools."

Now, I should come clean: I, too, have misspent time, money, and false hope. I have a box of unused mouthpiece parts to show for it that cost $500. Experimentation is fun and interesting and can lead to innovation, which, in turn, can lead to lasting improvement. But no equipment can take the place of calm, consistent, artistically inspired work.

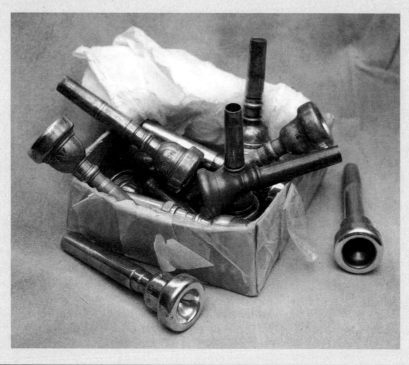

Looking for a Trumpet and Mouthpiece

When you're shopping for a trumpet, you want to do your research. This chapter is a great place to start. But it helps to have the advice of someone who knows you and your unique situation. Talk to people you trust, like your trumpet teacher or a pro you respect — that's the best kind of research you can do. Shop around. Look at music stores, and see what your band or school has available. In this section, I give you some tips.

Getting expert help

There are many experts in the trumpet world, some self-appointed and others universally acknowledged. Needless to say, advice from self-appointed experts should be taken with a grain of salt. The people to trust are your own teacher and professional players as well as trusted colleagues.

The Internet can be a great help in doing your own research. All the instrument and mouthpiece manufacturers have Web sites, and you can find commentary and reviews by individuals as well. I find that the Internet is most helpful in answering specific questions — for example, "What is the throat size of a Bach 7C?" or "What is the diameter of the Yamaha medium large bore, compared to the Benge 3X?" Use the Internet to supplement the expert advice you get in person. Sites such as www.trumpetmaster.com and www.trumpetherald.com are especially useful.

Talking to your teacher

If you're taking lessons, your teacher is your first and probably best source of information. In addition to having broad experience in the trumpet world, your teacher knows you and your specific interests and needs.

In fact, your teacher may be able to find an instrument *for* you — I've called my colleagues, searching for a trumpet for a particular student, with good results.

Your teacher also can try out a trumpet that you've located. It's worth your time and money to pay your teacher the cost of one lesson, and then use that time to meet at a music store for direct input. You can try the trumpet and so can your teacher. You also can play a few mouthpieces and get feedback.

From personal experience, I can say that having too many variables all at once can be very confusing. Find a mouthpiece that's comfortable and helps you make a clear, resonant buzz, and then stick to that mouthpiece when you try different trumpets. Stay in the same room, and aim the trumpet the same way in order to compare them accurately.

Reaching out to a pro

If you don't have your own private instructor, you can still get advice from a professional player. Professional trumpeters are often equipment geeks or at least knowledgeable about makes, models, and availability.

Making contact with someone can be as easy as waiting to introduce yourself at the stage door after a concert or calling the orchestra office and asking for a referral. High school teachers who are experienced trumpeters also can be very helpful, as can university professors.

Every player has a bias and most of us have a certain sound quality in mind and an expectation of the kind of response we like. So, you won't get truly objective advice — for that reason your own teacher, knowing you better than a stranger, is your best source for guidance in choosing equipment.

Shopping around

Getting your first trumpet can be a wonder and a fulfilling experience, a thrill that lasts a long time. I'll never forget my first trumpet — an old trumpet made by a small maker in Europe. My dad found it in a pawn shop for $35, but I loved that trumpet from the moment I opened the case and saw a deep gold lacquered trumpet nestled in green felt lining. That trumpet got me started on a satisfying career. So, do your research, get all the advice that you can, try as many trumpets as possible, and stay open to luck.

My dad did none of what I recommend today. Fortunately, the tone quality of my first trumpet was very good and there were no leaks or dents. To improve your odds of finding a great trumpet, follow the advice I offer in this section.

Getting an instrument for free

You may not have to buy your own trumpet, at least in the beginning. (If you eventually feel sure that you'll want to keep playing and you'd like to own your own trumpet, heed the advice in the following sections.) Here are some ways you can get your hands on an instrument without having to empty your pockets.

Community organizations

Most areas have community bands and orchestras. In fact, their numbers are growing, largely due to the huge number of people retiring with their health (and teeth) intact, looking for activities. (Dentists love trumpet players — trumpeters have a very strong reason to look after their teeth.) Some groups even admit only beginners and teach them how to play in a remarkably short time.

These organizations often facilitate the purchase or lease of instruments. Sometimes the ensemble owns instruments that they'll lend to you as long as you're a member; other groups have a relationship with retailers. Instrument manufacturers sometimes supply instruments to these groups as a community outreach project.

Schools

Policies on supplying instruments to students vary in different school districts, and even from school to school within a district. If you're interested in an educational music program, you or your child has a good chance of being supplied with a trumpet. These trumpets may not be any good — they may be cheap, old, and in poor condition. However, some schools have excellent instruments available for their programs, and many schools offer a lease or purchase arrangement with retailers that can save you a lot of money.

If you or your child is seriously interested in instrumental music, look around for the best program in your area. You first priority should be finding an excellent, charismatic teacher, who not only teaches correct techniques but also has a well-organized program with good instruments available.

Visiting music retailers

There are different kinds of music retailers. One kind to avoid is the small local store with guitars, amps, and keyboards in the window, with a few no-name trumpets or saxophones for accent. The sales personnel are rarely knowledgeable and the instruments that they sell are usually not well-known brands.

You're far better off at the kind of store frequented by professionals. You'll see prominently displayed a selection of well-known instruments; a mouthpiece rack; accessories such as valve oil, mutes, specialty instrument cases, and trumpet stands; and a good selection of study books, duets, and other printed material. The salespeople will be knowledgeable and there will often be at least one trumpeter on hand. The store will have a studio where you can try out the trumpets.

The advantages of a good retailer are many:

- ✔ You get more-informed advice.
- ✔ There is a good selection of instruments and mouthpieces.
- ✔ The retailer will often back up the manufacturer's warranty.
- ✔ There is usually an on-site instrument repair shop that can look after any minor problems or adjustments.

Some music stores even have a rent-to-buy program, so you can rent the instrument and your payments are deducted from the purchase price if you decide to buy.

Ask your teacher and professional trumpet players which music retailers they recommend in your area.

Surfing the Web and scanning classified ads

The online auction site eBay (www.ebay.com) is a source of used musical instruments. You can see photographs to make sure that the instrument isn't dented and that the finish is in good shape. But you can't tell how the trumpet plays from a Web site, so be careful. I've had some students who bought instruments online and the instruments were virtually unplayable. Other students have bought instruments that were fine — and sold for a reasonable price.

Be sensible. Stick to well-known brands, check the serial numbers to see how old the instrument is, and talk to experts before you make a purchase.

The classified ads in your local newspaper and on craigslist (www.craigslist. org) can both yield good results. I had a student who arrived at a lesson with a beautiful Bach Stradivarius that she had seen advertised in the paper. She paid $200 for it and it was a very fine instrument — but this is a rare occurrence.

If you buy a trumpet from a classified ad or through craigslist, you should be able to meet the seller in person. If you can, take your teacher or a trusted expert with you to check out the instrument before you buy. (Besides, you probably don't want to meet a stranger alone anyway.)

Chapter 4

A Primer on Music Notation

Many people would rather do anything than learn about music theory. Even music majors in colleges and universities resist the study of theory and have trouble getting through the courses. Why? I believe a lot of it has to do with the way theory is perceived, and with some mistaken ideas about music itself.

Music is a language. With our spoken language, we learn how it sounds first and gradually begin to make the sounds that we hear, before learning to read and write. But language literacy is not called *theory*. It's just the written version of our speech. In order to demystify the topic of music theory, a name change is in order: What's called basic music theory could be called simply reading and writing music.

In order to be musically literate, you need to understand some basic concepts. After that, learning music literacy is a matter of experience — just doing it.

Reading the Language of Music

If you think of music as a language, which I do, then certain things are true about it. One is that music is meant to be understood. Just what is to be understood, just what is being communicated, is much less clear than in spoken language, because in the musical language, there are no words. But just because we don't know what is being communicated doesn't mean that nothing *is*. A trumpeter plays a melody and communicates something — something hard to describe in words, and perhaps something different for every listener. But there *is* something.

The materials of music can't teach that something, any more than learning your ABCs can teach you to write a beautiful poem. But musical literacy is as valuable to a musician as reading and writing are to all of us.

The really good news about reading music is that the note names are the same as the first seven letters of the alphabet. You're pretty familiar with the first seven letters. You can say them quickly without much thought. But try saying them backward. Go ahead, give it a try. How did you do? It takes me a bit of thought and some practice to say those seven letters backward quickly.

You need to be very fluent with those letters. The key of C is basic in music so it's good practice to say the seven letters starting and stopping on C — C, D, E, F, G, A, B, C. And then say them backward, back down to C — C, B, A, G, F, E, D, C. If you learned your doh-re-mi-fa-so-la-ti-doh, the alphabet sequence that you just said can be sung to the same notes.

Now that you know the names of the notes, you have to see how those notes are written, because it's done in a kind of code. When you know the key to the code, reading music is a cinch.

The musical staff

Musicians use what's called a *staff* to help us locate the notes. Often, you need to read music very quickly, so just writing the alphabet letters in sequence is too cumbersome and also doesn't deal with rhythm, which I talk about later in the chapter. So, the staff is part of a kind of code in the form of a graph. It consists of five horizontal lines, numbered one through five from the bottom to the top (as shown in Figure 4-1). The spaces in between the lines are also numbered one through four, from the bottom to the top.

Figure 4-1:
The musical staff, with the lines and spaces numbered.

5 lines   *4 spaces*

Each of these lines and the four spaces between them is named by a letter, and the letters are always in alphabetical order, starting with the bottom line. Now comes the key to the code: You need to know the name of just one of those letters, and you can figure out the rest. The staff can have a different starting note, but it always has the same sequence. The music that trumpeters play is in what is called the *treble clef* (see Figure 4-2). Its other name is the *G clef*, because it's drawn so that G is identified. And there's the key to the code.

The French word for "key" is *clef*. So, the key to understanding note reading is the clef.

Figure 4-2:
The treble
clef.

You can see that in the lower part of the treble clef a little swirl encircles the second line from the bottom. That tells us where G is. And if G is the second line then the space below it is — drum roll, please — F! Yes, by George, you've got it! And the line below that, the first or bottom line of the staff is E.

So, you have the information required to figure out all the notes in the treble clef. You can even name the notes below and above the clef, using small lines through the notes, called *ledger lines*.

Now, it's time for a bit of practice. In Figure 4-3, you see little dots called quarter notes (see "Whole notes, half notes, quarter notes, and more" later in this chapter) on different lines and spaces. Try your hand at identifying these notes without peeking at the answers.

Figure 4-3:
Naming
notes.

Here are the answers: F, A, G, and D.

The scale

A musical scale is a sequence of notes, for our purposes, starting and ending on the same pitch, spanning an octave. It's called an *octave* after the Latin word for "eight," because the top of the octave is eight notes higher than the bottom of the octave.

The scale is named after the first note of the sequence. The C scale notes are: C, D, E, F, G, A, B, C. The sound of a scale is well known to almost everyone. The famous "Do-Re-Mi" song from *The Sound of Music*, uses the notes of the scale either in the normal alphabetical sequence or in a different order. ***Remember:*** Written music is just a visual description of what we hear.

Figure 4-4 is the C scale, using whole notes, which is the first kind of note most students encounter (see "Whole notes, half notes, quarter notes, and more" later in this chapter). As you can see, a whole note is simply a small elliptical sphere encircling the line or fitting in the space it occupies.

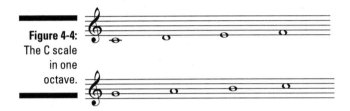

Figure 4-4: The C scale in one octave.

Scales can be longer than one octave. You just keep on going, continuing the same alphabetical sequence of notes. Figure 4-5 is a two-octave C scale. As a trumpeter, your basic range is the two-octave C scale, with a few notes on either end, so it's good to get familiar with it. You can see ledger lines below and above the staff.

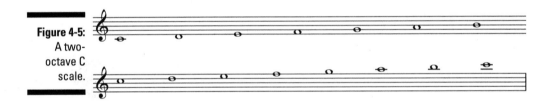

Figure 4-5: A two-octave C scale.

Intervals

An *interval* is the space between notes. Trumpeters need to know the sound of the various intervals to help them find the correct notes to play. The interval between C and D is called a *second* (because it includes two notes). The interval between C and E is called a *third* (because it includes three notes — C, D, and E). The interval between C and F is called a *fourth* (because it includes four notes — C, D, E, and F). And the interval between C and C is an *octave* (because it includes eight notes). Intervals go on getting larger, so C to D above octave C is a *ninth,* and so on.

In Figure 4-6 you can practice identifying intervals. Start with the bottom note and count up to the top one.

Figure 4-6:
Identify the
intervals.

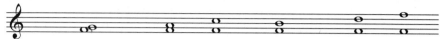

TIP

When calculating intervals, always include the bottom and top notes.

Here are the answers: second, third, fifth, fourth, sixth, and octave.

There are downward intervals, too. A down to C is a sixth, going backward in the alphabet (A, G, F, E, D, C), so six notes. Now, here's an interesting fact: A down to C (A, G, F, E, D, C) is a sixth, and A up to C (A, B, C) is a third. Six plus three is nine. From F up to C is a fifth. And F down to C is a fourth. Five plus four is nine. So if you add the interval of a note down to another note, to the interval between the same two notes inverted, you always get nine. Things like that make the mathematician that is supposed to be lurking in every musician very happy.

The piano keyboard

You've probably seen, and maybe even played, a piano. The keyboard (shown in Figure 4-7) is a very useful tool for understanding scales. There are white keys and black keys. The black ones are smaller, in between the larger white ones and set farther back. If you look closely, you'll notice that although most of the white keys have black keys between them, some of them don't — which has big implications for understanding scales.

The Piano Keyboard

Figure 4-7:
The piano
keyboard.

C D E F G A B C D E F G A B C D E F G A B C

C and D have a black key between them. From C to the white key, D, is a second, also called a *tone*. B and C have no black key between them. Without that extra key, the distance from B to C is only half the distance that C to D is, so B to C is called a *semitone*. It's also called a *minor second* to distinguish it from C to D, which is called a *major second*. There are different kinds of intervals, depending on the position of the black and white notes.

On the CD, the first two notes are a tone apart; the next two notes are a semitone apart.

Referring to Figure 4-7, you can see that there is a tone between C and D, a tone between D and E, and then only a semitone between E and F. From F to G is a tone, as are G to A and A to B. Then between B and C there's no black note, so it's a semitone. So, the scale has the following interval pattern: tone, tone, semitone, tone, tone, tone, semitone. This is the pattern of intervals of what is called the *major scale*.

On the CD, a major scale is played on a trumpet, up and down. Sing along, and then sing the major scale without the CD, while looking at Figure 4-4. Now you can describe it more fully as the *C major scale*.

The black key above C is called *D♭*. Take some time to look at the keyboard in Figure 4-7; you'll see that the note names are written in. Music has a system of altering the notes, using what are called *accidentals*. The three accidentals are naturals, sharps, and flats (see Figure 4-8). Flats lower the note they follow by a semitone, so B♭ is a semitone lower than B. Sharps raise the note by a semitone. And naturals are neither sharp nor flat.

Figure 4-8:
Naturals,
sharps, and
flats.

Let's go back to the language parallel: You can think of C as your first language, your mother tongue. But music is a universal language and musicians "speak" (sing or play) and read and write all the different translations. The same letters are used, but different spellings using those letters create a different language. You can have the same selection of notes, altered by accidentals (or "spelled" differently) playing different sounds. A major scale can start on any note, and with the same intervallic pattern, using accidentals to alter the notes up or down a semitone, still sounds like a major scale, but using different notes.

Figure 4-9 shows two scales: the F major scale, starting and ending on F, and the G major scale, both of which have the same pattern of intervals as the C major scale. In the F major scale, in order to keep the intervals the same, it's necessary to add a flat to the fourth note, B, so it becomes B♭, a semitone lower. In the G major scale, F has to be raised so it's only a semitone away from the octave, so a sharp is added.

Figure 4-9:
F and G
major
scales.

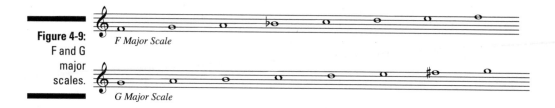

F Major Scale

G Major Scale

Key Signatures: Put Your John Hancock on It

There's another way to write different scales, easier than using sharps and flats. Instead of placing an accidental beside each of the notes that need to be altered, you can place the whole scale in a new *key*. Figure 4-10 shows another way of writing the F and G major scales. One is with accidentals (similar to Figure 4-9), and the other is with what is known as a *key signature*.

A signature identifies a person — it's what you sign on a contract or a check or anything else official. A key signature accomplishes the same thing for a key, identifying the particular scale that will be used for the music "signed" by the placement of the sharps or flats. Key signatures don't contain flats and sharps mixed — a key signature has either all sharps or all flats. Only one key signature has no flats and no sharps: C major.

Figure 4-10:
The F and
G major
scales with
key signa-
tures.

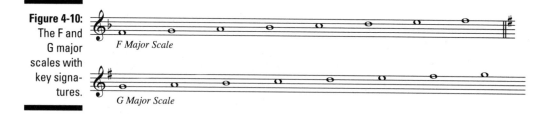

F Major Scale

G Major Scale

Finding and identifying the key signature is a useful skill for all musicians. In the following sections, I tell you how.

The degrees of the scale

In music, as in spoken language, there are many names for the same things, because we want different descriptions to suit various needs. The notes of a scale are called by their letter names. They're sometimes called doh-re-mi-fa-so-la-ti-doh. They can be identified numerically as 1-2-3-4-5-6-7-8. And finally, they're also known as the *degrees of the scale.* The degrees of the scale are tonic, supertonic, mediant, subdominant, dominant, submediant, leading tone, and octave.

The most important degrees for the purpose of finding the key signature are the tonic and the leading tone. The leading tone is one step below the octave, a semitone below.

The order of the sharps

Here's one of those time-honored sayings that help you remember the order of things: Father Charles Goes Down And Ends Battle. The first letter of each word of this little ditty gives you the order in which the sharps are written, as well as the note where the sharp is placed.

The list starts with one sharp, appropriately enough. Notice that each succeeding sharp is a fifth away, or five scale degrees. In Figure 4-11, you see the sharps written the way they appear in musical script. See if you can confirm the name of the line or space on which each sharp sits.

Figure 4-11:
The sharps
as they
appear in
music.

Now, when you want to find the name of sharp keys, just remember that the last sharp is the leading tone of the key. The leading tone is one semitone below the tonic. To find the name of the key, simply go up to the next scale degree. If the last sharp in the series is F, for example, go up one step to G; the name of the key is G major. Figure 4-12 gives you practice in identifying sharp key signatures.

Figure 4-12:
Name the
sharp keys.

Here are the answers: D major, E major, A major, B major, G major, F♯ major, and C♯ major.

Sometimes, you'll know the name of the key and you'll need to write the key signature. You simply reverse the process of finding the name of the key. If you know the key — for now, let's use G major — find the leading tone by going down one step to F. Therefore, F is the last sharp of your key signature. Because F is the first sharp in the list ("**F**ather **C**harles **G**oes **D**own **A**nd **E**nds **B**attle"), it's the only sharp. So, G major has one sharp: F.

The order of the flats

To name the flat keys, start with the order of the flats. Here's another helpful ditty: **B**attle **E**nds **A**nd **D**own **G**oes **C**harles's **F**ather. It sounds hauntingly familiar, doesn't it? That's because it's the reverse of the order of sharps (see the preceding section). Notice that after B, each succeeding flat is a fourth higher, or four scale steps. In Figure 4-13, you can see how the flats are written.

Figure 4-13:
How the
flats are
written.

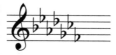

Here's the way you can use the order of the flats to find the name of the key: The second-to-last flat is the tonic of the key.

Look at Figure 4-13. The flats appear from the left, moving to the right. If there are two flats, the second-to-last one is B♭, and that is the tonic — hence, the name of the key.

There is a small complication, an addendum to this rule: If there is only one flat, it is B♭ and there's no second-to-last flat to name the key. The key of F has one flat, which is B♭.

Figure 4-14 gives you some practice in naming the flat keys. There are seven key signatures to identify using the above rules.

Figure 4-14:
Name the
flat keys.

Here are the answers: B♭, E♭, A♭, D♭, G♭, C♭, and F.

Figuring Out Note Lengths

Music is like a living body in that it has a pulse, or a steady beat underlying the sound. Sometimes, this beat can be complex and multilayered, but music generally has a clear beat. Just imagine the booming bass sound of car radios in the summer, and you have an example of a steady beat. All the note lengths that I introduce in this section relate to a beat, or pulse. They're measured by how many beats the note is held.

Whole notes, half notes, quarter notes, and more

Whole notes are the longest note value in common usage. There always are complications in any language, and music is no different, but for starters, the simplest way of defining a *whole note* is having a duration of four beats. If you see a whole note, for example, on the second line of the treble clef, it'll be a G and you'll hold it for four beats. You can count 1-2-3-4, and that's the duration of that note. Look at Figure 4-15 for some whole notes. You can also practice naming these notes.

Figure 4-15:
Whole
notes.

Here are the answers: G, C, C, F, G, F, and E.

Now, different people speak at varying speeds. My niece talks so quickly that I usually have to stop her and get a translation, whereas I had a history teacher whose soporific pace made staying awake a challenge (one that I usually failed to meet). So it is in music: The speed of the beats can be very different. The speed of the beats is called the *tempo*. A whole note at a slow tempo is held longer than a whole note at a lively, fast tempo.

Given that a whole note is held for four beats, you probably won't be surprised to learn that a half note is held for two beats. Figure 4-16 shows several half notes, on different lines and spaces of the treble clef. Notice the vertical line, called a *stem*, which, when attached to the side of the half note, identifies it. It's worth noting that two half notes are equal in duration to one whole note, at the same tempo.

Figure 4-16:
Half notes.

A quarter note is held for one beat, and four quarter notes are equal in duration to one whole note. The same elliptical shape is used for the quarter note as for the whole and half notes, but in quarter notes that shape is filled in, with a stem attached to the side. Figure 4-17 shows examples of quarter notes.

Figure 4-17:
Quarter notes.

An eighth note is one-eighth of a whole note, and it gets half a beat. A sixteenth note is one-sixteenth of a whole note, and it gets a quarter beat. Eighth notes are like quarter notes with a little tail on the stem, and sixteenths have two tails. Figure 4-18 has a selection.

Figure 4-18:
Eighth
notes and
sixteenth
notes.

There's no need to get out the calculator yet, if ever. Although theoretically this process of dividing the whole note into smaller note values could go on forever, and some music has some pretty small note values, wind players rarely play beyond sixteenth notes, at least in the beginning stages. Thirty-second, sixty-fourth, and one-hundred-and-twenty-eighth notes do appear, generally in piano music, where all the musicians have to do is wiggle their fingers. Okay, that's not fair, but there's a reason that brass players especially don't play quite as fast as pianists: We have to make every note with our lips, wind, tongue, and fingers, and that's pretty complicated already.

The whole structure is illustrated by Figure 4-19, a chart showing the relative note values.

To make reading and writing a series of smaller note values easier, a *beam* replaces the individual tails. Figure 4-20 shows tails and beams.

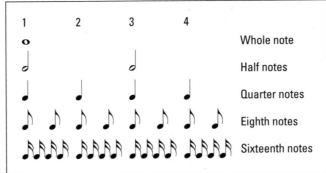

Figure 4-19:
Note values.

Figure 4-20:
Tails and
beams.

Ties and dotted notes

Duration of notes is a complex subject because of the variety of the sounds that must be written down and understood. A half note worth two counts may not be long enough for the musical need, but a whole note, four counts, may be too long. There are two methods of dealing with this:

- ✔ **Ties:** In Figure 4-21, a curved line connects a half note (two beats) to a quarter note (one beat), creating a note value of three beats. A half note could be tied to an eighth note (one-half beat) resulting in a duration of two and a half beats. Figure 4-21 shows examples of ties creating a variety of note values. A tie connects two adjacent notes of the same name. A slur looks like a tie but joins two notes of different names.

Figure 4-21:
Ties allow
you to
create notes
of the length
you need.

- ✔ **Dotted notes:** Musicians are lazy, just like everybody else. There's a more convenient method of reading and writing more complex note values. It's called the *dot,* and it is simply that — a dot following the note. A dot following a note increases its duration by half the value of the note. So, a half note (two beats) followed by a dot is held for three beats. Figure 4-22 gives examples of dotted notes and their equivalent in tied notes.

Figure 4-22:
Dotted
notes and
tied notes.

The sounds of silence

Imagine a great orator, not your history teacher (at least not mine). A good speaker uses all kinds of rhetorical devices, and musicians use the same ones. One example is the placing of silence within a speech, for dramatic effect. "If I am elected, there will be (dramatic pause) *two* chickens in every pot!"

In music, those silences are called *rests*. Rests must be written and read just as clearly as notes are, with an accurate expression of their duration — so don't try to rush through them. Figure 4-23 shows note values and their equivalents in rests.

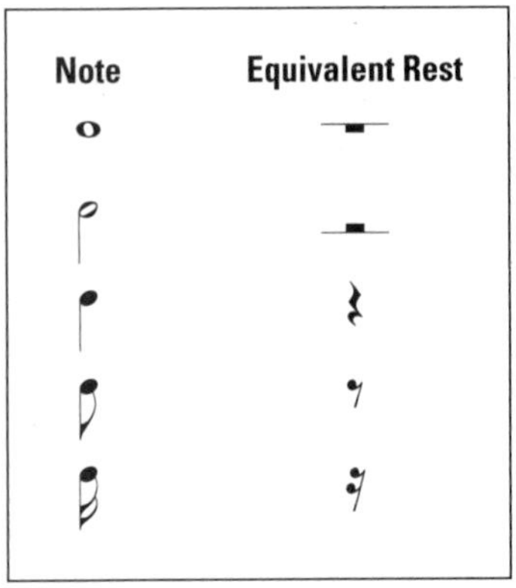

Figure 4-23: Note and rest values.

Note	Equivalent Rest

Signs of the Time

The language you speak has various functions. Sometimes you use it to comfort a crying child. Other times you use it to cheer for the home team. Still other times you may try to talk a buyer into signing on the dotted line or yell at the driver who just cut you off. And language is versatile enough to fulfill these and many other purposes. Music has the same need for variety: singing to a baby, belting out a Broadway tune, playing a fanfare, helping a parade get off on the right foot, and giving people music to dance to.

One of the means by which music shows its versatility is the use of *measures* or *bars*. Using what are called *measure lines* or *bar lines* — the vertical lines drawn through the staff that you see in many of the figures in this chapter — music can be divided into regular groupings, giving rhythmic emphasis and thereby greater communication. Measures can be irregular, especially in very modern music, but for most music, the measures tend to give a steady rhythmic pulse and energy to the sound. The organization of music according to rhythmic pulse, using bars or measures, is called *meter*.

Music is either in *duple meter* (two or four beats to a measure) or *triple meter* (three beats to a measure). In the following sections, I walk you through some of the more common meters in music.

Common time: Everybody's favorite

A bar of *common time* is the space between two bar lines containing four beats. Another name for this meter is by its key signature, which is 4/4 time — four beats to the bar, and the quarter note gets one beat. The rhythmic emphasis is strongest on the first beat of the bar, known as the *downbeat*. The second beat is weak, beat three is stronger (though not as strong as the downbeat), and the fourth beat is weak. Common time is also indicated by a capital *C*.

In a time signature, the top number is the number of beats in the bar, and the bottom number is the type of note value that gets one beat.

Here's an illustration: Sing the popular song, "Yankee Doodle" (shown in Figure 4-24), with the stress as indicated. The horizontal lines and accents over or under some of the notes indicates a stronger pulse.

YANKee *Doo*dle **WENT** to *town,* **RID**ing *on* a **PO**ny

There are four bars of common time, and the most stress is on the first beat of each bar, which falls on the first syllable of *Yankee,* on *went,* and on the first syllables of *riding* and *pony.*

TRACK 3

Figure 4-24: "Yankee Doodle" in common time.

Cut time: Looks the same, but it's twice as fast

Cut time is one of the trials faced by music students. Why should a note that used to be worth four beats sometimes be worth only two beats? The answer lies in the rhythmic emphasis created. In cut time, 2/2, the half note gets only one beat, not two, and only the first beat of the bar is emphasized. It usually goes with faster music, but not always. It's the rhythmic pulse, or feel, that is different.

To adjust the previous example (see Figure 4-25):

YANKee Doodle **WENT** to town, **RID**ing on a **PO**ny

Because there are fewer emphasized beats, the feel is lighter.

TRACK 4

Figure 4-25:
"Yankee
Doodle" in
cut time.

Waltzing around the topic

Music and dance are closely related, so much of the rhythmic aspect of music can be described in terms of dancing. The waltz is the most famous dance associated with triple meter. In 3/4 time (three beats to the bar, and the quarter note gets one beat), the notes are divided so there are three quarter notes in each measure and the emphasis is on the first beat. Imagine Fred Astaire and Ginger Rogers gliding across the dance floor, and the feeling of the waltz may become clear. The dancers move on beat one and only their feet lightly lift for beats two and three: **ONE**-two-three, **ONE**-two-three.

Figure 4-26 is an excerpt from Tchaikovsky's ballet *Sleeping Beauty*.

TRACK 5

Figure 4-26:
The theme
from
*Sleeping
Beauty* is an
example of
a waltz.

It's polka time!

The polka is a rather muscular dance in duple meter. If you've been lucky enough to dance the polka, as I have, you know that the emphasis is on the first beat of the bar, and it's a strong emphasis. Hurtling around the dance floor trying to avoid destruction at the hands, or feet, of your larger, more aggressive friends, it may be hard to discern the beat. But it's there, a strong **ONE**-two, **ONE**-two. A little bit of the famous "Beer Barrel Polka" will give you the idea (see Figure 4-27).

Figure 4-27:
A bit of the "Beer Barrel Polka," also known as "Roll Out the Barrel."

TRACK 6

Part II
The Noble Sound of the Trumpet

The 5th Wave   By Rich Tennant

D. BOYD
TRUMPET
LESSONS
2ND Floor

"Okay, did you feel that rhythm on the way down?
That's the rhythm I'm looking for."

In this part . . .

1 cover the strange art of making questionable sounds with your lips in Chapter 5. I introduce all the foundations for successful trumpet playing, including good posture, relaxed breathing, and mouthpiece buzzing. You finally get to play a note — two notes, actually — on the trumpet in Chapter 6. Flushed with success, you continue in Chapter 7 to find out about more notes and different ways to play them. Understanding articulation occupies Chapter 8, as you continue to add to the range of sounds and styles that a trumpeter can produce. Chapter 9 is a description of a good warm-up routine, something that every trumpeter needs.

Chapter 5

Making Buzzing Beautiful

Trumpet sound is created by a very simple thing, and that is the vibrating of the lips as air passes through them. It's basically a rude noise, civilized by the mouthpiece and trumpet, producing the glorious sound that is trumpet tone. But in order to make that glorious sound, you need to know a thing or two: how to breathe, how to form an embouchure, and how to buzz on the mouthpiece. In this chapter, I tell you how.

The Art of Breathing

We breathe a lot. At rest we inhale and exhale about 12 times per minute on average. So, someone who's 20 years old has already taken 126,144,000 breaths. That's a lot of breaths. You'd think we'd be pretty good at it. And we are, for normal living. A normal conversational breath is fairly shallow, but trumpet playing requires a very deep breath, like the way you inhale before diving into water. But a trumpet breath must also be relaxed, with a smooth inhale and flowing exhale. In this section, I explain how to take a good breath for the trumpet.

Posture perfect

Good posture is an important prerequisite for good breathing. A slumped posture makes it very difficult to take a big breath, because the torso isn't free to open up with the breath. Standing with your weight unevenly distributed is less stable and leads to a shallow, tense breath. In Chapter 6, I describe good playing posture in detail. For now, just stay relaxed with your weight distributed evenly between both feet (whether you're standing or seated) and with your chest up naturally and open to receive the air.

A way to set yourself up with good posture is to stand against a flat wall, with your heels, your butt, your shoulders, and the back of your head all touching the wall. Standing this way feels awkward at first, but you'll get used to it. Of course, you aren't rigid and immobile in good posture — you need to be supple but strong, straight but not stiff. Like a tree, you're rooted to the ground but able to be flexible, taking big relaxed breaths.

People's shoulders tend to be stiff and tense, largely because of stress. You probably aren't even aware that your shoulders are raised up several inches from the relaxed position. Try rolling each shoulder backward a few times, finally allowing the shoulder to drop at the bottom of a roll. You'll find that that shoulder is lower than the other one. When you repeat with the other shoulder, they look balanced. This little routine can help you discover a new, more comfortable posture.

Keeping it natural

The best advice I was ever given about breathing was to take a breath like a big sigh. Sighs have a flow, relaxation, and rhythm that make them a perfect model for trumpet breathing. Besides, what's more natural than a sigh? You already know how to do it, so you can avoid the self-consciousness that's so often a part of trumpet breathing instruction.

The sound that you make as you inhale is very important. The unforced, easy (like a sigh), windy sound of a good breath helps produce a trumpet tone with those same qualities. In fact, I tell my students that their tone is a mirror image of the breath preceding it.

Here are a few tips for practicing for good trumpet breathing:

- **The exhale of a practice or warm-up breath should be flowing and consistent.** Think of blowing out a candle — the flame should go out immediately, which will help produce a very good *attack* (the start of the note). The trumpet sound should have a very direct and quick start, with full tone right away.

- **Practice breathing with a sheet of paper in front of you.** Hold a sheet of paper a few inches in front of your face, with just a couple of fingers holding the top of the paper. Take a breath, and blow toward the paper with the goal of blowing it so the page is horizontal, parallel to the ground. Make sure to blow a relaxed stream of air — don't force it. When you succeed at that distance, move the paper a little farther away until finally you can achieve the horizontal goal when you're holding it at arm's length, as is shown in Figure 5-1.

Figure 5-1:
Blowing
a sheet
of paper
is good
practice.

- ✔ **Imagine a pendulum of a grandfather clock, swinging back and forth without stopping at either side.** Your breath should be smooth and even, just like the pendulum, with no pause between the inhale and the exhale. A good golfer knows about this rhythmic back-and-forth motion, and many trumpeters imagine a golf swing as their breathing model.

- ✔ **Breathe around the mouthpiece.** One problem that many trumpeters have is taking a big breath with the trumpet and mouthpiece right at the lips, blocking the airway. You have to breathe *around* the mouthpiece, and a good way to practice that is to place your index finger on your lips, right in the center. Open your lips a bit and inhale past your finger with an *oh* sound. Avoid stretching the corners of the mouth back in a grimace or smile. When you exhale, pretend you're blowing your finger away, pointing it outward.

Flow, not force

Just as professional athletes don't seem to be working hard out on the field or court, your goal is to make trumpet playing look and feel easy. What you're striving for is *flow,* a natural and efficient movement, like the kind that athletes, dancers, or animals in the wild have. A resonant, clear tone is the result of relaxed, flowing air, not excessive force or strain.

TRACK 7

You can tell by the sound of your breath whether it's relaxed or not. On the CD, you hear two examples of breath: The first is of a forced, strained breath; the second is a relaxed flow. Try to match the sound of that second breath.

The Embouchure: How to Hold Your Mouth

The word *embouchure* comes from the French *bouche,* for mouth. The lips and all the muscles around the mouth and cheeks are part of the embouchure. All wind-instrument players use an embouchure to guide the breath from the mouth through the lips and the mouthpiece. Embouchure shape varies a little bit from instrument to instrument and from player to player. Some general principles apply, though, and the main one is that the embouchure should be firm and stable. In this section, I tell you how to form and maintain a good trumpet embouchure.

Taking a dim view of an embouchure

Say the word *dim* and leave your lips closed: *dimmmm.* You've formed a basic embouchure (see Figure 5-2). Like many things about playing the trumpet, simple is good when it comes to forming an embouchure. The *dim* formation is the starting point and the most important thing about it is that the lips are touching.

The opening between the lips is called the *aperture.* When playing many instruments, there should be space between the lips in the basic setup. But when playing the trumpet, the aperture only forms when the lips vibrate to create the sound. The lips must start in the closed *dim* position; otherwise, the tone will be breathy and things like *range* (higher and lower notes), *articulation* (connecting notes in songs and studies), and *endurance* (how long you can play before getting tired) will all suffer.

Form a *dim* embouchure, and then blow out to your open hand. After an initial *pooh* sound, you'll notice that the muscles at the sides of your mouth firm up as a response to the flow of air. The harder you blow, the firmer these muscles will get, as long as you remember not to let the cheeks puff as you blow. Try it in front of a mirror and see how it feels and looks. That firm feeling in the cheeks beside the mouth is the beginning of your embouchure development.

Figure 5-2:
The basic embou-
chure.

Buzzing the lips for a clear sound

Now it's time to make a sound with your lips. The noise you make could be construed to be somewhat rude, but trumpeters learn to put up with this misconception. We know that it's a buzzing sound, and it can sound better or worse. You want it to sound better, and the way to do that is to keep blowing a relaxed flow of air while keeping your lips together. The air passing through your lips will create exactly the right aperture.

Form the *dim* embouchure (see the last section), and blow toward your hand. This time, keep the lips touching as you blow, lightly pressing them together. If you're lucky, you'll get a buzz right away, but I have to warn you that this step can take a few tries. Some people do well if they think of the sound *pooh* as they blow — this keeps the lips together.

TRACK 8

I can also put your mind at rest and say that there are very fine players who can't buzz their lips without the mouthpiece. In fact, some teachers discour- age buzzing the lips, and other equally qualified teachers advocate it. On the CD, you hear the sound of a good buzz. Look in a mirror as you try the buzz, watching for the embouchure firming up.

How *not* to form an embouchure

I may as well talk about Dizzy Gillespie right now and get it over with, because people ask about him all the time. He was one of the greatest musicians of the 20th century, a magnificent jazz artist, and an amazingly skillful trumpeter. But he had just about the worst embouchure of all time. He puffed his cheeks out, only a little when he started, but by the end of his career his cheeks and even his neck puffed out like a bull-frog because his face and neck muscles were damaged by years of playing.

How could he play so well with such a poor embouchure? The answer is that his musical genius was so strong that it enabled him to play brilliantly even though his technique was not at all what any teacher would recommend. His distinctive tone and amazing high notes were a product of his embouchure as well as other unique attributes. The point is: Set yourself up for success by learning to play with a strong, well-formed embouchure. No two players are exactly the same, but Dizzy Gillespie was an extreme example of uniqueness in human creativity.

If you can discover the buzz at this stage — even a slight vibration — you're ready to go to the mouthpiece.

Playing the Mouthpiece Alone

You can establish the foundation of good tone with musical mouthpiece playing. Buzzing on the mouthpiece gets you far — you can achieve good tone, accurate tuning, clear articulation, and good endurance. Beginning players find that holding the mouthpiece alone is easier than holding the trumpet. Plus, the mouthpiece is very portable, and not very loud, so you can practice on it practically anywhere.

Always play with a strong musical idea. If it's just one note, make it the most beautiful sound you can. If it's a song, make it sound tuneful and in the style of the original music. If it's a march, or a lullaby, make it sound like one.

You'll feel some resistance to the air caused by the small opening in the mouthpiece, called the *throat,* but keep blowing out easily — without forcing it. A good preparation for buzzing on the mouthpiece is to blow air through the mouthpiece, toward your hand.

Ready to make some noise? Here's how to make a clear, attractive sound — not a harsh noise.

1. **Hold the mouthpiece in your left hand and bring it up to rest on your lips.**

   The mouthpiece should rest firmly on the lips but should not press too hard.

2. **Take a big breath and blow through the mouthpiece.**

   Make sure that the rim of the mouthpiece is above the fleshy part of the upper lip (as shown in Figure 5-3). Do this several times for a few seconds each time.

TRACK 9, 0:00

3. **Listen to the CD.**

   You'll hear the first mouthpiece note demonstrated. Listen several times before you go on.

   Note: Track 9 also includes the note played on the trumpet, for a sneak peek of what's to come.

4. **Take a big breath and, as you exhale, bring your lips together and think of the *pooh* sound you made when buzzing the lips by themselves (see "Buzzing the lips for a clear sound," earlier in this chapter).**

   The combined effect is something like *oh* when you breathe in, *mm* as the lips come together, and *pooh* as you exhale: *ohmmpooh*.

   As you blow and buzz, make sure you're hearing the sound that you want, the note you heard on the CD.

Figure 5-3:
Where to
place your
mouthpiece.

Playing long tones

Musicians call long-held notes *long tones*. Long tones are practiced by all wind players, but especially by brass players. Playing long tones helps build strength in your embouchure as you make the best sound you can. Good mouthpiece tone is clear, without excess breathiness, and consistent, maintaining the same sound for the entire note.

Playing one long note can be tedious, but playing along with the CD can make it more interesting. Start by listening to the CD for a reminder of the correct pitch of the note. Make sure you're playing that pitch. (It's a G, which is the first note you'll play on the trumpet.)

TRACK 10

The piano accompaniment on the CD sounds very nice as you play the long tone. Before the CD track begins, you'll hear four clicks that give you the speed of the music, called the *tempo*. Hold the note for four counts. The piano will play with a steady tempo, clearly indicating the beats. Rest for four, and then play for four again — or for eight if you feel able to. Repeat this as often as you like, remembering to rest as much as you play. If you want to try playing other notes, feel free. Experiment. Let your ear be your guide.

Make sure your stereo is turned up loud when you start playing along with it. Otherwise, you won't be able to hear it over your own playing.

Sliding around

Imitating the sound of a siren is a useful technique for a trumpeter. Imagine sliding down to a lower note in a smooth sound, or sliding up, without any break in the sound. The musical term for this is *glissando*.

TRACK 11

After you've rested for several minutes or more, practice sliding up and down. I like to imitate various sounds — for example, a siren and a car revving. Play a G and then try to slide up or down. Listen to the CD for examples.

Keep the breath blowing smoothly as you hear a higher sound in your head. This inner hearing can be a tremendous help in becoming a good player. Think also of blowing faster air when you slide up. For a downward glissando, it helps to think of slower air while hearing the sound you want.

Using the tongue for clarity

Just as you use your tongue to talk, trumpeters use their tongues to clearly start notes and often to help connect them.

Chapter 6 devotes a lot of attention to this subject, but for now, you can keep it simple. Instead of *ohmmpooh* to start a note, change the *p* to *t*. The result is *ohmmtooh.*

TRACK 12

The CD has two examples, one with the tongue and one without the tongue. Listen carefully and then match the sound of the note started with the tongue.

TRACK 13

The tongue also helps connect notes, in what's called *articulation*. To articulate means to connect, and trumpeters connect notes without the tongue sometimes (called *slurring*) and with the tongue. Repeating *tooh* several times while blowing out a steady breath is the first step in tongued articulation. Then try it while playing a note on the mouthpiece. Listen to the CD, and copy what you hear.

The Musical Mouthpiece

The best way to improve on the mouthpiece is to play familiar songs. Because you know the song well, you have the sound in your ear. You also have a clear idea of the style — a march, a love song, a polka, a lullaby. . . .

Pick a distinctive song that has real character. If you know the music and it's interesting to play, you activate your musical ear and your focus intensifies. The songs you play shouldn't be too difficult or complicated — simple folk songs, children's songs, and easy pop tunes are great places to start.

Imagine the sound of a phone ringing. Can you hear it? Now imagine a dog barking or a cat meowing. You can hear these sounds in your head, in your imagination. That amazing ability to imagine sounds and hear them in your own inner hearing is one of the best assets that you have as a trumpeter. If you actively bring the sounds of a trumpet or a buzzing mouthpiece to your inner hearing, you have a good chance of reproducing that imagined sound as you play.

Following are examples of easy, playable mouthpiece songs. They're written out and also recorded on the CD so you can access them aurally and visually. You can play along with the CD or play them on your own, but either way, make sure to listen to the CD track first, then sing or hum the song, and finally play it on the mouthpiece. Your main goal is to have fun playing them, and play them with lots of gusto and style!

A metronome marking appears at the start of each of these songs. The marking will give you an idea of how fast or slow the piece goes. You may use a metronome if you want, or just play along with the CD. You may also just hear the music and play it the way you feel it! (For more on metronomes, see the nearby sidebar, "Marking time: The metronome.")

Take a big breath before each song, and take enough time during the songs to breathe deeply. A breath mark (either a comma or a *v*) is at each place in the music where a breath would work well. Rest between songs, too. You should rest for as much time as you play, especially at the beginning stage when your lips are getting used to buzzing.

 TRACK 14

Twinkle, Twinkle, Little Star

This famous melody was originally composed by Mozart. Use the tongue for clarity as described earlier.

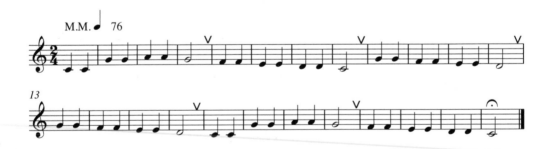

 TRACK 15

Ode to Joy

Another famous song is "Ode to Joy," from Beethoven's Ninth Symphony. It's written in a style called *cantabile,* or singing, so it should be very smooth.

Listen to the recording, and sing along, matching the smooth style, sometimes called *legato*. The curved lines under some of the notes indicate that you don't tongue at those spots, but slide to the next note.

 TRACK 16

Hot Cross Buns

This song is a popular starting tune for beginning instrumentalists. It has a smooth line and some repeated notes for tonguing practice. Keep the air blowing as you repeat the sound *tooh*. Focus on one line of air lightly tapped by the tongue.

 TRACK 17

Mexican Hat Dance

This is a lively tune. A combination of tonguing and slurring is prevalent in the music that you'll be playing on the trumpet. Whether using the tongue or not, always maintain a steady exhale.

Marking time: The metronome

The metronome is a mechanical or electronic means of setting a constant tempo and indicating that tempo aurally. Tempo is measured in *beats per minute*. The inventor of the metronome was *Maelzel,* who is remembered in every piece of music with a tempo marking: *M.M.* stands for *Maelzel's metronome.*

The old-fashioned pendulum metronomes are still used, but electronic models have taken over. Electronic metronomes have the advantage of more precise measurements of the beat, and a variety of sounds, from clicks to recorded voices. They also feature a light that flashes in time with the beat, providing visual reinforcement. The simplest option is to use an online metronome, like the one at www.metronomeonline.com.

Remember: The metronome is a tool that can give you information, but because music is played by human beings, tempos tend to vary. Don't think of a metronome as the ultimate authority on keeping time. It's really just a guideline for choosing your tempo, and a metronome can help you stay steady as you play.

Chapter 6

Sound the Trumpet!

. . . .

In This Chapter

▶ Paying attention to posture

▶ Getting a hold of the trumpet

▶ Playing your first note

▶ Working on tone and tuning

▶ Using your tongue to articulate each note

▶ Joining notes together

▶ Playing your second note

. . . .

I can remember everything about playing my first note: how it sounded, of course, but also how it felt to hold such a beautiful instrument and make such a strong sound. Everything about the trumpet was wonderful to me — *especially* the sound — and I hope you feel that way, too.

In this chapter, I show you the proper posture for playing the trumpet, because posture is critical to making the best sound possible. Then I walk you through holding the trumpet, explaining where to place both your hands. You play your first note and find out about tone and tuning. You begin to use the tongue for clear articulation. You string notes together using air, punctuated by the tongue. And finally, you play the second note, concert B♭.

Posture for Playing

Posture is important — not just because you look better when you're standing or sitting up straight, but because it helps you breathe fully and easily and hold the trumpet comfortably. In this section, I fill you in on the correct posture when you're standing up and sitting down.

Standing tall

Trumpeters often stand when performing — especially when playing a solo, in front of an orchestra or in a jazz band. The standing position is the best one for developing good breathing habits. Most trumpeters practice while standing about half the time, and sitting properly for the other half.

Here are some tips for achieving great posture when standing:

- ✔ **Stand straight yet supple, with both feet planted firmly on the floor, about shoulder width apart.** Think of a tree — a tree's roots are firmly planted, but the tree sways a little with the breeze.

- ✔ **Raise your chest in a normal, healthy position.** The sternum, or breastbone, should be in an up position. You should feel relaxed. Avoid military-style stiffness.

- ✔ **Keep your head level.** Tuck your chin down to your chest, and then tilt your head way back. Settle on a position halfway between these two extremes as your trumpet-playing position. If your head is raised too high, you'll feel tension in the neck. Looking down too low feels constricted and reduces the flow of wind as you play. You want to look expectant and ready for action.

A positive, confident posture will not only help you breathe freely but also help with your self-image as a performer. You should feel comfortable when standing.

So, how do you look and feel? Go to a full-length mirror and see, or ask someone to take a photo of you. Try to match up with the posture you see in Figure 6-1. You should feel relaxed, secure on your feet, straight but not rigid. You should look outward confidently.

Standing while seated

Sometimes I confuse my students by asking them to "stand while seated." (The great tuba player and teacher Arnold Jacobs coined this term.) My students' reaction is often, "Huh? Which is it — standing or sitting?" It makes them think a bit and they come up with the answer, which is that you should sit almost as if you were standing. "Stand while seated" helps people avoid slumping against the back of the chair.

Figure 6-1:
Proper
standing
posture.

People learn to slouch at an early age in response to the boredom and frustration of being confined to a chair for too long. If you want to see perfect posture, look at preschool kids sitting on the floor, backs straight and heads level. By first or second grade, the damage has begun — but the good news is that it's never too late to improve your posture.

To establish a good seated posture, follow these tips:

✔ Sit toward the front of the chair, without leaning back.

✔ Plant both feet firmly on the ground, about shoulder width apart.

Sitting tall, as if standing, keeps the torso open to receive a full breath. This position also ensures that the bell of the trumpet will be pointed outward, rather than down at the floor. Proper sitting posture helps produce good tone by encouraging a deep breath and focusing your sound directly toward the listener.

Figure 6-2 shows you the front and side views of a good seated posture.

Figure 6-2:
Proper
seated
posture,
front and
side views.

Holding the Trumpet

After you've perfected your posture, you're ready to hold the trumpet. The way that you hold the trumpet has a big impact on how you play. A relaxed hand position helps your arms and shoulders stay supple, leading to a more relaxed breath and better use of the valves.

You'll be holding your trumpet for many minutes at a time in the playing position, so the more relaxed and comfortable you are, the better.

Placing the left hand

The left hand bears most of the weight of the trumpet, because the right hand has to be free to manipulate the valves. If you think of cradling the trumpet with the left hand, you'll have the right idea.

The following steps will set up your left-hand position:

1. **Make your hand into a *V* shape, as shown in Figure 6-3.**

   Your fingers are together and the thumb is extended so you form a right angle between your thumb and fingers.

2. **Put the left hand against the valve section, with the thumb and fingers under the bell, as shown in Figure 6-4.**

Figure 6-3:
The left
hand
making a
V shape.

Figure 6-4:
The thumb
and fingers
under the
bell section,
against
the valve
casing.

3. **Curl the fingers in around the valve casing and leave the thumb in the up position.**

    This position will keep you from gripping the valves too hard, which leads to tension in the arm and shoulder and, ultimately, in the sound.

    On most trumpets, there is a ring soldered onto the third valve slide. For most people, the ring finger goes comfortably through this ring (refer to Figure 6-7). If you have large hands, you might instead put your middle finger through the ring, with your ring finger and pinky underneath (see Figure 6-5). If you have smaller hands, you might put your middle finger through the ring and the ring and pinky finger on top (see Figure 6-6). Experiment to see what's comfortable and which position enables you to move the slide (see Chapter 7 for information about using the slide).

4. **Bring the trumpet up so the mouthpiece touches your lips, remembering not to lean forward toward the trumpet.**

    Your arm should be at about a 45-degree angle, not too horizontal (which is much too tiring) or too vertical (which is tight and confining). Figure 6-7 shows the left hand and arm position.

Always bring the trumpet to you. This sounds obvious but many players seem to bend toward the trumpet, wrapping their hands tightly around it as if trying to keep it from escaping.

Figure 6-5:
If your hands are larger, you may want to put your middle finger through the ring.

Figure 6-6:
If your hands are smaller, you can put your ring and pinky finger on top.

Figure 6-7:
The left hand holding the trumpet, with the correct arm angle.

Placing the right hand

Your right hand's main job is not to hold the trumpet, but to play the valves, so the fingers need to be free to move quickly up and down, positioned so that the index finger is over the first valve cap (the one closest to you) and your middle and ring fingers are on the second and third valves.

Here's how to place the right hand on the trumpet:

1. **Curve your index, middle, and ring fingers, resting the pads at the tops of the fingers on the valves.**

2. **Hold your little finger curved in the air.**

   Imagine you're holding a fancy teacup at the queen's garden party.

   Don't put your little finger in the little finger hook. It'll add tension, and you'll be inclined to pull the trumpet toward you, pressing against your lips too hard. (When you're turning pages, inserting or removing a mute [see Chapter 19], or just holding your trumpet, you can put your little finger in the hook. That's its real purpose.)

3. **Curve your thumb, with the tip resting between the first and second valves, just under the leadpipe.**

   As you look down at your hand, you should see a backward C made by your thumb and fingers.

The little trumpet in your head: How to always sound great

Playing the trumpet, like any skill, can't succeed without an idea of what you want to achieve. Imagine being led into a dark room, holding a dart in your hand, and being told to hit the bull's-eye. Well, *what* bull's-eye? Where's the target? Your chances of success wouldn't be great — in fact, they'd be just about zero. But if the lights are on and you see the target, your chances increase exponentially.

You see where I'm going with this: If you have a clear idea of the sound you want to make on the trumpet, your chances of making it are dramatically better than if you aren't hearing anything in your head.

Arnold Jacobs, the great brass teacher and tuba virtuoso with the Chicago Symphony Orchestra, summarized this learning strategy of developing a clear mental image, by telling his students to "Play the little trumpet in your head." Jacobs advised his students to avoid overanalyzing their playing, focusing instead on the sound they wanted to make.

The better that you imagine your trumpet sound to be, the better your chances are of producing an actually great tone. So, listen to a lot of fine players, on recordings, at concerts, on TV — wherever you hear trumpets. Do this very diligently and you'll develop your inner trumpet sound. The results will be heard every time you play.

Figure 6-8 shows how your right hand should look when holding the trumpet.

The result of all your preparation is that the trumpet is firmly but comfortably supported by the left hand, and the right fingers are resting on the three valves, curved like a backward C, with the thumb under the leadpipe and the little finger floating in the air. If the right hand is too involved with carrying the weight of the instrument, it'll be tense and not supple enough to efficiently work the valves.

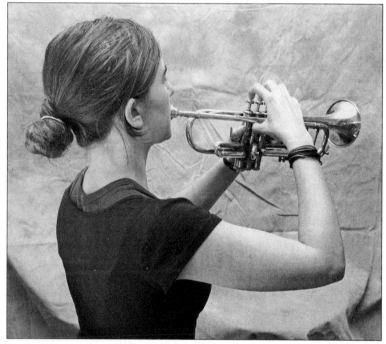

Figure 6-8:
Proper
right-hand
position.

First Note G: Home Base

The second line of the treble clef is G. (Refer to Chapter 4 if you need a musical refresher.) The treble clef is also called the G clef, because the little curl at the bottom encircles the second line. The note G is a great place to start because it's neither too high nor too low. G also can be the starting point for warm-ups and practice sessions because it's relaxing to play and very secure.

You don't have to push down any valves to play G, either, so you can concentrate on the sound. (When you have no valves down, this position is called *open.*) You can practice your excellent hand positions, both left and right. Because there are no valves down for this note, your right hand can rest lightly on the valve caps as I describe in the section, "Holding the Trumpet," earlier in this chapter.

This is the moment you've been waiting for: You're almost ready to play your first note, to join the trumpeters' club. Take these steps before you play your first note:

TRACK 9, 0:06

1. **Listen to the G on the CD and buzz that note with just the mouthpiece (see Chapter 5).**

   Your lips should be well together, as in the word *dim*.

2. **Place the mouthpiece into the mouthpiece receiver. Insert the shank of the mouthpiece and rotate a quarter turn.**

   Never jam the mouthpiece into the receiver — it can become stuck, requiring a trip to the repair shop.

3. **Sit tall, as if standing, with a straight back, both feet on the floor and a level head.**

4. **Hold the trumpet firmly but without tension.**

5. **Take a big, relaxed breath, like a sigh.**

6. **Listen again to the G played on the CD (see Step 1).**

Now you're ready to play. Holding the trumpet correctly, take a big breath, put your lips together (think of the word *dim*), and play the note shown in Figure 6-9.

The dot with the curved line over it is a musical device called a *fermata*. Notes under a fermata are held until your conductor cuts you off (it's sometimes called "the conductor's eye"), until you want to stop, or until need to take a breath.

Figure 6-9:
Your first
note, G.

Bravo! Welcome to the trumpet world!

The next exercise (see Figure 6-10) will help you to gain consistent control in playing G. Make sure to take time to rest as indicated in the figure.

Play with a sound that is neither too loud nor too soft. A nice relaxed tone is what you're after.

Figure 6-10:
G with different note lengths and rests.

Rest as much as you play, especially at the beginning stage, but even as you become more experienced. Your lips will become too tired to buzz properly, and you can even do serious damage to the muscles and nerves of your lips if you don't rest enough. At first, you may feel a tingling sensation in your lips, even after just a few seconds. That's perfectly normal at the beginning stages — it's a signal to you to take a little break, and let your lips rest. You may put the trumpet away for several hours or even for the day. Gradually, your lips will get used to buzzing and your embouchure will strengthen.

While you're resting, you can listen to the *Trumpet For Dummies* CD or another recording of an inspiring player. You can also take a few deep, relaxed breaths, imagining yourself blowing out a candle. Short practice sessions, a few times a day, will gradually help your lips get used to playing.

Repeat the short exercises in this section once or twice a day for several days, making sure that you're sounding clear and relaxed. It's important that you try to play with a beautiful sound right from the beginning, but of course your first sounds may be rough or pinched. You may even have some difficulty getting a sound at first.

I know you may want to charge ahead and play more notes right away, but you're building a foundation and it takes time and patience. Physical development is required in playing these and the later notes. Your embouchure muscles have never been required to work like this before, and the lip tissue in contact with the mouthpiece needs to get toughened up a bit. So, don't try to rush this early stage of your trumpet career.

Tone and Tuning

After you've played the exercises in the preceding section a few times, with plenty of rest in between, you're ready to start thinking about two things: tone and tuning. *Tone* is the sound that you make, your personal voice on the trumpet, and *tuning* means playing in tune. I cover both topics and their relationship to each other in the following sections.

Good trumpet tone

Musical instruments were inspired by the human voice, so a beautiful singing or speaking voice can be a guide in understanding what good tone is on the trumpet. Like a lovely voice, trumpet tone should be clear, melodious, strong, and never harsh.

Don't try to play too loudly — think of wind flow not force.

Keep your lips close together. If your lips are too far apart, you'll hear breathiness, like static on the radio. Bring the lips together as if saying *dim*.

As always, take a full relaxed breath and blow out smoothly, as if blowing out a candle.

How to tune your trumpet

Tuning, also called *playing in tune,* is something that most people can recognize, even without musical training. Another way of saying "accurate tuning" is the term *good intonation.*

What you need to know as a trumpeter is how to play a sound slightly *sharper* (higher) or *flatter* (lower). A flat note tends to have an unpleasant sound, which many teachers call "tubby." A sharp note sounds tight and constrained, or "pinched." So, tone and tuning are united in the way they sound — if you play in tune, your sound will be better, and vice versa. The CD gives you the pitch to aim for, so when I give you a track number, listen to it closely and try to match it exactly.

TRACK 18

On the CD, you hear some examples of sharp and flat notes. The first note is in tune, with a centered sound, the second note is flat and tubby, and the third note is sharp and pinched. Finally, the well tuned and centered note is played again.

Here are some tips to keep in mind to help you play in tune:

✔ **Try to keep the lips close together.** The *dim* shape works very well. If your lips are too far apart, you'll sound flat. You can experiment with this by bringing your lips closer together and then farther apart while holding your G. See if you notice the pitch going up and then down.

✔ **Remember to blow freely.** You'll tend to sound flatter if you aren't blowing enough wind. A way to think of it is to imagine the speedometer of a car. If you blow faster wind, you can think of the speedometer as showing a faster speed. This technique helps your tuning, as well as your tone.

✔ **Hold your trumpet roughly parallel to the floor.** I say "roughly" because everyone holds the trumpet at a slightly different angle depending on the teeth and jaw. Make sure you're comfortable and that the trumpet is pointing out, or slightly angled down, but not aimed at the floor.

✔ **Play with a medium-loud sound.** The musical term for that is *mezzo forte,* and it's a good place to start when developing good sound. If you play too loudly, your tone will sound forced and you'll probably play sharp.

Another way to tell if your tone sounds good is to watch the people in your vicinity. If they quickly move farther away, you probably need to listen for a nicer tone!

✔ **Adjust the tuning slide.** In Chapter 2, I describe the tuning slide, which connects to the leadpipe. The tuning slide must be pulled slightly out, about ½ inch. You'll learn to adjust this slide more carefully as you play more, but the position I describe is the place to start.

Starting Notes with the Tongue

When you play any wind instrument, you use your tongue to clearly start notes, just as when you speak you use your tongue to articulate consonants. If you say *too-too-too-too-too-too-too* with one breath of air, you have the perfect model for trumpet tonguing.

Blow a consistent stream of wind through the lips, tapping the tongue against the *hard palate* (the spot behind the teeth where you put your tongue when you say a word like *two* or *heat*) as you blow. Hold your open hand a few inches in front of your mouth, and aim the wind toward the middle of your palm. You should feel the pulsating air. Practice this preparation for clear tonguing until it feels comfortable.

Breath attacks

Starting the tone with breath alone is an important step toward learning to start with the tongue. The air must be moving well enough that it can start a good sound. If you rely on the tongue to release the air, you'll get tonguing that's too heavy. This is a very common problem with young trumpet students, so the breath attack is a valuable technique.

Blow the air as if you're blowing out a candle. Make the flame go out instantly, but without undue force. (You don't want to splatter candle wax all over the place!) Repeat this exercise on G (see Figure 6-11), with lots of candle blowing, many times, until you produce a clear tone each time. Make sure that your lips are touching. (Think *dim.*)

Figure 6-11:
Breath
attacks
on G.

Adding the tongue

After you achieve consistent, clear starts with breath attacks, you can begin to add the tongue. Instead of *whoo,* make it *tooh* (rhyming with Winnie the Pooh). Repeat the pattern *whoo-whoo-tooh* many times, as in Figure 6-12.

Figure 6-12:
Adding the
tongue.

Your guide as to whether you're doing it correctly is the sound. Is it clear? Does the tone start immediately? If you have an airy start or a delayed attack, your lips could be too far apart. A big accent at the beginning of the note could mean that your air is too powerful, almost an explosion, or that your tongue is holding the air back before the start of the note. Finally, coordinating the start of the wind with the stroke of the tongue is one of the early challenges in trumpet playing.

Repeat this exercise many times, remembering to rest at least as much as you play. You may experience a tingling sensation in the lips — that's the time to rest. Lip strength builds up slowly and gradually.

Don't play loudly. A relaxed medium-loud tone *(mezzo forte)* just like what you hear on the CD is what you're aiming for.

Connecting Notes

There are two basic ways that we connect notes: *slurring* (without the tongue) and *tonguing*. Both are vital to the tool kit of a good trumpeter. When you slur two notes together, you blow smoothly, hear the new note, and move the valve quickly. If the slur is between two notes with the same fingering, you hear the notes and blow — simple as that! A curved line over or under the notes tells you that a slur is called for.

You're now ready to connect notes together, using breath, while tonguing each one. This is a basic skill that will let you play a lot of music. The term *articulation* is the overall word for connecting notes. Just as in speaking, the trumpeter's tongue taps the hard palate. Remember to prepare for this technique by holding your hand about 6 inches in front of your face and blowing a stream of air toward it. When you add the tongue, you'll feel the wind pulsating against your palm. I tell my students to say "twenty-two thousand two hundred and twenty-two" or "tooh-tooh-tooh-tooh-tooh."

A long tone is simply a sustained note. Because you're playing only one note, you can focus on making your most beautiful sound and staying nicely in tune.

When you tongue, you're simply tapping a long tone. On the CD, you hear a single tone held for two counts and then the same tone with the addition of four taps of the tongue, followed by another half note. After you listen to the CD, play the same exercise (shown in Figure 6-13) several times, aiming for a clear *mezzo forte* sound and consistent taps of the tongue. Keep the tone just as clear and in tune when you tongue as when you play a simple long tone.

TRACK 19

Figure 6-13: Repeated notes.

When you tongue, you may find that your embouchure moves with each stroke of the tongue. If you suspect that this is happening, just go to the nearest mirror and check. The goal is to move the tongue in a fast stroke, saying *tooh* without the jaw and lips moving. Looking in the mirror can help.

The Second Note: Low C

Life as a trumpeter is about to get more diverse and interesting. You've established a clear tone on the note G and learned to start the note and start repeated notes using the tongue. Now you get to add a new note: low C. Like G, low C is played with no valves down.

You need to hear the note before you play it, so start by listening to the CD (see Figure 6-14). Blow slower air, and remember to keep the embouchure firm. After you've listened to the CD track, play the exercise shown in Figure 6-14.

TRACK 20

Figure 6-14:
Playing low C.

TRACK 21

The other thing that you can do is buzz on the mouthpiece alone, sliding down from G to C. You can use a keyboard or piano to help you with the pitch. The CD demonstrates that technique.

Figure 6-15 is a little exercise using the first two notes, low C and G. Keep the embouchure firm and listen for the correct pitch. It helps to sing the music first.

TRACK 22

Figure 6-15:
Music for home-base G and low C.

Chapter 7

Adding More Notes, Making More Music

*I*n the previous chapter, you learn to play G and C, but making music on the trumpet (or any other instrument) is pretty difficult with only two notes. In this chapter, you add several new notes and play some more songs and *etudes* (tuneful pieces written to address a particular technique). I explain how to connect notes with just air, and how to use the valves to increase the number of notes you can play. Playing scales is something that all musicians do, and I introduce you to that part of trumpeting. Finally, I invite you to play some well-known tunes that have been part of the trumpet world for generations.

Repetition is key when learning an instrument, so going over the material from Chapters 5 and 6 will help solidify your technique and strengthen your embouchure. Each day as you begin to practice, it's a good idea to go through the steps of buzzing the mouthpiece and playing G and C. You can play the mouthpiece songs in Chapter 5 any time, and you can always add your own favorite songs.

Sit or stand with good posture (see Chapter 6) and breathe deeply and easily.

He's the boogie-woogie bugle boy of Company B

The bugle and its forebears have been around a long time. The bugle (see the photograph) is a compact, tightly wound, conical-bore, trumpet-like instrument, with a mouthpiece and a bell. As soon as brass could be shaped into tubes and folded, bugles became the army's chosen signaling instrument, replacing the animal horns and wooden or bone lip-reed instruments of antiquity. The pitches used in signaling are the notes of the overtone series (see Chapter 2). The familiar "Taps" of the U.S. Army and "Last Post" of the British and Canadian armies both have their counterparts in all countries of the world.

How those cavalry buglers managed to play while riding a galloping horse is a miracle! Believe me, playing a brass instrument while marching or riding a horse takes a lot of practice, and even then it doesn't sound very good. We can thank the great studio trumpeters in Hollywood, sitting in very stable chairs, for those bugle calls we hear in the movies.

Signaling wasn't just for the military, though. Post horns announced the arrival of the coach carrying the mail. Hunting horns helped locate the poor fox. These instruments share the same overtone series and many of the same calls as the bugle. One of the most popular bugle calls is the fanfare announcing the next horse race at the track. After the call, we hear "And they're off!" — that's if we frequent racetracks. (Trumpeters generally are at home practicing and far too busy for that sort of thing.)

Changing Notes Using Wind

Blowing faster wind will help you play higher notes. By propelling air out of your mouth at a faster rate, you speed up the vibrations of your lips and enable the sounding of higher pitches. Trumpeters call exercises in which you change notes using wind *flexibilities.*

Faster wind is half the requirement; the other half is hearing the note you want to play. For example, if you're playing a low C and you want to go up to a G, hear the G clearly and blow faster wind. Try it! If you were successful, bravo! If you had some trouble, make sure that your lips are firm and that your low C has a centered tone. Then hear the G and blow faster wind.

TRACK 23

In this section, you add a third note to your repertoire. This is a third-space C, an octave above the low C that you've already played. First, to prepare you for the trumpet technique, take your mouthpiece alone. Listen to the CD to get the pitches, and then play a mouthpiece G, hear the higher C, and blow faster wind. Listen for the siren sound (glissando) that you play in Chapter 5 as you ascend to the C.

Some trumpeters call third-space C "high C," but it isn't high — it's actually in the comfortable middle range of the trumpet.

Playing these two notes on the trumpet is easy in one way: You don't have to change the fingering. But it also can be difficult, because you'll feel some resistance to changing notes. This is where hearing the new pitch comes in. If you hear the pitch in your head and blow faster wind, just as you did with the mouthpiece alone, the small adjustments in embouchure and oral cavity will happen naturally and appropriately, enabling the change.

The exercise in Figure 7-1 will help you gain confidence and consistency in changing notes using wind. Starting on G should feel comfortable to you by now, because it was your first note.

Figure 7-1:
Your first
flexibility
exercise.

TRACK 24

TRACK 25

Take some time to rest your lips, and maybe listen to some great trumpet playing from your ever-growing CD collection. Then take the mouthpiece again and slur from a G down to a low C, and back up to the G, again after listening to, and even playing along with the CD.

Here's another flexibility exercise (see Figure 7-2): Listen to the CD first, and then copy the sound. Your home base, G, is the starting point. Then you slur down to low C, back up to G, and then to third-space C.

TRACK 26

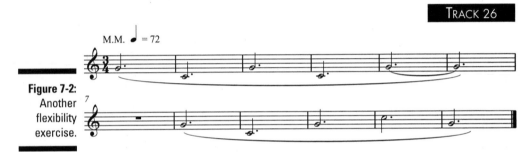

Figure 7-2: Another flexibility exercise.

Adding Notes Using the Valves

This is the fun part — you finally get to use the valves! You've established a good tone on the mouthpiece and on the first three open notes that trumpeters use. These three open notes are part of the overtone series (see Chapter 2). The addition of the valves adds much more scope to trumpet playing.

Hold your home-base G for a long tone — say, 10 seconds. After you have a nice steady tone, lower the second valve. Be sure to push the valve down all the way, very quickly. Don't change anything else, just the valve. You'll hear a very nice F♯. Now look at your valves. Notice that the slide connected to the second valve is the shortest one. By lowering the valve, you open a channel into that slide, lengthening the trumpet and, with it, the vibrating column of air. A longer tube means a lower note.

Each valve lengthens the trumpet by a specific, fixed amount. The second valve lowers any open note by a semitone. This is the smallest pitch measurement used in almost all the music we play. The first valve is twice as long, so it lowers any open note by two semitones or one tone. The third valve is the longest — it lowers any open note by three semitones, also called a minor third.

Having only three valves means that using them in combination is necessary. Lowering, no valves, or one, two or all three of the valves at the same time gives you a total of seven different combinations. (The third valve is not normally used by itself.) Figure 7-3 shows the seven valve combinations. This sequence has been used by trumpeters for about 175 years.

Figure 7-3:
The seven valve combinations.

Now it's time to practice the valve combinations. In the next exercise, you'll start on home-base G, and add valves to play different notes. Listen to the CD before you play the exercise shown in Figure 7-4.

Press the valves straight down, very quickly. Moving the valves slowly produces a bending of the pitch that is used by jazz trumpeters and others for expressive effect, but the basic technique is a quick stroke so the valve depresses instantly. Keep a steady flow of wind as you change the valves. The effect should be as smooth as a singer changing notes.

TRACK 27

Figure 7-4:
Practicing the valve positions.

The valves have to move quickly, but the sound has to stay smooth. This requires some practice: A fast stroke of the valves could cause a change in the trumpet position and a resulting disruption of the sound. The quickness of your finger stroke on the valve has to be accompanied by steady wind flow and by a very firm left-hand hold on the trumpet against your lips. The stable left hand and embouchure, plus the consistent flow of wind, are crucial in every aspect of trumpet playing. The right hand has to be relaxed, not gripping the instrument in a tense way, but stable enough that the finger action is efficient.

You can practice the valve changes without playing. This is a good way to rest your chops for a while and get some necessary practice on the fingerings. (Trumpeters call their lips and embouchure muscles their *chops*. In fact, having chops has become a widely-used term for being able to do anything well. Everybody copies trumpet players.)

Here are some tips to keep in mind as you practice:

✔ **Put the thumb of the right hand between the first and second valve casings, just under the leadpipe.**

✔ **Curve the fingers, resting the pads on the valve caps.**

✔ **Keep the little finger free of the finger hook, as contrary as it sounds.** The finger hook is there for holding the trumpet with the right hand only, while turning pages or putting a mute into the bell or just standing around. But when you play, keep the little finger free!

Filling in the Gaps: The Chromatic Scale

You now have a lot more scope as a trumpeter. Instead of being limited to just the open notes, as is the case with the bugle, you can connect those open notes with the help of the valves.

The overtone series is also known as the harmonic series of overtones. The terms *overtone, partial,* and *harmonic* tend to be used interchangeably in music, even though their meanings are slightly different. The fundamental and each of the overtones are all partials, but a harmonic is very specifically a multiple of the fundamental frequency. Because trumpeters use these terms a lot, and not strictly accurately, it's helpful for you to realize that an overtone, a harmonic, and a partial are the same thing for a trumpeter.

Connecting the open notes

The first three open notes, or harmonics, that trumpeters use are middle C, G, and third-space C. You can join those harmonics and play a complete scale in semitones; this is called the *chromatic scale*.

The chromatic scale consists of 12 semitones. A musical scale fills in the gap between an octave. The first chromatic scale that a trumpeter usually learns connects middle C and third-space C. You've learned the necessary fingerings to fill in the octave, but the extra requirement for a trumpeter is to blow a steady flow of wind and maintain a firm embouchure. The way that you practiced joining the open notes with air has to be continued while you manipulate the valves.

The exercise in Figure 7-5 will enable you to learn the fingerings of the chromatic scale while maintaining the necessary wind flow.

TRACK 28

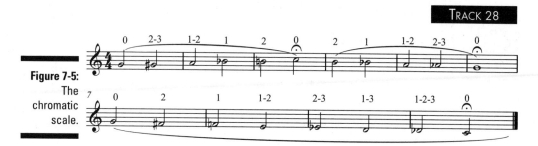

Figure 7-5: The chromatic scale.

Combining valve positions with the overtone series

Trumpet players love to practice, and one of our favorite pastimes is playing open-note slurs, or *flexibilities* (see "Changing Notes Using Wind," earlier in this chapter). You can combine the chromatic fingerings with flexibilities to further develop your trumpet skills as well as your embouchure and wind production. When you become proficient at the exercise that follows, you can start inventing different patterns of your own.

Even though you're moving to higher or lower notes, you can always think of a horizontal flow of sound. Musicians are very concerned with the musical line. Even though there are high and low notes, a connected line is the most important consideration. If you blow a steady flow of air, thinking of a horizontal direction, with the sound always moving farther away from you, the changes from higher notes to lower notes, or vice versa, become much more playable and sound better, too.

In the exercise in Figure 7-6, your inner hearing is your most important guide. If you hear the intervals clearly and, of course, blow a steady flow of wind, you'll be able to smoothly connect the notes in the repeated musical figures. This exercise is not great music in itself, but if you can play these combinations of notes smoothly, you'll be able to use this technique to play many lovely tunes.

Listen to the CD before you play the exercise shown in Figure 7-6 — this will help you hear what you want to achieve.

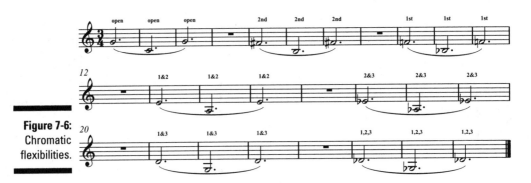

Figure 7-6:
Chromatic
flexibilities.

Scaling the Heights of Technique

Included in the heading of this section — "Scaling the Heights of Technique" — are three aspects of playing the trumpet. Each is important to your development, and they're combined in the practice of scales.

✔ **Scales:** A *scale* in music is a series of notes, usually connecting octaves. Your first scale was a chromatic scale connecting middle C and third-space C. There are different types of scales. In this section, I introduce the *diatonic scale* to add to the chromatic one you've just played. In a chromatic scale, each step is a semitone, but in a diatonic scale, tones and semitones both appear. This sounds very technical, but if you think back to doh-re-mi-fa-so-la-ti-doh, it'll be much more familiar. (You can find more information on how music is organized in Chapter 4.)

✔ **Heights:** *Heights* refers to increasing your range. Playing higher on the trumpet is a skill that takes time. Hearing the higher notes before you play them is very helpful, as is remembering to blow faster air as you ascend. Through regular practice the muscles of the embouchure will get stronger.

✔ **Technique:** *Technique* is an all-encompassing term that basically means "how you play the trumpet." The quick fingers on the valves that you've been working on are included in technique, as is moving those valves efficiently while blowing a steady stream of wind.

In this section, I introduce three scales — C, F, and G — which go a long way toward helping you play some interesting and fun songs. Some scale studies, which use the notes of a particular scale to form an interesting technique-building piece, are followed by some songs using the notes of your new scales.

The C scale

Let's prepare for the C scale gradually. Home-base, G, is always a great place to start, and G is the middle of your new scale. So, why not start in the middle?

Some beginning trumpeters have trouble getting from a G up to a third-space C. In the "Changing Notes Using Wind" section, earlier in this chapter, you play from G up to C using faster wind. Review this technique, playing from G to C several times, just using the wind.

It's also good to fill in the interval between G and C with the chromatic fingerings, remembering to keep blowing faster wind as you go up. So, practice the top part of the C chromatic scale a few times, from G to C.

The next step is to go from home-base G down to middle C. First, slur down, blowing out smoothly while hearing the notes clearly in your head. Then play the bottom half of the chromatic scale, down to C. Remember to blow out with a horizontal image of the air stream. Think out, not down.

Now you're ready for a C scale. You're going to play a major scale, which is a diatonic (not a chromatic) scale.

All these terms may be confusing, but it's important to understand what you're playing. Remember that diatonic scales employ a combination of tones and semitones, while chromatic scales use only semitones.

Slurring the C scale

I remember when I played my first C scale. It was very exciting, especially when I realized that I could play a lot of songs with those notes!

Have fun with the exercise in Figure 7-7. Learning to play scales with a consistent sound and accurate intonation is a major step in becoming a good trumpeter. It's the musical equivalent of learning the alphabet — after you've mastered some scales, a whole vocabulary of music-making awaits you! *Remember:* Hear the sound that you want and remember to blow consistently. And listen to the CD to help guide your inner concept.

TRACK 30

Figure 7-7: The C scale, slurred.

Playing a scale study

A scale study uses the notes of the scale you're working on and gives you more experience with the scale. The scale study in Figure 7-8 starts on a G, goes up to a C, and then goes all the way down and back up again. The whole exercise is played without tonguing, with a slurred articulation. You only tongue the first note, and then the first notes after a breath.

Take lots of time with the exercise in Figure 7-8, making sure you have the correct fingerings. Always remember to breathe deeply and in a relaxed way, just like a big sigh. The CD track will help guide your efforts.

TRACK 31

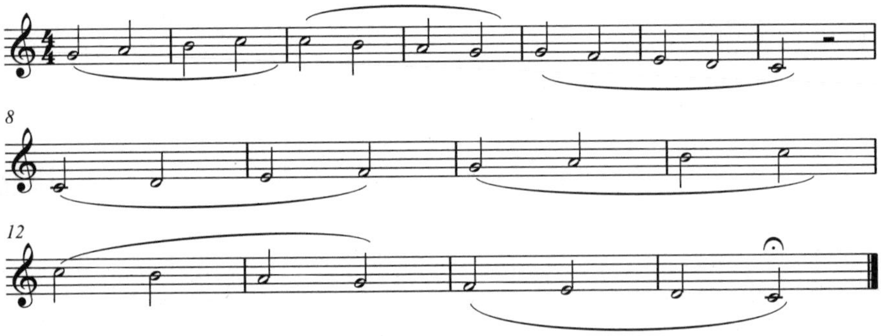

Figure 7-8:
Scale study
in C.

F and G: The closest neighbors

As I mention in Chapter 4, the key of C has no sharps or flats. The next two scales will be the keys that are closest to C — F, with one flat, and G, with one sharp. As you learn more scales, you're expanding your range higher and learning a few new notes. You're also continuing to improve your tone and intonation.

Learning the trumpet involves physical as well as musical development. Take time to rest. While resting, you can read other parts of this book and listen to the accompanying CD, or listen to a CD of a performer you admire. Listening to great trumpeters will inspire your efforts.

Going up: The F scale

First-space F is a comfortable note to start on — plus, it's very familiar to you. The upper half of the F scale goes into uncharted territory, however, and you need some preparation. Take your mouthpiece alone and buzz an F, after checking pitch with your trumpet or on a piano.

F on the trumpet is an E♭ on the piano.

Then slide upward, with the siren sound you worked on in Chapter 5. With a firm embouchure and faster air, go as high as comfortably possible, and then slide back down. Do this several times. The only note that is different from the key of C is B♭.

Practice the scale study in Figure 7-9, but be patient. If you're having trouble going up to the F, play only as high as feels and sounds good. If the sound is strained and you aren't blowing freely, it's time to rest and then work slowly toward your goal. Feel free at this stage to play the lower octave, jumping down to the low D, E, and F.

TRACK 32

Figure 7-9:
Scale study
in the key
of F.

Going down: The G scale

Balance is important in trumpet playing, as in most things. If you've been trying to extend your upper range for a while, the next thing you can do is move downward toward the lower register. The lower notes are physically easier and somewhat less stressful, so some low-register work can help you relax.

The G scale (see Figure 7-10) shares most of the notes of the C scale, except for F♯. I want to warn you that distinguishing between F and F♯ (first valve versus second valve) is a challenge for some students. The best approach is to listen for how you want the music to sound. Choosing the correct fingering is much easier when the decision is based on what you want to hear as opposed to simply trying to remember a valve position.

When you're descending, continue to blow outward in a horizontal line of sound. This helps you to keep your embouchure firm and consistent, and gives the low notes lots of air.

TRACK 33

Figure 7-10:
Scale study
in the key
of G.

The key of D adds one more sharp, with the notes F and C being raised a semitone. The fingering 1-2-3 for C♯ needs the extended third slide to be in tune. Push your ring finger in the third slide ring out about ½ inch to make it sound right.

Playing Around with Songs in C, F, and D

You work to learn new notes and scales so that you can enjoy the fruits of your labor. Scales are the alphabet of the language of music. The more musical "words" you can say and spell, the more stories you can tell.

 TRACK 34

Oh, When the Saints

"Oh, When the Saints" is a song in the key of C that you've probably heard many times. Originally a hymn, this is a famous jazz standard.

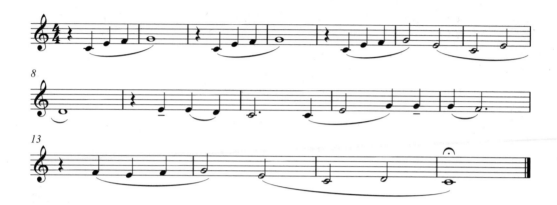

TRACK 35

Prince of Denmark's March

"Prince of Denmark's March" is a song in the key of F. It's a famous trumpet tune, very popular as a wedding favorite. Remember to play B♭ with the first valve.

Jeremiah Clarke

All through the Night

"All through the Night" is a familiar song in the key of D. This will explore the lower register of the trumpet. Listen to the CD carefully to establish your concept of the song before you play it.

Chapter 8

Becoming Articulate on the Trumpet

*T*his chapter is aimed at developing your articulation, both slurring and tonguing, and both techniques in combination. Joining notes together in music is like speaking in smooth sentences; both increase good communication. Different styles of tonguing are included here, with some songs at the end so you can apply what you've learned.

Tapping the Flow: Basic Tonguing

In Chapter 7, you use the tongue to start some notes. In this section, you focus more on that skill.

Keep in mind the following pointers:

✔ **A steady stream of wind is the most important element of tonguing.** Keep the wind blowing steadily while the tongue taps the spot where you say any *t* sound like *two* or *heat.*

✔ **The stroke of the tongue needs to be very quick.** For initial attacks, your breath in and out sounds like *ohhtoo* — in (ohh) and out (to) without a pause between the inhale and the exhale, just like a big sigh.

- ✓ **For repeated notes, think of two parallel systems: a stream of air and a tapping tongue.** Start with a stream of air, and add the tongue, using the palm of your hand as a target, and feeling the pulsating wind on your palm. The tongue must move independently, without influencing the steady air flow.

- ✓ **Make sure that the jaw and lips don't move when you tongue.** Practice some air trumpet (see the nearby sidebar) while looking in a mirror to ensure that your tongue stroke is efficient. You can use a mirror when practicing trumpet or mouthpiece alone.

- ✓ **Coordinating the tongue with the valve changes takes slow, deliberate practice.** Imagine that your tongue is located in your fingers as they bang down the valves. And, of course, you must maintain the steady flow of air.

Tonguing on one note

You can now combine the *long tones* in Chapter 5 (on the mouthpiece) and Chapter 6 (on the trumpet) with repeated note tonguing. Figure 8-1 is an exercise that you can play on air trumpet, on the mouthpiece, and on the real trumpet.

Always take a big, relaxed breath and blow out steadily, remembering that the inhale and exhale should have a pleasant, windy sound. Take plenty of time to rest in the bars with the fermata (see Chapter 6) over the rest. Rest for as much time as you took to play the preceding part of the exercise. Listen to the CD several times before playing the exercise in Figure 8-1.

For more practice, you can play the same pattern with each of the seven valve combinations: 0, 2, 1, 1-2, 2-3, 1-3, and 1-2-3.

Rocking out on the air trumpet

You've seen kids (and adults) playing the air guitar, right? It's a way to get into the music without the challenge of playing the real instrument. You can use the same technique and motivation to practice articulation. If you just blow air, while pretending to hold a trumpet and moving the fingers as if they were on the valves, you can "play" any song and get the tongue, fingers, and wind all working together. "Happy Birthday" works well for this technique, but many other tunes you like will do the trick. And you can play the air trumpet late at night or even in public (as long as you don't mind people thinking that you're weird) because it makes very little noise. There's just the quiet sound of a relaxed sigh, punctuated by articulation.

TRACK 37

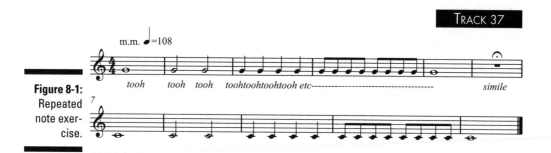

Figure 8-1:
Repeated note exercise.

tooh   tooh   tooh   toohtoohtoohtooh etc----------------------------------   simile

Changing notes while tonguing

You need to learn how to tongue on more than one note, because, thankfully for the survival of music as we know it, music is written with changing pitches.

Changing the speed of the wind, keeping a firm embouchure, and hearing the new note give you a clear tone and clean change of notes.

Adding the tongue and learning to coordinate the changing of the note with the stroke of the tongue (see Figure 8-2) is an important task requiring slow practice. Starting on home-base G and slurring down to middle C refreshes the skills found in Chapter 7 and sets you up for successful tonguing in the second half of the exercise. Listen to the CD a few times to form a clear sound image of what and how you're trying to play.

TRACK 38

Figure 8-2:
Changing notes and tonguing.

Different Strokes: Tonguing Techniques

There's more than one way to tongue, and a good trumpeter should learn at least three basic styles:

- **Legato** is the basic style that you've been working on. Most of the music that you'll play is in this smooth, connected style.

- **Marcato,** or accented, is like legato in that the notes are connected, but different in a well-marked, weighty style.

- **Staccato** means literally half the length of the written note, so a written quarter note will sound like an eighth note, and an eighth note like a sixteenth. Staccato usually is found in light, nonaccented music.

In this section, I give you more specifics on these three styles of articulation.

Legato: Smoothly does it

Learning a good legato style is important because it's very common in music of all kinds. If you compare music to a spoken language, legato corresponds to the smooth way we normally speak. In legato tonguing, the flow of sound continues nonstop, while the tongue lightly punctuates the sound.

The exercise in Figure 8-3 starts with a slurred passage, and then adds the tongue. The slur technique helps establish a good flow of wind; I often practice a tongued passage without the tongue, or slurred, to set up the proper flow. Listening to the CD will guide your approach to this exercise.

The jaw and cheeks should not move while tonguing. Only the tongue moves, lightly and quickly. Look in a mirror to make sure you're not moving when tonguing.

TRACK 39

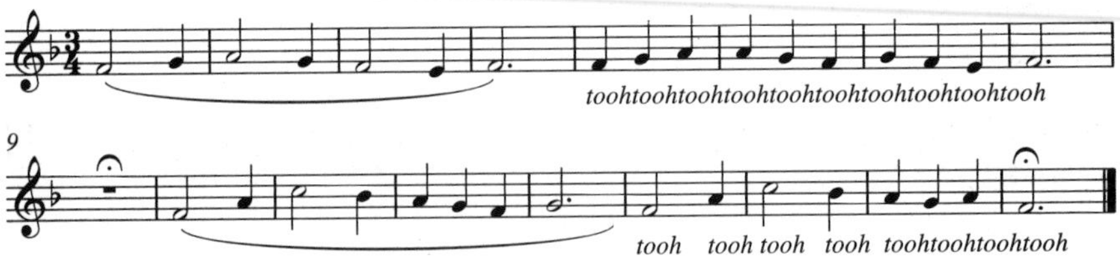

Figure 8-3:
A study
for legato
tonguing.

toohtoohtoohtoohtoohtoohtoohtoohtoohtooh

tooh   tooh tooh   tooh   toohtoohtoohtooh

The study in Figure 8-4 is mostly quarter notes an a scale pattern. Because quarter notes are usually fairly slow it's easy to forget to keep blowing all through each note into the next. Strive for the smooth connection as you hear on the CD.

Figure 8-4: Another study for legato tonguing.

Marcato: Very serious tonguing

Continuing the spoken-language analogy, marcato is like very serious, emphatic speech. Imagine a particularly moralistic politician lecturing on public safety: "We must reclaim our streets!" There is a heavy emphasis on every note in marcato tonguing, but the notes are still connected. The > that you see in Figure 8-5 stands for *marcato*.

The important thing is not to tongue too hard — the flow of sound is still central. As always, the best teacher is your ear. Listen to the CD carefully and try to match the style.

Figure 8-5: Marcato articulation.

Staccato: Quick and light

Staccato means half the value of the written note. Sometimes a composer will put a little dot over each note, and sometimes the word *staccato* appears. Either way, each note is detached from the next one, while still giving the sense of a coherent line of music.

Staccato is like very deliberate, clearly enunciated speaking, for special effect. Imagine a parent telling a young kid not to touch something: "Do-not-touch-that!" Luckily, music played in staccato style is often light and quick: "We-are-hav-ing-so-much-fun!"

Stopping staccato notes with the tongue is a trap that many students fall into. Some jazz styles include tongue stopping, and it works very well there, but as a general approach to articulation, tongue stopping is not helpful because it impedes the flow of air, creating a choppy effect. It also leads to inferior sound and endurance, because the supply of air is compromised. Plus, it just sounds bad!

Hold up your hand and imagine your fingers are five candles. Blow each one out in sequence, first without using the tongue and then with the *tooh* sound. That is your basic staccato technique. The air stops between the notes because you stop blowing. Now, blow against your palm in a long-short-short pattern: *toooh-tooh-tooh, toooh-tooh-tooh.* You can repeat this pattern on the mouthpiece, on home-base G, and then on the trumpet, on the same note.

Make sure you don't tongue too hard. The impetus for the sound is the breath that you're blowing out, not the stroke of the tongue. The tongue just adds the sound of *t* at the start of each note.

The exercise in Figure 8-6 is a scale study that you can use for articulation practice. Play the exercise without tonguing the first time, as if the eighth notes were full quarter notes. Then repeat with the same full sound and continuity, only with the tongue in staccato style. Listen to the CD to get a sense of what staccato should sound like.

Because *staccato* means "half the value of the note" a quarter-note staccato can also be written as an eighth note with an eighth rest.

The repeat sign — two dots, like a colon, appearing at the beginning and end of a passage — indicates that the music in between the two dots is to be played twice. Basically, it saves the copyist from having to write all those notes and rests twice. Figure 8-6 contains an example of this shortcut.

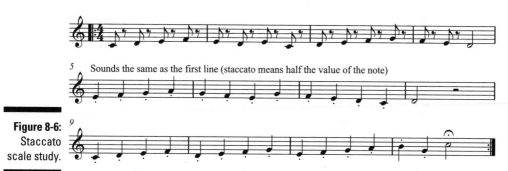

TRACK 42

5 Sounds the same as the first line (staccato means half the value of the note)

Figure 8-6:
Staccato
scale study.

Combining Slurring and Tonguing

Most of the music that we listen to and play involves different tonguing styles and a combination of tonguing and slurring. As always, it's vital to keep blowing a steady stream of air in all the various articulations that trumpeters use. Here's where the air-trumpet technique (see the "Rocking out on the air trumpet" sidebar, earlier in this chapter) can really help with coordinating your tongue stroke with the fingers on the valves.

Imagine repeating F to G many times. The first finger moves quickly to push down the valve as you blow out smoothly and tongue each note. When playing air trumpet, you can focus on the timing of your tongue stroke and valve change without the other parts of trumpeting to distract you.

Here's a little trick to help you keep blowing smoothly without the tonguing disrupting the flow: Blow toward your left palm while tapping the stream of air with your right index finger. Don't go right through the air, but just lightly and quickly tap the flow. This illustrates and reinforces the way that you can keep the blowing and tonguing separate.

The scale study in Figure 8-7 starts with slurring, gradually adds articulation, and combines slurring and tonguing. Sing the exercise with the articulation as marked, and then do some air trumpet. Practicing the study on the mouthpiece is a great idea.

Figure 8-7:
Scale
study for
slurring and
tonguing.

Practicing Scales and Songs with Different Articulations

Music, like speech, is full of contrast. Sometimes we speak emphatically by raising our voices; other times we drop our voices to a dramatic whisper. Articulation is also varied, as I point out in "Different Strokes: Tonguing Techniques," earlier in this chapter. The reason for variety in speech and music is identical: effective communication. If we always sound the same, it's boring and we lose our listeners. Through variety, we maintain the attention of our audience.

The studies and songs in this section give you a chance to be expressive on the trumpet, using different articulations. Both the scales and the songs have headings or titles and style indications to help you interpret the music. Through variety, you can become more than just a sounder of notes; expressive music is the goal.

Before playing the pieces in Figure 8-8, listen to the CD to nourish the inner sound ideal that will guide your playing. In the second piece in Figure 8-8, the horizontal lines over some of the eighth notes indicate *tenuto* (a reminder to hold the note for its full value). The third piece in Figure 8-8 is in the key of D major. The two sharps are F♯ and C♯. The expression marking is *Marcato but lively,* indicating a strong but bouncy attack.

Figure 8-8:
Songs and
scales with
slurring and
tonguing
combined.

Skipping around with scales in thirds

So far, you've practiced scales and harmonic changes and added different articulations. Scales can be played in another way, giving more variety to your trumpeting and making articulation even more interesting and challenging.

When music moves up or down to the next note, it is said to be *scalar*. Doh-re-mi-fa-so-la-ti-doh is by far the most famous musical phrase, but there are many other configurations of those notes. One way that you add interest to songs and studies is to play scales in thirds. This means that instead of doh-re-mi-fa, you could play doh-mi-re-fa. The challenge to a trumpeter is to connect notes that are a little farther apart than direct neighbors — you need more wind when notes are farther away from each other.

Wind and *air* aren't the same thing. *Air* could be the kind of smooth flow that we trumpeters need, or it could be the kind of pressurized hiss that opening the valve on a tire produces. *Wind* has the association of freely blowing, unrestricted flow. Of course, wind can be ferocious — as in a hurricane or tornado. A gentle breeze, freely blown in a flowing manner, like a sigh, is the most helpful image for a wind instrument player. When I talk about a "flow of air" or a "windy breath." I mean the same thing — the relaxed inhale and directed exhale of a good breath.

The distance between two notes is called an *interval* (see Chapter 4). The scale in thirds in Figure 8-9 will give you experience with different intervals. In a scale passage, the notes played are separated by the interval of a second. Ascending a scale in thirds, you play up an interval of a third, and then down by a second, up by a third, and so on. Figure 8-9 is a C scale, in thirds. Keep the wind flowing and listen for the coordination of the valve and tongue strokes. The CD gives you the idea.

TRACK 45

Figure 8-9: Scale in thirds.

Songs with seconds and thirds

In this section are some musical examples of different scale patterns. You can apply the steady flow of wind and the quick valve stroke and the coordination of fingers and tongue as you enjoy playing some songs written especially for you, by me!

Listen to the CD to guide your playing.

TRACK 46

Stepping Smoothly

This song is in C major and in legato style, so connect the notes as you play the different articulations. The word *stepping* in the title can be a help in playing legato. When you walk, you take steps while your weight moves from foot to foot, but there is always a connection to the ground. Legato playing is like that, and the connection while you change notes is the steady, consistent air.

TRACK 47

Ceremonial March

This song is in marcato style. The title is "Ceremonial March," so it shouldn't be played too quickly. Imagine a procession of elderly academics filing in to convocation — very serious. It's in F major, so make sure you play a B♭, not a B♮! Listen to the CD for connected and yet strongly accented articulation. The flow of sound, propelled by wind, is the main ingredient here. Some different markings are introduced. The > accent with a tenuto line is a reminder to play weighty and yet connected. The term *Rallentando* at the end tells you (politely) to slow down.

 TRACK 48

Laughing, Singing

This song is cheerful and light. Children skipping and laughing come to mind. Even though many of the notes are played in a detached style, separated from each other, there is still a melodic line that needs a flow of wind. The CD gives you an idea of the style and "windy" approach to articulation. As you listen, you can play air trumpet, practicing both the fingerings and the breathing in and blowing out.

Before playing, practice some repeated notes, first on air trumpet, and then on the horn. (All brass players call their instruments "horns.") Make sure that you aren't tonguing too hard or causing your jaw to move when you tongue. (Practice the exercise in Figure 8-1 a few times.) The model is, as always, one stream of sound, lightly tapped by the tongue.

Chapter 9

Warming Up for Greater Success

*W*arming up is a very important part of your trumpet day. Just as a baseball pitcher needs a physical warm-up, and needs to fine-tune the release of the ball, the coordination of the legs and arms, and something almost intangible, a feel for the ball, so it is for a trumpeter. You need to establish physical relaxation and flow, as well as the response of the lips and tongue, and something intangible, a sense of music.

The greatest trumpeter I ever heard was Adolf Herseth of the Chicago Symphony Orchestra. He said that a warm-up is a good practice session, gradually approached. It's important not to rush things, not to play high or loud too soon in your practicing, so the idea of a gradual start in Herseth's statement is certainly true. And a good practice session covers all the necessities of trumpet playing.

This chapter describes a warm-up routine that starts gradually and covers all the basics. Having a regular routine to start your playing builds your technique and nourishes the inner trumpet that guides your playing.

Relaxing the Body and Mind

Playing trumpet is a physical activity, as well as a mental and emotional one. Starting a warm-up with some deep, relaxed breathing not only establishes good breathing habits but also relaxes your body.

Breathing for tone and technique

The wonderful thing about deep, relaxed breaths is the calming effect they produce. If you're trying to relax, the best thing you can do is take a few big sighs. Trumpeters need the relaxation afforded by deep breathing and we also need the air as fuel for our playing. Quantity and quality are both important, so the breath has to be deep *and* relaxed.

Here are some breathing exercises to start a great warm-up. You can do a few of these each time you warm up, alternating them as you see fit.

- Clear enough space in your practice area so that you can wave your arms around without hitting anything. Move freely, swaying from side to side. Swing both arms in front of you like a pendulum. Breathe in deeply as your arms swing one way and exhale as they swing the other way. You should feel very free, making large relaxed swinging gestures, as you breathe deeply and freely.

- Take some breaths in exaggerated postures. Raise one arm as high as you can over your head and take a big breath in and out. Then raise the other arm up and do the same thing with that arm. Then do both arms together. Now bend over at the waist, as relaxed as possible, and inhale and exhale deeply in that position. Repeat that last one a couple times, because it feels so good.

- Hold your hand out and, as you inhale, imagine that you're sucking your hand toward your mouth, allowing your hand to move in close to your face. Then exhale and imagine that you're blowing your hand away from you.

- Hold your index finger at your lips in the "shh" position, and breathe in past your finger with a pleasant breezy sound. Exhale, imagining that you're blowing your finger away. Do this several times.

- Hold a small sheet of paper, the size of a Post-it note, very close to your lips. Breathe in and out easily and aim for the paper, watching it move out to the horizontal as you blow. Then get a regular sheet of paper and hold it farther away, again aiming for that horizontal position as it waves in the breeze. Finish with the piece of paper held at arm's length.

✔ To build up your lung capacity, try exhaling for gradually longer breaths. Start with four counts in and four counts out, then four counts in and six counts out, then four counts in and eight counts out, and so on. You'll find yourself taking deeper breaths as you go along. You can use your metronome to help keep a steady beat — set it at about 60 beats per minute.

✔ "Play" a few pieces on the air trumpet (see Chapter 8). It'll help you breathe deeply. Don't try to conserve the air as you play "Happy Birthday," for example. Instead, waste the air, get rid of it quickly, and take a fresh breath.

Stretching and getting supple

A good warm-up can include some physical preparation. The arm swinging that you can do as part of a breathing exercise is a good start. Here are a few more exercises to help get you ready to play the trumpet:

✔ Go for a walk. Yes, some old-fashioned cardio in the form of a brisk walk gets the body awake. If there's no one around, or if you don't care if people think you're weird, sing a nice walking tune as you go.

✔ Make some silly faces:

  • Purse your lips tightly together, and then relax them. Do this several times.

  • Open your mouth wide a few times, returning to a normal position.

  • Scrunch up your whole face and relax, repeating this a few times.

  • Yawn widely a couple of times.

  • Grin and then relax your mouth a few times.

  All these silly faces — and any more that you can think of — help you relax and serve to wake up the embouchure muscles. If there's a baby available, just hang out with her and copy her facial expressions. That's a good workout.

✔ Stretch whatever feels like stretching — touch your toes, reach for the ceiling, swing your arms, do some knee bends. All these free-form stretches can feel good and are helpful in a warm-up.

Listening for inspiration

Warm up your imagination by listening to some great trumpet playing while doing these stretches and breathing exercises. The stronger imagined trumpet sound that you have, the better you'll play. Casual listening while exercising lets the sounds enter your inner hearing, nourishing the trumpet sound in your imagination.

Making Music on the Mouthpiece

In Chapter 5, I cover mouthpiece buzzing in detail. The warm-up routine is a wonderful time to do some very musical, tuneful mouthpiece playing.

Letting it sing

Singers seem to be the most natural music-makers. There's no piece of wood or metal getting in the way, just the breath and the voice. The mouthpiece comes close to that kind of freedom. I like to play very singable tunes on the mouthpiece, and I have to confess that I usually sing them before I buzz them. (You may want to be alone when you warm up, or at least with very tolerant people.)

Be as expressive as possible when you play these songs. If it's a march, make sure it has energy and motion. If it's a lullaby, try to put someone to sleep.

It's always fun to play the mouthpiece for a small child. His reactions will tell you how convincing your music-making is.

Making a sound like a siren

TRACK 49

At first listen, imitating a siren isn't much of musical statement, but if you make it a very clear, beautiful siren, with a perfect octave glissando, or slide, you're preparing your lips and mind for trumpet playing. (See Chapter 5 for more on the glissando.) Listen to the glissando on the CD and then imitate it. Home-base G is a great note to start on. Make the glissando perfectly consistent, without any breaks or changes to the sound quality.

There are some wonderful warm-up mouthpiece songs that connect well with the glissandi that you've been buzzing. "Oh What a Beautiful Morning" and "Over the Rainbow" both contain lots of glissando possibilities. Listen to recordings of singers performing them, and then create your mouthpiece interpretation.

Sounding the First Trumpet Note of the Day

Our good friend home-base G is a great choice for your first note. It's very comfortable and familiar, like an old broken-in pair of blue jeans. Play G a few times, in a moderate dynamic level, *mezzo forte*. In a way, every day that you warm up, you're revisiting your very first trumpet note (see Chapter 6).

Sometimes I like to start with a breath attack, the G sounding as result of relaxed air flow. Then I add the tongue, with the *whooh-whooh-tooh* exercise in Chapter 6. Figure 9-1 shows a different version of that exercise that works very well as a warm-up. Use breath attack for the first time and tongue attack on the repeat. Listen to the CD to get the idea.

Figure 9-1: Breath-attack and tongue-attack routine.

Hearing it, breathing it, and blowing it

Flexibilities are part of a good warm-up, and it's great to play them soon after practicing your glissandi on the mouthpiece. The same connection to the sound while changing notes is vital in mouthpiece glissandi and flexibilities. Because you're changing notes, you want to be sure to listen to the recording initially, and then to "the little trumpet in your head" (see Chapter 6). The process that eventually should become a deeply ingrained habit is to listen for the sound and style that you want; take a deep, relaxed breath; and blow freely, guided by the little trumpet in your head.

The exercises in Figure 9-2 change notes using wind, and move back and forth between lower and higher notes, but they also encourage a horizontal flow of air and sound. Hear the changing pitches and keep blowing outward.

TRACK 51

Figure 9-2:
Warm-up
flexibilities.

Flowing is the way to go

Vincent Cichowicz was a wonderful trumpeter with the Chicago Symphony Orchestra, and an amazing teacher as well. He wrote a series of what he called "flow studies" that trumpeters all over the world play every day. The exercises in Figure 9-3 are based on Mr. Cichowicz's concept.

Blow steadily without using the tongue. This articulation is called slurring, and a constant flow of wind is essential. A slur marking is a curved line over or under the changing notes. It should sound as if you're playing one note, changing notes with lightning-fast valve action and a clear inner hearing of the sound. Take a break between each line, using the time to take a few deep sighs and stretches. If your notes connect smoothly and instantly as they do on the CD, you're doing it correctly.

TRACK 52

Figure 9-3:
Flow con-
nectors.

Adding Range

In a warm-up, it's good to start in the middle register and then expand up and down, keeping your lips fresh with frequent rest breaks. The first range exercise I suggest (see Figure 9-4) moves outward in semitones from home-base G. Listen to the CD to get the pitches and continuity of sound established in your inner hearing.

Figure 9-4: Chromatic range expander.

The next range exercise (shown in Figure 9-5) uses the diminished seventh chord (see Chapter 4) to move through the registers. Diminished seventh chords are enjoyable to play because they're made up of the intervals of a minor third, or three semitones. The minor-third interval is just one step more than a second, so it's very close, and a comfortable interval on the trumpet. As you do in scale steps, keep the air flowing, hear the next note, and bang the valves down quickly (but not so hard as to disrupt the sound). Breathe deeply when you need to fill up, and blow freely. Never try to conserve the air. Get rid of it — waste it, as Arnold Jacobs used to say.

Blow out in a horizontal flow, not up or down as the notes change. Hear the new note and blow consistently out.

Figure 9-5: Diminished seventh chords.

Now for some lower-register work, with a balancing upward line (see Figure 9-6). This exercise will help you play the low notes with a full sound and still be able to play up a scale after the low register.

The problem that some players have is that they open up their embouchure too much in order to more easily get the low notes. In doing so, they produce an uncentered, often flat tone that can easily get stuck in the low register. Listen for a centered sound, keep the embouchure firm, and blow freely with a large volume of air doing the work. The CD has a performance of the first part of the figure, which will give your inner hearing the musical image.

TRACK 55

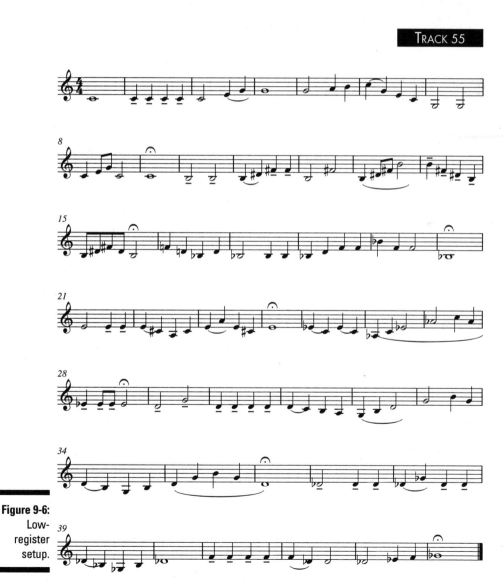

Figure 9-6:
Low-
register
setup.

Adding Articulation

Tonguing needs to be warmed up, too. And because tonguing relies on a good flow of wind, each of the following tonguing setups starts with a long tone and a slurred passage before adding the tongue.

In articulation, the tongue taps the flowing wind. The wind is more important in tonguing than the tongue is! Always keep blowing as if you're playing a long tone, whether you're slurring or tonguing.

Figure 9-7 is an F major scale study patterned after the famous trumpet "bible," *Clarke's Technical Studies,* by the famous cornet virtuoso Herbert L. Clarke. A continuous horizontal flow of air will give you the proper support for this exercise.

TRACK 56

Figure 9-7:
Scale study
tongue
setup.

Now for some tonguing in arpeggiated figures (see Figure 9-8). These chords are played in different configurations, so hearing the next note in the series requires a bit more attention, as does the flow of wind. Make sure that the wind starts quickly when you blow, not taking time to get up to the speed that you want. Work on the coordination between the stroke of the tongue and the quick wind. As always, the CD provides an aural guide.

Finally, we can set up the tongue for quickness. No surprise, a fast tongue relies on wind. The tongue bounces off the flow of wind like a rope off the back of a speedboat, bouncing off the waves.

First, some warming-up without the trumpet or mouthpiece. Blow out *whoooh,* and then start tapping the tongue against the wind, as if saying *tooh-tooh-tooh-tooh-tooh-tooh-tooh.* Don't let the jaw or embouchure move — don't "chew" the notes. You want the tongue to be quick, light, and efficient. You can inhale and let the tongue flap against that inward flow as well. Try rolling your *r*'s as a further means of relaxing the tongue.

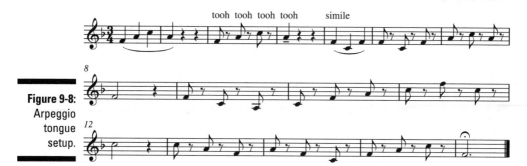

Figure 9-8:
Arpeggio
tongue
setup.

After you feel that the tongue is moving quickly and easily, listen to the CD to nourish your inner trumpet, before playing the setup for speed, in the key of G major (see Figure 9-9). The metronome marking is set as 100 to the quarter note, speeding up to 144 as your fluency improves. Just the first part is demonstrated, to give you the idea.

Figure 9-9:
Speeding up
the tongue.

Soft and Loud, Gentle and Robust

Think of a musical character, a feeling, rather than simply "soft and loud." Musical dynamics are an important part of your ability to be expressive, to tell stories with your music. Thinking only *soft* usually leaves your sound with insufficient air and no real musical direction; thinking *loud* as an end in itself can produce a forced, ugly sound. Instead, *gentle* has a story of some kind and no necessary restriction on air supply, and a word such as *robust* conjures up an energetic image.

In these long notes and slurs, the dynamics — the softs and louds — are added using divergent lines for *forte* and convergent ones for *piano*. Focus on maintaining your beautiful, clear sound and staying in tune as you *crescendo* (get louder) or *diminuendo* (get softer).

First, some simple long tones with dynamics (see Figure 9-10). An accidental is carried to all affected notes within the tie.

TRACK 59

Figure 9-10: Long tones with dynamics.

The next warm-up exercise (shown in Figure 9-11) gives you the opportunity to play scales and arpeggios with dynamic variety. Listen to the CD and follow the dynamics closely.

TRACK 60

Figure 9-11: Scales and arpeggios with dynamics.

Lyrical Playing

The last part of a good warm-up gives you the chance to apply the beautiful tone, clear articulation, and dynamic variety in some melodies. Take a few big sighs before you start to refresh your breathing concept.

TRACK 61

Blowing with the Breeze

Listen to the CD for a performance of this piece with piano accompaniment. A click track will give the tempo at the start, and you'll hear the piece a second time with just piano for you to play along with.

TRACK 62

Lyrical Scale Tune

This tune is just a scale pattern, in the key of F, but if played with a gentle flow and a relaxed sound, it's fun to play. I hope you enjoy it!

Easy and Flowing

Play as if singing

Most trumpet teachers encourage their students to "play it like you're singing." Basically, we're a lot more musical when we sing than when we pick up these heavy pieces of machinery and try to blow through them, while buzzing the lips, tapping the tongue, hearing the notes and style that we want, reading strange markings on a sheet of paper, breathing deeply, and somehow not passing out from the effort of concentrating on all that. When I put it like that, it seems miraculous that people can play the trumpet at all! But we *can* play! And we *can* make beautiful music! And we *can* enjoy it!

Singing the pieces and exercises that you're working on is a good way to tap into your musical soul. Singing the music also can help you learn the pitches and rhythms and the style so that when you play them on the trumpet they come with some musically helpful feelings and concepts. Mostly, singing reminds you that it's fun to make music, and that the trumpet can be just as much fun as singing — or even more.

Part III
Developing Your Technique

The 5th Wave   By Rich Tennant

"I know the kazoo is easier to play, but I miss the Royal Trumpeters."

In this part . . .

Expanding the range into the lower notes is the subject of Chapter 10. Everyone loves a trumpeter (at least that's what trumpeters think), and one reason is because we play the highest notes of the brass family. We're like the tightrope walker at a circus and, luckily, we have a net. Chapter 11 guides you through the principles of the upper register.

In Chapter 12, you get a chance to apply the music theory that I introduce in Part I. Using scales and arpeggios to play more interesting music will add a lot to your playing.

Because playing the trumpet is a physically demanding activity, you need to approach it sensibly, and Chapter 13 helps you do that. Articulation, introduced in Chapter 8, has many facets, and Chapter 14 adds to your knowledge and skill in this important area of trumpeting. Finally, in Chapter 15, you apply these techniques to different styles of music.

Chapter 10

Lower! Slower!

• •

• •

Trumpeters love to play high. It's a big part of the trumpet identity, the sound riding above everyone else, like the army trumpets leading the charge. Famous trumpeters like Cat Anderson and Maynard Ferguson became known for their amazing prowess in the extreme high range. There's no doubt that the upper register is exciting to listen to, but too much attention to the upper register can lead to problems, especially before you've developed a strong set of chops and a healthy breathing habit. Your tone will suffer, becoming thin and tight, and you can even injure your lips.

The middle register is the place to establish tone and build good habits. Moving down into the lower register from the middle gives you a secure base; a good, firm embouchure; and relaxed exhale. In this chapter, I offer some ideas, songs, and exercises to prepare the middle register for moving downward.

Starting in the Middle

Middle G, the second line in the treble clef, is a great place to begin practicing. It's an easy note to pitch, because it's a fourth away from the next open note. You aren't likely to *mispitch* (hit the wrong harmonic in the overtone series) with middle G. Because it's not too low, your embouchure will be firm and properly formed. Sometimes, starting in the lower register leads to a loose, open embouchure, because you can play a note below low C without a good setup. G does require some firmness but none of the tension that can accompany the high range. As in all things, moderation is the best policy.

Long tones and slurs

Figure 10-1 is a slow slur exercise starting on middle G that helps to establish a good, centered sound. It's based on exercises found in a famous book by Max Schlossberg called *Daily Drills and Technical Studies for Trumpet*.

A basic principle of good trumpet playing is established in these exercises: Don't move your embouchure when you move from one note to another. Keep a consistently firm setting and use wind speed and valves, as well as a very clear inner sound idea. The first eight bars are recorded for your reference. Listen for a clear start to the note and a consistent tone quality.

TRACK 63

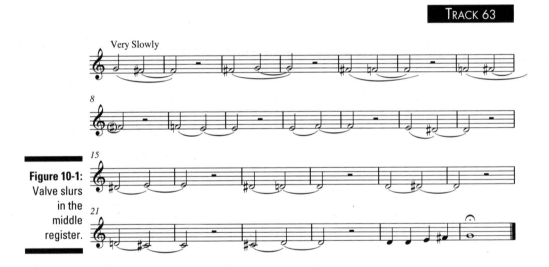

Figure 10-1:
Valve slurs
in the
middle
register.

Trumpeters make use of alternate fingerings for wind slurs. The middle G is played open — with no valves. But, because the notes of the overtone series get closer together as they go higher, fingerings that were necessary to lengthen the tubing and the air column in the lowest register aren't needed in the middle and upper ranges.

Let me give you an example: Low D is a fourth below G, so the first and third valves combine to lower the pitch by that interval and produce a D. But a fourth below third-space C is open G, so one and three are not required. But they *are* available; if you play an open G and, while sustaining it, lower the first and third valves, you'll still play a G.

There are many examples of this throughout the trumpet range, and many jazz soloists — from Louis Armstrong to Wynton Marsalis — have used this trill-like effect in their solos. One of the main practical uses for this phenomenon is in wind slurs, or *flexibilities.* You use this fingering alternative in the exercise in Figure 10-2.

There are various kinds of slurs. For example, wind slurs move from one harmonic to another using only air; valve slurs require a constant stream of wind and quick valve changes. Figure 10-1 is a study in valve slurs. Figure 10-2 gives you practice in wind slurs.

Blow a very strong and steady stream of air, keep your embouchure firm, and hear the notes you want to hit. Listen carefully to the CD. The first two patterns are there to guide you.

TRACK 64

Figure 10-2:
Wind slurs
in the
middle and
low
registers.

Steady wind, firm embouchure

You need to have a steady flow of wind and a firm embouchure. Luckily, these two pillars of good trumpet playing encourage each other: A good exhale helps to firm up the embouchure muscles. As you blow out with a smooth flow of wind, the cheek and lip muscles naturally contract. But notice that if you blow very hard, your cheeks will puff. The great brass teacher Arnold Jacobs used to say, "Use flow not force" — and good embouchure formation is one of the reasons for that advice.

A good illustration of the difference between force and flow involves blowing a sheet of paper. Try holding a piece of paper against a wall; then let go and keep it from falling by blowing on it. You'll find that it takes a lot of force to do that. Now, hold the top edge of the paper in your hand about a foot in front of your face. Try to blow the paper so it's horizontal to the floor. As you achieve success, move the paper farther away from you until it's at arm's length. This technique works very well with a relaxed flow, and it's a good basic model for playing the trumpet.

Both a firm embouchure and a steady flow of wind are necessary for valve slurs, with the extra requirement of very quick and decisive finger action on the valves. Figure 10-3 is a study in valve slurs that is based on a drill from Herbert L. Clarke's famous book *Technical Studies for the Cornet*. The CD contains the first part of the study and demonstrates a consistent tone and quick valves for the clean note changes required for good trumpet technique.

TRACK 65

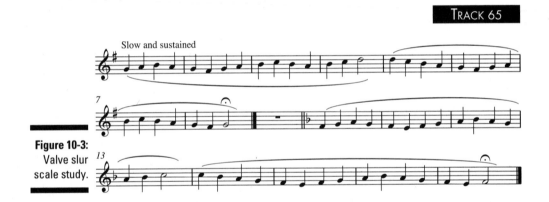

Figure 10-3:
Valve slur
scale study.

Buzzing the Mouthpiece for Low Notes

The mouthpiece should be a regular part of your practicing, and developing low-register proficiency is one of the results. Because there is less resistance when you play the mouthpiece, you have to blow more freely in order to get a clear sound.

Sliding down

Use the glissando technique that I introduce in Chapter 5 to maintain a consistent tone quality as you descend to the low register. Think of a siren as you buzz. If a visual image helps you, try imagining driving your car down a hill — you're still moving forward, but you're also going down at the same time.

Start on home-base G and slide down to a C; then slide back up again. Coming back up to the G is very good for embouchure firmness and tonal consistency. Too often, trumpeters will let the embouchure sag in order to get the low notes. Returning to the middle register encourages the firmness of the lips and cheeks that will give you a good sound in all registers.

Figure 10-4 is the written-out glissando, with the irregular line indicating a constant sound as you descend and return. The CD shows you what I mean and gives you the pitch of the first two sets of glissandos.

Many players drop their heads down when playing lower, in a kind of sympathetic gesture. Don't do this — keep your head up and blow a steady stream of horizontal wind.

TRACK 66

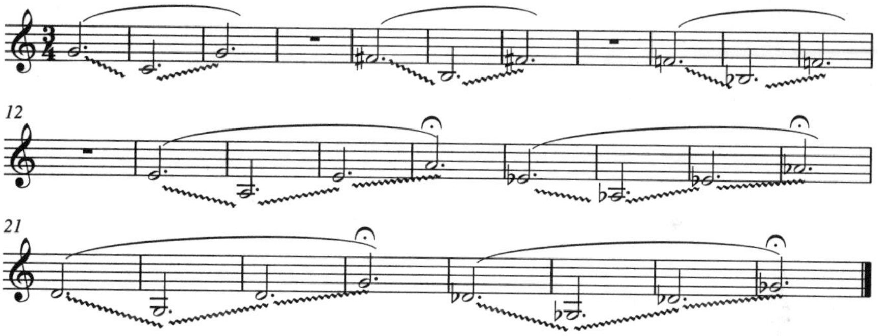

Figure 10-4:
Mouthpiece
glissandi
from the
middle
register
to the low
register and
back.

Playing low and mellow mouthpiece songs

Low-register mouthpiece songs are enjoyable to play and very good for tone, air, and embouchure development. The low register requires much more air than the middle and high ranges do. When you're playing in the low register, you'll find yourself needing to breathe almost every other note — and that's fine. Breathe as often as you need to, and blow freely.

Try recording yourself. It's good a way to see whether you're staying on the right pitch — when you're playing, you can't always tell. Listen for the right notes and also for a clear tone.

Excess breathiness in the sound is a sign that your lips are too open. Remember to think of *dim* for the right placement of the lips (see Chapter 5). Go back to a middle G and slide down, bringing that nice tone with you.

Tonguing is sometimes a challenge in the low register, and buzzing on the mouthpiece will really show whether you're connecting well. Figure 10-5 is a good tonguing setup for the lower register. Keep a steady stream of air flowing as you tongue. The CD contains the first pattern and illustrates the correct approach.

TRACK 67

Figure 10-5:
Establishing
clear tongu-
ing in the
low register.

TRACK 68

A Variation of Twinkle, Twinkle Little Star

This version of the famous song by Mozart adds some glissandi to help you get to the lower register with a full sound. Remember to blow lots of wind, but not too hard. Try to tongue very clearly, just as you would in the middle register.

Playing the Low Register on the Trumpet

When you pick up your trumpet to play after a good mouthpiece session, you'll notice that the tone is clearer and seems to speak more easily. The trumpet adds a little more resistance than you feel on the mouthpiece, because of the additional tubing.

One of the benefits of mouthpiece playing is how good the trumpet sounds afterward. This may sound a bit like advising you to bang your head against a brick wall because it feels so good when you stop. But mouthpiece playing is a far more positive (and less painful) activity than banging your head against a brick wall, and your trumpet playing will definitely benefit.

The first thing you'll notice when you play low notes on the trumpet is how much air you use. Just take as many breaths as you need and keep blowing.

The clarino and the principale roles: High and low

In baroque music, the trumpets were divided into the high parts, called the *clarino*, and the low parts, known as the *principale*. Of course, then as now, the high-note specialists were more popular and had more dates than the lowly principale players. (Okay, I just made that up, but it was probably true.)

Most modern trumpeters want to be more versatile, and the equipment and training enable us to play in all registers and styles. However, there still is that distinction — unofficial though it may be — between the flashy high-notes player who gets more dates and the grunts who toil in the more obscure low range.

The fanfares that were the staple diet of the principale player make excellent practice for the modern player in establishing the low register. Fanfare figures need very clear tonguing and tone. The following figure includes several principale-style pieces that will give you practice in low-register accuracy. The CD will give you the idea.

TRACK 69

The following section deals with the low register in various ways. The concept of horizontal direction works very well in retaining a clear and focused tone as you go lower. Think of an escalator going down; you stay standing straight and move forward as you descend. I also include exercises, including a few more slurs, and some songs that will make the basement seem interesting.

Going low, blowing slow

One way you can get more air for the low register, so you can sound stronger and play longer phrases, is to think of slower air. The upper register is facilitated by a faster stream of wind, and the lower register benefits from a slower stream.

Imagining a speedometer needle moving as you change speeds can help. Also, try holding a sheet of paper at the top, very close to your face, and blowing out just enough to slightly move it. This is slow air and it's a good model for how to play in the low register.

If you blow too hard, the lips resist, vibrating less instead of more. As you begin to get a consistently clear tone you can blow more strongly, resulting in a louder sound. But the starting place is slow air.

Figure 10-6 gives you some exercises to help develop your lower range. Notice that the exercises start in the middle and go down to the lower register. After sustaining a low note, the notes come back up again. Listen to the CD to establish the kind of sound you're after.

TRACK 70

Slowly and smoothly

7

Figure 10-6:
Exercises
in the low
register.

13

Thinking out, not down

There's a lot of room for imagery in trumpet playing. The way that you hear the sound is an inner, aural imagery. The way that you imagine the style or the kind of musical expression can be very influential on your playing of the music. And a visual image can help technique, especially with changing registers.

In the preceding section, I mention visualizing a speedometer needle to help you change wind speed. Another helpful image is a horizontal line — a stream of sound that goes out, rather than up or down. Lean forward a little, or walk forward as you play downward. Focus your gaze on an object across the room and think of your sound aiming right at it. Imagine a thread extending outward from the bell of your trumpet, all the notes connected to it. All these images will help your lower range stay vibrant and energized.

Figure 10-7 starts with a descending G major scale, played very slowly, with an upward figure at the end. This is a great opportunity to practice thinking out, not down. Listen to the CD for the kind of sound you want to emulate.

TRACK 71

Figure 10-7:
Descending
G major
scale study.

Another great low-register concept is warm air. Blow hard against your hand. It feels cold, right? Now blow warm air. There will be a difference in your tone if you think of warm air as you play the lower notes.

Longing for long tones

Holding one note for a long time can be kind of boring. I don't play a lot of long tones — I'd rather add a slow musical line to the mix. But the low register is one part of trumpet technique that does profit from sustaining a note for a full breath.

To add interest and work on maintaining good tone and tuning at different levels of loudness, called *dynamics,* I like to play louder and softer while holding the note. The music in Figure 10-8 shows two diverging lines, meaning *crescendo* (louder), and two converging lines, meaning *decrescendo* (softer). The CD contains the first phrase, giving you the idea of dynamics while sustaining a consistently clear tone. Be sure not to let the tone go flat. This might be a good time to look at a tuner and keep the indicator right in the middle. Blowing too hard will force the tone, and both quality and tuning will suffer. Hear a beautiful sound and match it when you play.

TRACK 72

Figure 10-8: Long tones in the low register.

Sliding down to the basement with slurs

More slurs. Trumpeters can't get enough of them! Slurs are so good for developing embouchure and air flow — plus, they're fun. Buzzing the lips against a metal ring seems to please trumpeters.

Keep the embouchure firm — the less motion in the lips and jaw, the better. Blow in a straight line. Keep the lips close together, as in *dim.* And make a nice tone.

Figure 10-9 shows some slurs starting on a D♭. You can play the G♭ at the end of the exercise with the alternate fingering of first, second, and third valve. In the following measure, you can play the G with first and third valves. These two examples are included on the CD.

TRACK 73

Figure 10-9: Wind slurs in the low register.

Making music in the low range

I'll finish this chapter with a song for the trumpet in the low range. Of course, you can play it on the mouthpiece, too — in fact, I strongly recommend that you play it on the mouthpiece.

TRACK 74

Diving to the Deep End

This somewhat mournful tune very smoothly explores the low register. Keep your sound light, never too loud, and always flowing horizontally forward. The lowest note played on the trumpet is contained in this piece, low F♯. For both the low G and F♯, move your third valve tuning slide out about three-quarters of an inch so it will be in tune with a buoyant tone.

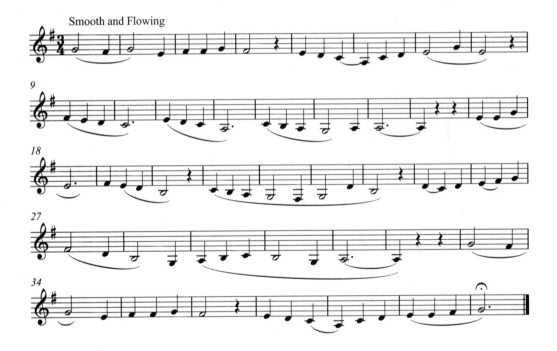

Chapter 11

Higher! Faster!

In This Chapter

▶ Blowing faster versus harder

▶ Buzzing on the mouthpiece for high notes

▶ Connecting the middle range to the high notes with wind

▶ Moving higher with scales and leaps

▶ Playing music in the upper register

*T*he middle register is the best starting point for the higher notes, as it is for the low range (see Chapter 10). On home-base G, you can blow freely and with confidence, nurturing a good embouchure and a clear tone. Moving upward toward the high notes with the solid, comfortable tone of a G makes a lot of sense.

But how do trumpeters play higher notes? The answer is — or should be — that they play very much as they do in the middle register. Extreme mouthpieces, stretching or pressing on the lips, blowing excessively hard . . . you want to avoid all these. In order to play a clear, relaxed upper register you have to hear the note that you're after, take a big breath, and blow *faster* air.

In this chapter, I give you more ideas about faster wind for the higher notes and the importance of hearing the note you want to play before and while playing it. It's also very important to be confident and I give you some ideas about developing the "no fear" approach that can make a big difference in your high register. Scales and leaps go along with flexibilities in a comprehensive approach to playing in the high range and I cover that in this chapter also. Finally, I offer some songs to play that give you the chance to move toward the high register in a musical way.

When playing in the upper register, make sure to take time to rest. Let the lips relax and get the blood flowing again. If you notice that your lips are tingling, it's time to give them a break — wait until they feel normal before playing any more. Balance higher playing with some low-register work. Slide down from a high note to the low range if you're buzzing the mouthpiece. If you're on the trumpet, play down a scale periodically and play some repeated, soft, low notes with a clear tongue.

Windy Work

Exhaling with faster wind or air is quite different from simply blowing harder. The ancient Romans blew as hard as they could, needing leather straps tied around their heads to hold their cheeks in, and they still couldn't play higher. All they did was play louder, with the goal of terrifying their enemies. If the extent of the Roman Empire is any indication, they must have succeeded. You have the somewhat different goal of making beautiful music, so you need another way.

When you're trying to blow faster, it can help to hold a sheet of paper a few inches in front of your face and blow gently. The paper slowly moves outward toward the horizontal. Now, speed up the wind as you blow. The paper will quickly move to the horizontal position. Compare this to just blowing hard at the page and you'll notice something: When you just blow hard, the paper moves outward quickly but immediately falls down again, and it seems less focused. Now, blow an immediately fast stream of wind toward the page; you should see a smooth, even flow, and a sustained horizontal trajectory. There's also a difference in the sound of the wind between blowing faster and blowing harder — when you blow faster, it's a breezy sound, not a hurricane. Hard blowing sounds forced, with a sense of working against yourself.

The visual image of a speedometer also helps with faster air. With your hand acting as the speedometer needle, blow 10 miles per hour, then 40 miles per hour, then 80 miles per hour. Again, compare this to just blowing as hard as you can, and you'll notice that the quality of the wind is different. The sound of faster wind is clear and consistent, and the tone that you produce will reflect the quality of that wind. The inhale can have a relaxed, easy sound or a strained quality. Aiming for a nice-sounding breath in will help your exhale.

Sliding Up on the Mouthpiece

The mouthpiece is a great tool for learning technique on the trumpet. Upward glissandi (see Chapter 9) help you increase wind speed while keeping the lips firmly in the *dim* position.

Imitating the sound of a siren is a good plan, focusing on the upward sound especially. The sound of any machine speeding up does very well. A racing car, for example, with the sound of changing gears, provides some entertainment value, even if only for yourself. Whatever image works for you, use it to help you buzz higher.

Playing songs on the mouthpiece in the higher register is another excellent technique for increasing trumpet range. Choose tunes that have upward leaps, like "My Bonnie" or "Here Comes the Bride." Listen to the CD for excerpts of these songs.

Moving between Registers with Wind

Trumpeters need not only to be able to play high notes and low notes, but also to move between the extremes of range with an even tone quality. A firm, consistent embouchure is a big part of this, as is a flowing stream of wind. Mouthpiece playing as described in the preceding section will help you develop both of these aspects of trumpet technique.

Rest at least a few minutes after you finish the mouthpiece work. Go for a walk or have some tea, but whatever you do, let your lips rest. Then, when you pick up your trumpet, start in the middle register and gradually move up. It's a good idea to return to the middle register after your foray into the high range.

Using the overtone series

The overtone series is very handy for moving from the middle range to the higher range because you focus on wind slurs and stay on the same fingering. A good trumpet player can reliably play in all registers, and overtone slurs are a great way to move toward that goal.

The firmness of the embouchure is vital — you may achieve a few higher notes by stretching or squeezing the lips, but you sacrifice good tone and reliability.

Figure 11-1 is an exercise using the notes of the overtone series. Keep a consistently firm embouchure and blow faster wind as the notes ascend. I like to think of a very well-tuned racecar — the touch of your foot on the accelerator is all you need for instant speed. As always, hearing the notes clearly in your head before you play and as you're playing is crucial. The CD contains the first two phrases. Listening carefully will help you strengthen your aural imagination.

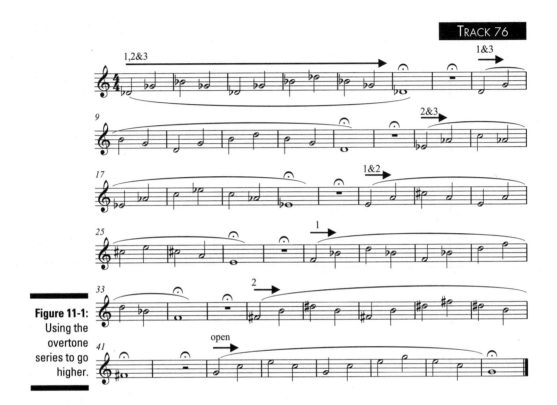

Figure 11-1:
Using the
overtone
series to go
higher.

Fourth-line D: The door to the upper register

Even though D on the fourth line isn't particularly high, it's an entry point to the high range. Maybe it's more like the gate to the front yard — you have to get past it to reach the house. The interval of a second between C and D is an important one for achieving high-note success.

Scales are excellent for fluency in this register. Figure 11-2 is based on an exercise by the great trumpet teacher, James Stamp, using the F major and G major scales. Here's a chance to use the wind speed that you've been working on. Before you play, take your handy sheet of paper and practice speeding up the wind, blowing the paper toward the horizontal plane. Then listen to the first two lines played on the CD. Buzz this exercise on the mouthpiece before playing it on the trumpet.

Figure 11-2: Scale studies for the C-to-D connection.

Approaching the High Notes in Different Ways

When you play real music in any style, from baroque fanfares to popular ballads, you'll encounter high notes, sometimes appearing as the end of a scale, sometimes by a larger interval (even by an octave leap), and sometimes as the first note of a phrase. You may slur to the note or tongue it, and it may be played softly or *forte*. So, practicing for the upper register should include all these approaches. In building technique, there's room for scale exercises; repetitive drills for tone studies; and fast, slow, technical, and lyrical music.

In the following sections, I give examples of the different ways in which trumpeters approach the high range.

Scaling the heights

Scales by their nature go up and down, and because music is comprised to a great extent of scale figures, practicing them is smart. The scale studies in Figure 11-3 start in the middle register and move up. The CD performance gives you the idea of the first set of scales, in F major.

Even though the notes are higher, you want to play them as if they are *not* high — in other words, with a full, relaxed air stream and a stable embouchure.

Your attitude toward the upper register matters a lot: If you think of the high notes as high — and, therefore, hard and risky — you'll have trouble. But if you keep your mind full of the sound you want and blow freely, lots of good things will happen.

TRACK 78

Figure 11-3:
Scales for
the upper
register.

Think of the way you push off a trampoline before you leap. All the power you need is collected in your poised legs and the stretched trampoline. Similarly, the note before the upward scale gives you the momentum to fly into the higher range, so hold it for full value and make sure it's a strong sound. You can even crescendo as you approach the leap to heighten the feeling of flowing forward and up.

The CD will let you hear this concept. Doing some mouthpiece work before you play each of these exercises will be a big help, too. Each of the scale studies begins by establishing a full sound on the first note, to give you a solid base for your upward flight.

Leaping tall buildings

All trumpeters are superheroes, at least in their own minds (and what else matters?). Learning to leap into the higher range with confidence is something that every trumpeter needs to do. A very clear aural image will guide your leap. Hear the note you want to play before and as you play it, in all the rich detail that you can manage. If you don't make that effort of imagination, the upper register is unknown and somewhat risky, and your odds of playing accurately diminish.

The higher you go in the overtone series, the closer together the notes are (see Chapter 2). Because the notes are closer together, you can easily miss the one you want. The good news is that the more you listen to the sound in your head, the stronger your aural concept is, the greater, by far, are your odds of success.

The exercises in Figure 11-4 start with fairly easy leaps and work toward the more challenging ones — the ones that are farther away. The second exercise introduces the key of Bb major. The CD includes a performance of the first of these exercises. Listening carefully will help you succeed.

This isn't really the upper register. Most trumpeters think of the high register as starting on the A above the staff. But the techniques here will serve you well as you ascend even more.

I recommend that you practice your air acceleration with a sheet of paper a few times, and then do some upward glissandi on the mouthpiece before you play the exercises.

Focusing on flexibilities

A wind slur can be any movement between overtones using faster or slower wind, but a flexibility study repeats the overtone slur many times on the same breath. Flexibilities really focus on keeping the wind stream flowing freely and maintaining a stable embouchure as you change notes.

Figure 11-4:
Leaping
toward the
upper
register.

The great thing about flexibilities is the way you get set in a good embouchure formation and repeat the slur many times. This reinforces the way you want to feel when you approach upward slurs. Building strength is another benefit, as is wind continuity.

In the exercises in Figure 11-5, hold the starting note for a brief long tone, establishing a strong, secure sound. Then the slurs begin gradually, again setting up the wind and embouchure. Listening to the CD will help you get a sense of how to play a flexibility drill. Only the last phrase, in C major, is demonstrated.

Keep the same flow of wind as the slurs speed up. Be sure to take many breaks, especially between exercises. Start with the first one and only continue when you're playing it smoothly at a medium dynamic, with clear, quick overtone slurs.

Play at a medium dynamic. If you play too loudly in flexibility studies, you can end up forcing the sound rather than developing a fluent approach.

Figure 11-5:
Flexibilities
for the
upper
register.

Music for the Upper Register

I once told Arnie Chycoski, the brilliant lead player for Rob McConnell's Boss Brass, that I was having trouble with the high notes. He said, "Well, do you play up there?", and I admitted that I didn't very much. He just laughed and shook his head. We all tend to avoid what's difficult for us, or what we *think* is difficult. But it's clear that if you want to play well in the upper register, you have to practice up there. In this section, I give you some music to lead you toward the higher notes.

Rest as much as you play. The upper register especially requires some downtime to let the lips relax.

A clarino fanfare

Figure 11-6 presents two fanfare etudes written to recall the clarino style of the baroque. (An *etude* is a particular kind of piece, a combination of a song and an exercise. A musical line can be expressed in a composition while working on technical skills.) These etudes were especially composed to help you approach the upper register with confidence. Very clear articulation and brilliant tone are features of clarino style.

A fanfare is intended to convey a warning or other important announcement over a great distance. A wonderful example is the offstage fanfare from the opera *Fidelio* by Beethoven. The CD will give you an idea of the style.

TRACK 81

Figure 11-6:
Two fanfares in clarino style.

A melody

It's not all fanfares for trumpeters — we get to be romantic, too. Melodies are usually slower and softer than fanfares. But articulation is also subtly different: A fanfare features marcato tonguing, with a very clear tongue. A ballad needs to convey a different feeling, so the approach is gentler. The articulation style called for is legato, meaning smooth.

 TRACK 82

Flowing toward the Upper Register

This little song moves toward the upper register, going to A above the staff. Playing from G to A involves hearing the notes clearly, increasing the speed of the wind, and having a very firm embouchure. Start with a relaxed, easy breath and a lovely tone.

 Hearing the note in your head before you play is a cornerstone of trumpet playing. It's especially important in the upper register because the overtones are separated by ever smaller intervals as you ascend, making it easier to hit the wrong note.

Although singing everything that you play as a way of getting familiar with the sound is a very good idea in the practice room, testing the pitch by humming under your breath just before you play isn't usually helpful, in my opinion. Sitting onstage before an entrance (nervously) humming what you hope and pray is the right note is not a confidence builder. Be brave: As you take a deep, relaxed breath, hear the note, or what you think is the note, and go for it.

An etude

Following is an etude that requires all the approaches covered in this chapter. You'll use the valves to slur up, and you'll do overtone slurs, leaps, and scales. Adding complexities such as dynamics makes scales, flexibilities, and etudes more interesting and useful, because you have to learn to play well at quiet levels. You'll notice dynamic markings in this etude.

Here's a play-by-play commentary on how to best approach each challenge:

- The measures are numbered above the staff on the first line, and then at the beginning of each line after that.

- In the first bar, it's great if you aim through the held note toward the moving eighth notes, like water flowing more quickly as it draws nearer to a waterfall.

- In measure 3, keep a steady stream of horizontal wind blowing through the eighth notes. When slurs are adjacent to tongued notes, always be sure to connect with wind when you tongue, as if you're still slurring.

- Measure 8 gives you a chance to try the trampoline concept. Play strongly on the A half note, and leap from that position of strength to the D.

- Crescendo in measure 11, toward the G (even though it isn't marked), and keep the horizontal flow moving as the figure descends to the G in measure 12.

- Measure 13 is a change of style; this is a brief fanfare, so it's louder and more accented. It's closely followed by a gentler figure in measure 14, and then bars 15 and 16 have the same contrast. Really exaggerate the difference in style and dynamic level.

- In measure 16, there's an upward leap of a fifth, so blow lots of air and hear the note clearly. You can practice a glissando on the mouthpiece as a warm-up.

- In measure 19, there's an overtone slur, G to E, repeated twice, like a flexibility. Again a horizontal flow is the best concept.

TRACK 83

Floating Up

This etude is not actually in the upper register, but prepares you for higher playing. If you can move easily up to G with a clear and relaxed tone, then you're ready to move higher. Never compromise the smooth breathing and lovely tone that you can achieve when playing in the middle register. The high notes will come as a result of solid playing habits in the middle range. The CD demonstrates the first 12 measures of this etude.

 Rest after playing each of these pieces, and for a longer time when you've finished all the exercises in this chapter. Play some quiet low notes to help your lips relax, and then put the trumpet away for at least an hour. See Chapter 16 for tips on helping your lips relax after a strenuous workout.

Chapter 12

Arpeggios: Leaps of Faith

An *arpeggio* is a different configuration of the notes in a scale, using the first, third, and fifth degrees. In this chapter, you have a chance to play exercises and etudes using arpeggios. You discover how to keep a connected horizontal line of music going forward even while going up and down arpeggios. Finally, you play some music that combines arpeggios and scales, the building blocks of music.

Picking Your Spots: How Scales Become Arpeggios

A *scale* is a series of notes, identified by the letters of the alphabet from A to G. In Chapter 4, I define the major scale as notes separated by the following intervals: tone, tone, semitone, tone, tone, tone, semitone. The piano keyboard can be a visual guide: The white notes between C and C an octave away make up a major scale. An *arpeggio* is a series of notes based on that scale.

The C major arpeggio takes the first, third, and fifth notes, plus the octave, from the C major scale. So, you have C, E, G, and C. If you remember your elementary school music classes, you can sing "doh, mi, so, doh," and you'll have it. Find a keyboard and experiment. (See Chapter 4 for an illustration of a keyboard — you can check the names of the notes on that illustration.)

For a trumpeter, an arpeggio is a little more of a challenge than a scale because of the different spaces between the notes. The first interval is between C and E, or doh and mi. It's a *major third* and requires a little more wind speed, as well as a clear idea of the sound of the note. The next interval, between E and G, or mi and so, is a *minor third*. It's called a minor third because it's smaller than a major third by one semitone, yet it's still two notes away (E, F, G). Minor thirds are usually a little easier to play than major thirds, just because they're a semitone closer, but they still need more wind than a second. Then you have G to C (G, A, B, C), which is called a *perfect fourth*. There are other kinds of arpeggios, but in this chapter you work mostly with the major arpeggio and briefly with the diminished seventh arpeggio.

Singing these musical figures is very helpful; if you sing some music, it's planted in your musical inner hearing very directly. I encourage you to hang around a piano and sing scales and arpeggios whenever the spirit moves you.

Combining the Upper and Lower Registers

Because arpeggios contain leaps, they travel a long way in a short time. In four notes, you're an octave higher or lower, which is eight scale steps. So, part of playing arpeggios is traveling between registers, making them a challenge. Arpeggios are very good practice vehicles for this reason.

The arpeggio studies in Figure 12-1 travel higher and lower. Notice that they all begin with a fermata, so you can establish a secure sound, before moving up or down, and returning to the starting note.

A sense of balance is very helpful when you're playing arpeggios — just as core strength is helpful to a practitioner of yoga or martial arts. Strength and security in the middle makes the upper and lower registers more reachable — friendly neighbors you can drop in on any time and be sure of a hospitable welcome.

Connecting from note to note is one of the fundamentals of trumpet technique. How you get from A to B, or C or G, matters a lot because that's primarily where your ability to communicate resides. Sure, beautiful tone is an end in itself to some extent — and it's a powerful aspect of playing a musical instrument — but tone isn't everything.

The foundation of connecting notes is slurring. That's where the energy and flow in your playing come from. Tonguing is added for clarity — and that's very important, too — but good tonguing is based on a smooth flow of wind, and slurring is the pure form of that. Scratch any technical problem you're having playing the trumpet and it turns out to be a wind problem. So, practice everything slurred first to make the connections, and then add the tongue for clarity and variety. "Tongue while slurring" is a pithy little reminder to help you keep your priorities in order.

ON THE CD

Go with the flow

How does flow differ from force? Both bring to mind energy and motion, but the idea of force is that something is being overcome, some resistance that must be defeated. What you have to learn is that the resistance that can invite force is supplied almost completely by you. If you tense up, you work against yourself, and you become the obstacle that force is required to overcome.

Sounds kind of tiring, doesn't it? The great trumpeter and teacher Vincent Cichowicz compared the approach of some trumpeters to driving with their foot on the brake and the gas at the same time. You can easily see how pointless it is to play that way, but changing to a more relaxed, flowing way of playing isn't easy. The key is to practice that way every day, so that it becomes a habit. When you've nurtured a healthy playing procedure, you'll revert to that approach even when you're trying for high notes or playing in any kind of stressful situation.

Remember: You can never go wrong by taking a few big sighs and blowing a sheet of paper, and then playing a mouthpiece song or two.

The establishing of healthy playing habits is why you warm up every day and play a lot of music in the middle-register, no-stress category. Yes, you need to challenge yourself in practice, playing fast notes, high notes, low notes, low to high notes, and so on. But you establish your home base of secure, relaxed tone production before, during, and at the end of a more strenuous practice session, and that repeated nurturing of a flowing, not forceful, playing procedure stands you in good stead.

The following study is based on Mr. Cichowicz's concept of flow studies, using scales and arpeggios. The CD focuses your attention on the kind of tone production resulting from a flow of wind.

TRACK 85

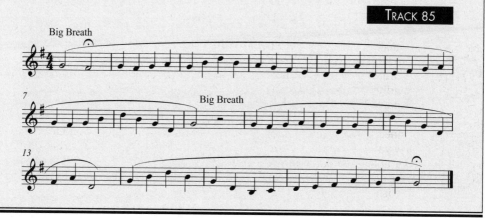

Figure 12-1 is based on the third study from Herbert L. Clarke's *Technical Studies for the Cornet.* Although it was written for the cornet, the principles are exactly applicable to the trumpet. (Clarke's book is used by every trumpeter I know.) Play with one smooth flow of wind, as if you're holding a long tone. You can establish that long-tone feeling on the first note, sustained as long as you want under a fermata. The CD will give your inner trumpet some nourishment.

TRACK 84

Figure 12-1:
Arpeggio
study.

Putting Scales and Arpeggios Together

The etudes in this section combine scales and arpeggios in ways you'll encounter in solos and ensemble music. One of the purposes of practicing is to prepare for any eventuality, any challenge that emerges in the music you play. I recommend a lot of variety in practice repertoire. But the key is to have a consistent approach based on a flow of horizontal wind (see the nearby sidebar, "Aiming horizontally, not vertically") and a clear idea of what you want to sound like. Playing from a secure base gives you the confidence and good basic playing procedure to meet the challenges that will present themselves as you continue to improve as a player.

Figure 12-2 is an etude that is very lyrical, with a flowing melodic line. The CD will prepare you to play the piece well.

In this lyrical study, the emphasis is on beautiful, flowing tone. A big, relaxed breath is essential. When tonguing is called for, it should be smooth, legato, to go with the basically slurred style. Here are some more tips for playing this etude:

- ✔ In the third bar, a subtle crescendo as you ascend is in order. It shouldn't be obvious that you get louder, but you should have a sense of direction toward the top note.

- ✔ In measure 7, there's a leap of a sixth, F to D. Lots of faster air will propel you up. Of course, remember not to think too much about going up — think instead of a horizontal flow, and hear the destination note.

- ✔ Measure 15 contains an arpeggio formed by an overtone slur, B♭, D, F. Remember to keep blowing outward and to keep the embouchure very firm and stable.

All the slurs in this etude can be played with a strong forward moving stream of wind. Whether tonguing or slurring, it's the wind that connects the notes in a smooth line of sound.

Smoothly (legato)

Figure 12-2: Lyrical study in scales and arpeggios.

Connecting Registers with the Diminished Seventh Arpeggio

Arpeggios in their simplest form consist of the root, third, and fifth notes of the scale, with the octave repeating at the top. There are other kinds of arpeggios, and the *diminished seventh* is one of them. The diminished seventh is very helpful for connecting the middle, lower, and upper registers.

The diminished seventh arpeggio has four notes, plus the octave. Each note is a minor third away from its neighbor. Because the scale this arpeggio comes from is not the major scale, accidentals (sharps and flats, which raise or lower the scale tones) are used. The C diminished seventh arpeggio consists of C, E♭, G♭, and A, with C repeating at the top. Look at the piano keyboard in Chapter 4 to find these notes, and sing them.

Aiming horizontally, not vertically

Pick a comfortable note in your good singing range and sing *ah*. Make sure that the vowel is really *ah* and not *uh*. Now, begin to sing up and down, starting with small glissandi, and then gradually expanding the range, always returning to your first note. Here's the important part: *When you sing up, think down, and when you sing down, think up.* The effect is to produce a horizontal flow with a consistent sound. After

you've sung this little warm-up, you can buzz it on the mouthpiece. You'll have set yourself up for a successful performance of the following etude.

After listening to the CD, play the following etude on the mouthpiece. Then perform it on the trumpet, with a big breath and a smooth flowing sound.

TRACK 87

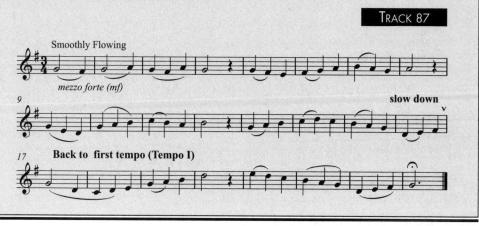

ON THE CD

Figure 12-3 shows a simple arpeggio. Listen to the CD to get used to how it sounds.

Figure 12-3:
C diminished seventh arpeggio.

TRACK 88

The etude in Figure 12-4 starts in the middle register and goes lower and then higher, gradually increasing the range. Slur all the notes, using a firm embouchure and a steady flow of wind. As the notes descend, think slower air, but in a horizontal direction. When the notes ascend, blow faster, again horizontally. Breathe wherever you need to, using the breaks in the slur marks as guides.

Throughout this book, the advice I give is to breathe deeply and in a relaxed sigh. You're most able to think of that advice at the beginning of a passage, when you have the time to collect your thoughts. In the middle of playing, you'll need to take breaths, too, and these breaths should be modeled after the first breath as much as possible. When you feel the need to breathe, but before you're desperate for oxygen, take the time for a breath. If it's a lyrical phrase, you have time to let the phrase relax, slowing down a bit before you inhale.

Listening to the CD will help you hear the sound of a diminished seventh arpeggio. Because the notes are all a minor third apart, the connections are able to be made quite smoothly. As always, buzzing the exercise first on the mouthpiece alone will help you produce the kind of wind flow necessary for a smooth performance.

TRACK 89

Figure 12-4:
Exercise
on the C
diminished
seventh
arpeggio.

Making the Connections

Thinking musically and coordinating your musical ideas with your wind, fingers, lips, and tongue need practice to become natural for you. The unifying force is the musical image, your inner hearing of the piece. When you play, hear what you want to sound like, it's as simple as that! Making connections in your thinking will help you make the connections from note to note, and you'll sound smooth.

TRACK 90

Connecting the Dots

The last music in this chapter puts together many of the ways in which you connect notes. There are scales, arpeggios, slurs of different kinds, and intervals large and small. There are slurred and tongued passages, soft and loud. Blow smoothly throughout! Pay close attention to the markings, and listen to the CD. I hope you enjoy playing it!

Chapter 13

Developing Strength and Endurance

*W*hen I was a teenager, I was fortunate to have a conversation with the great trumpeter Albert Aarons, of the Count Basie Band, after a concert. I asked him about endurance — being able to play all night seemed amazing to me. He was very nice and wisely said to me, "Just play, man. Play." But what should you play in order to build the strength *necessary* for trumpet playing, and how should you play it? This chapter covers some concepts and offers some musical selections to answer those questions.

But before I dive in, I want to define what I mean by *endurance* (or chops, as brass players call it). The presence of strong muscles in your cheeks doesn't necessarily mean you have good chops, any more than a body builder's bulkiness implies athletic ability. Here's the parallel: A body builder trains to have a developed musculature; trumpeters need to train to be able to play for a whole evening or to get through an etude or solo, still playing well at the end. And the way to achieve that goal is to play well, with good breaths and a strong *inner sound concept* (the little trumpet in your head; see Chapter 6).

To a large extent, endurance just comes from playing regularly, and it develops over years. But some specific kinds of playing and approaches can help you build endurance. In this chapter, I fill you in.

A Mighty Wind

When it comes to endurance, the single most important part of trumpet playing is wind. Wind that is freely blown — not tightly released, compressed air, or a forcefully produced hurricane — will help you produce the kind of sound that you want to make, the kind of sound that you're hearing in your mind. Wind also helps to form and strengthen your embouchure.

Time spent developing better use of wind is always time well spent. In this section, I offer exercises designed to increase the amount of air you can inhale and help you use wind more efficiently.

Blowing up a storm

The amount of air that your lungs can hold varies according to your physical size and your overall health. But the amount of air that your lungs can hold, although important, is *not* the most important aspect of good wind use. *How you breathe in and out — how relaxed, smooth, and flowing your breath is —* matters more than how much air you can hold.

Still, making good use of your lung capacity can be a big help with how much wind you have to use (your capacity) and how you use it (your efficiency). I explore both aspects of breathing in this section.

If you start to feel dizzy at any point during the following breathing exercises, which is a good possibility, rest. You probably don't want to try this or any other breathing exercise while walking a tight rope.

Increasing your capacity

Most average-size adults have a vital air capacity of 4 to 5 liters. Bigger people — people who are broader, taller, or who have longer torsos — have a greater capacity. Some people have vital air capacities of 10 liters or more. On the other end of the spectrum, the famous teacher and tuba virtuoso Arnold Jacobs, whose concepts I reference throughout this book, was said to have a capacity late in his life of only 2.5 liters because of various lung illnesses he suffered. Even so, Jacobs was able to play the instrument requiring the largest amount of wind, in the best and loudest brass section in the world. He's the exception that proves the rule, however. On balance, the more air you can comfortably breathe into your lungs, the better.

If you take the time to do breathing exercises every time you start a playing session, you'll feel the benefits in improved sound and endurance.

Exercise #1

The following exercise helps you increase your lung capacity. Before you try this exercise, read this section all the way through so that you know what to expect.

1. **With your finger at your lips, as if to say "shh," breathe in with a comfortable *oh* sound for two counts, about 1 second per count.**

   This is a metronome marking of 60, if you want to use it.

2. **Exhale freely for four counts.**

   As you blow out move your finger outward, as if you're blowing it away.

3. **Repeat steps 1 and 2 several times.**

4. **Now inhale for four counts, and exhale for four counts.**

   Make sure you're empty at the end of four counts, not gasping or doubled over with the exertion of emptying your lungs, just comfortably at rest. As Arnold Jacobs said, "Waste the wind — get rid of it."

5. **Repeat Step 4 several times.**

6. **Inhale for six counts, and exhale for six counts.**

7. **Repeat Step 6 several times.**

8. **Inhale for eight counts and exhale for eight counts.**

Throughout this exercise, your breathing should be relaxed and should sound free and breezy, not strained or tense. As in all breathing for the trumpet, there should be a smooth in-and-out feeling, with no pause between the inhale and the exhale.

Exercise #2

A little stretching while taking deep breaths can result in greater expansion of your torso, enabling your lungs to fill more easily. Find a large, airy space, with plenty of room to move, and follow these steps:

1. **While standing, reach up with your arms as high as you can, and take a big, easy breath. Then blow it out with a windy sound.**

2. **Bend over with your arms swinging loosely, and again take a big breath and blow it out.**

3. **Stand up and open your arms wide, embracing the world and all its possibilities, and breathe in and out in that posture.**

Feel free to add to this exercise any other position that works well for you. Do some freeform breathing and stretching.

The sound of the breath really is important. If you hear a gasp or rattle as you inhale, put your finger at the front of your lips in the "shh" position and focus on the wind moving past that place. Arnold Jacobs used to say that breathing should be thought of as happening outside the body, avoiding the tension of a constricted throat or oral cavity. Suck the wind toward you, and blow it away from you.

Exercise #3

Sometimes having some visual reinforcement can help you increase capacity. Here's what you need:

- A plastic bag, about 1 gallon to start with.

- A plastic tube, about 3 inches long with a 1-inch diameter. (Hardware stores sell them as plumbing connectors.)

- Heavy-duty masking tape or duct tape.

Now, tape the opening of the plastic bag to the tube, gathering it around the tube evenly, and sealing it tight.

When you've assembled the contraption, put the tube to your mouth, inhale deeply, and exhale into the bag, trying to fill it. If you easily fill it, get a bigger bag — you want to challenge yourself. After that first inhale and exhale, you can breathe in and out through the tube two or three times. Then stop.

Breathing your own exhaled air actually keeps you from hyperventilating, but only breathe in and out through the tube two or three times so you don't inhale too much carbon dioxide.

As you're able to breathe more deeply, increase the size of the bag.

Becoming more efficient

When you're playing music on the trumpet, you won't always have all the time in the world to breathe. Sometimes it seems as if the composer or conductor has no understanding of the fact that wind players actually need to breathe. You have to get used to that and learn to be very efficient with how you breathe.

The following exercises, based on one that Arnold Jacobs taught, helps you breathe quickly without gasping. The breath that you take when you first start should be the template for all the breaths that follow, even though you'll have much less time for some of those later breaths.

1. **Set a metronome to 60 counts per minute.**

2. **Inhale for four counts.**

3. **Exhale for six counts.**

4. Breathe in on count seven, exactly in the time of one beat.

5. Exhale on the next count again for six counts.

You can repeat steps 4 and 5 several times.

Don't begin your breath before beat seven — you want to begin right on the beat, and breathe out exactly on the following beat. The idea is to start to teach yourself how to take a quick breath, but one that is free and deep and still sounds easy and windy.

Now the goal is to speed things up a bit. So, still with seven-count units, speed up the metronome to about 72 counts per minute, and repeat the preceding exercise. You can increase the speed a few more times as you get better at the quick inhales.

Now to increase the speed, and the challenge, even more, try this exercise:

1. Set a metronome to 72 counts per minute.

2. Breathe in for one count.

3. Smoothly exhale while counting to four.

4. On the second half of the fourth count (on the *and* of four), inhale and then exhale on the next beat.

Repeat this exercise several times.

Now you have less time to breathe — only half a count — but you still want it to be free and deep, with a pleasant, windy quality to the sound. As you feel that you're improving, you can increase the speed, always making sure that your breath is relaxed and free and, thus, efficient.

Playing on the mouthpiece

Playing on the mouthpiece alone can help improve your wind capacity. Because no trumpet is attached to the mouthpiece, there's much less resistance, so you use much more wind. Practicing on the mouthpiece encourages you to take bigger breaths, especially if you try to increase the length of the phrases that you play.

Always play musically on the mouthpiece, expressing the feeling of the piece of music. Whether you play an exercise or a song, make sure that your tone is clear, the tuning is consistent, and the articulation is precise.

Figure 13-1 is a long tone and sliding exercise that you can play on the mouthpiece. It's designed to encourage you to breathe deeply and easily, so make sure to do exactly that. Don't try to conserve the wind — blow freely and inhale when you need to, taking four counts for your inhale. The CD will give you the idea by demonstrating the first part of the exercise.

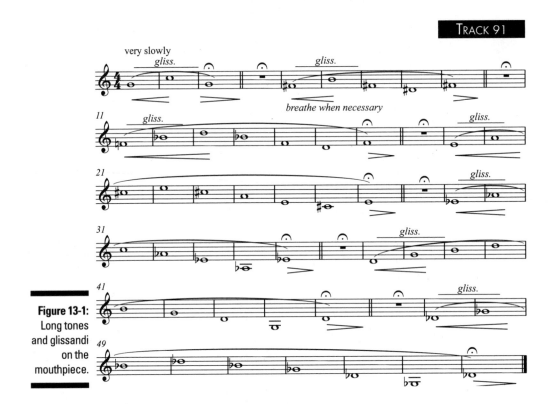

Figure 13-1:
Long tones and glissandi on the mouthpiece.

Speeding Up the Valves

Pushing down a trumpet valve doesn't take a lot of muscular strength, but you wouldn't know it by watching a group of beginners. Beginners tend to grip the trumpet tightly and clench their right hands as if for mortal combat. The feelings of anxiety you feel when you're learning a new skill may express themselves in tension all over your body, with your hands leading the way. So, a big part of developing skill in fingering the valves is understanding the *kind* of strength needed. You need fluidity, suppleness, speed, and coordination to play the trumpet, not brute force. When you're trying to develop well-coordinated speed, start slowly.

Slowing down for speed

Strange as it may seem, practicing slowly, with great precision, will lead to excellent fast playing. The exercise in Figure 13-2 is based on H. L. Clarke's *Technical Studies for the Cornet.* Your fingers should rest lightly on the valve caps, but lift a little before descending very quickly. You have to bang the valves down, while maintaining a steady breath of wind (and not jarring the trumpet). This technique creates the smooth connection that all trumpeters strive for.

Each phrase is slightly longer. Playing them all slowly, at a moderate dynamic, will help build embouchure strength. Take the time indicated in the rests with the fermati. Listen to the CD performance of the first part of the exercise before you play it. Remember that the point of this study is to play with a very slow tempo and quick valves.

Figure 13-2: Scale study for the fingers.

Accelerating the finger action

Now it's time to *gradually* increase the speed. The metronome can be very handy here. Set it at 60 to the quarter note to start with, and only start moving it up by no more than 4 beats at a time when you're playing with clarity and accuracy. You'll find that the speed increases without a lot of effort on your part. Don't go faster than the metronome and keep the brisk finger action and the smooth windy connections between the notes.

The scale studies in Figure 13-3 are again based on H. L. Clarke's *Technical Studies for the Cornet*. The performance on the CD is played at a tempo of 120 to the quarter note to give you a sense of where you're headed. Start at the slower speed as marked.

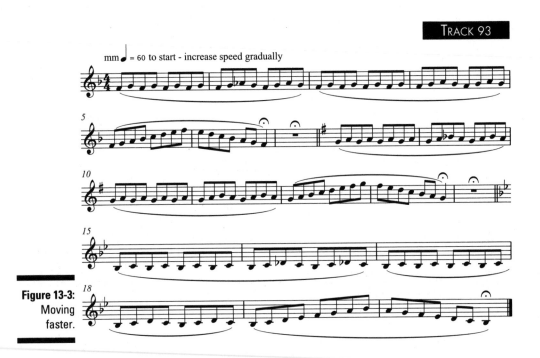

Figure 13-3:
Moving
faster.

Strengthening the Embouchure

Strong chops are the result of good playing — and a lot of it. The trouble is, developing embouchure strength takes time. When a certain threshold of strength and confidence is reached, a player can be said to have *gig chops* — meaning, she's strong and confident enough to get through any playing demands. There is strategy involved in gig chops, too:

✔ You need to know when to take it easy, even drop a bar or two if another player is covering it or if the other parts are so strong that nobody will notice if you take a few seconds' rest.

✔ You need to refrain from overblowing. If your lips have to work too hard to stay together because you're forcing too much air through them, they'll get tired very quickly.

Musical and sensible approaches to playing, along with specific practice techniques, will help you gain strength and confidence. In this section, I give you some ideas.

Holding on longer

Playing long tones is one way to strengthen your embouchure. Holding one note can get boring, and long tones lack the demands for making connections that are so important for a trumpeter. But there is a place for long tones as part of a comprehensive practice routine.

The long tone study in Figure 13-4 contains variety in dynamic level and a few extra notes thrown in to keep you musically involved. Play with a beautiful sound, clear and unforced, and remember to take lots of rest — at least as much rest as playing time. The first and last sections of this exercise are demonstrated on the CD.

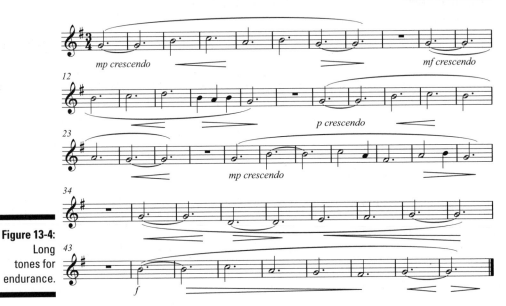

TRACK 94

mp crescendo   *mf crescendo*

p crescendo

mp crescendo

f

Figure 13-4:
Long tones for endurance.

Slurring for strength

Wind slurs are very good for improving a trumpeter's *flexibility* (the ability to play all over the range of the instrument reliably with a consistent tone). Wind slurs are also excellent for strengthening the chops. The wind slurs and flexibilities in Figure 13-5 require you to play for a little longer at a time, thus building strength. Performing a rendition on the mouthpiece alone is a great idea. The CD demonstrates both a mouthpiece version and the trumpet performance of the first bars of each series.

Play this exercise softly — you don't need to play loudly to build endurance. It's better to let the musical demand of the piece you're playing dictate the dynamic level. Maintain a firm embouchure throughout — the less your embouchure changes, the better your chances of playing with consistent tone. As always, take some windy breaths in and out before you start.

Wind speed is one of the key ingredients for changing notes smoothly. Hear the note you want to change to and then blow the appropriate air speed: faster for the higher notes and slower for the lower ones.

These wind slurs will build endurance by requiring you to play for a sustained time. The first phrase of each section is demonstrated on the CD.

Figure 13-5:
Wind slurs for endurance.

Etudes for Endurance

I've been preaching frequent rest during a practice session. You need to build strength and then let the body recover, absorbing the new situation. But sometimes you do have to push yourself, and etudes are a great way to do that. Playing in an ensemble is great for building strength as well, but if you don't have a gig or a rehearsal, etudes are always there for you. A good etude is an attractive, interesting piece of music, with technical challenges woven through it. An etude is wonderful for endurance because, if you think of it as a piece of music, you're inspired to play it through from beginning to end, strengthening the embouchure by using it appropriately.

An etude usually focuses on one or two technical challenges. The first of the following two etudes is concerned with developing your fluency between low and middle range, with some forays into the near upper register; the second of the two etudes works on clear articulation as you move throughout the low and middle ranges. Because both etudes are intended to help you develop endurance, I suggest employing both practice strategies I mention in the "Strengthening the Embouchure" section, earlier in this chapter.

- ✓ Focus on any technical challenges — for example, spots where you have to slow down in order to play.

- ✓ Then devote some practice time to performing these pieces from start to finish, without stopping to replay or work on anything. Make it a performance. You can up the ante a little by recording yourself and listening afterward for the good things and for the places that you need to polish.

Use the pauses that I've written into the etudes to get a relaxed breath and let the lips rest for a second or two. And remember that you're playing a piece of music — not Beethoven perhaps, but music with expression in tempo, dynamic, and articulation.

TRACK 96

Etude in a Flowing Style

This next etude is in 3/4 time, which always seems to me to flow along very well. Use that flowing style to guide your playing, and remember to breathe deeply and in a relaxed way. This etude is accompanied by the piano. The last note, D, under the fermata, is held for 6 clicks; then you'll have 12 clicks, or four measures, to get ready to play with the accompaniment.

It's all in your head

You can build your endurance with all the exercises I offer in this chapter, but if you allow negative thoughts or excessively controlling thoughts to take hold, none of it will matter. Negative thoughts do nothing to help a trumpeter become a stronger player, capable of playing for long stretches with consistent accuracy and artistry.

The trouble with trumpeters is the chatter that goes on while we play. The minute you say to yourself that your chops feel good and that endurance won't be a problem, your clever little brain gives you a signal that isn't the image of the music you want to play, but instead how great it is that you aren't tired. So, of course, you start getting tired.

The key to endurance on the trumpet is, first, to get in good shape by playing well and sensibly, finding the balance between challenging yourself and allowing yourself some rest time. But maybe even more important is to stay in the musical moment, to keep making the music that's in your mind. The great trumpet performer and teacher James Thompson says that we have to stay in the present time — not in the past ("Oh, that went well" or "I could've done that better") and not in the future ("I think I've got the chops for this next part" or "Do I have the chops for this next part?"). The present tense, the *now* of music, is filled with the sounds you want to make. There's no room for anything else.

TRACK 97

Etude in Staccato and Marcato Style

This etude for endurance involves staccato and marcato tonguing, with legato tongue and slurs mixed in for variety. Avoid a heavy stroke of the tongue for staccato and marcato. *Staccato* simply means short, not accented, and marcato accents should be played with a strong, windy breath rather than a hard tongue.

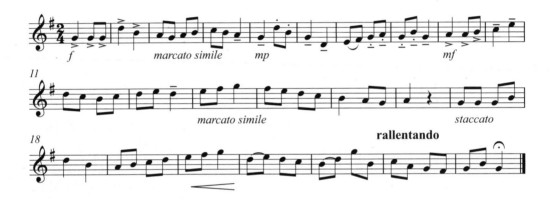

Strengthening with artificial aids

When I was a young player I was advised to strengthen my embouchure by gripping a pencil between my lips and holding it there with my embouchure while I tugged on it. I haven't heard that one for a long time, but new devices have appeared that are elaborations of the basic pencil trick. They're basically body-building for the embouchure and I have some reservations about that approach. In my opinion, the embouchure should be strengthened by doing what it's supposed to do and doing it well (in other words, by playing the trumpet). Performing isometric exercises using devices like the kind you see advertised could damage the lips and cheek muscles. Many well-respected players and teachers have endorsed these products (although not too many that I know and work with), but still, I have serious reservations about them. I think that Albert Aarons had it right when he said, "Just play, man. Play."

Chapter 14

Becoming More Articulate

. . . .

. . . .

*B*ecoming articulate on the trumpet is just as important as it is in speaking or writing. Clarity is a major goal when working on *tonguing* (adding the stroke of the tongue as in the sound *tooh* as you change or repeat notes), *slurring* (changing notes without the tongue), and combinations thereof. The extra ingredient for trumpeters is the development of tonguing speed. Trumpet music calls for all sorts of tempos and articulations, and you have to become fluent, just as you are in your native language.

The main principles of quick tonguing are

✔ A smooth, consistent flow of wind

✔ A concise, quick stroke of the tongue, as if saying *tooh*

✔ A firm, stable embouchure that doesn't move with each tongue stroke

You want to follow a practice method that starts with slow tonguing, increasing in speed, while maintaining these three principles. Lucky for you, that's exactly what I show you in this chapter.

After you've gotten acquainted with the rapid single stroke of the tongue, I introduce you to multiple tonguing.

Starting with the Basics: Single Tonguing

The basic form of tonguing is the single tongue. In Chapter 6, I introduce what the master teacher and trumpeter Vincent Cichowicz called the *basic legato* form of articulation. The basic legato is the style of tonguing enabling you to clearly articulate each note without an accent or a gap between them. Most of the music that you play calls for this basic form of articulation, so it makes sense to spend time establishing good habits.

The other reason to practice your single tonguing is that the faster and more efficiently you're able to do the basic tonguing, the better your multiple tonguing will be.

You can work on increasing tonguing speed by practicing wind patterns. Look in a mirror as you blow freely while tonguing *too-too-too-too-too,* slowly at first and then faster until you reach your fastest speed. Looking in the mirror helps you make sure that your jaw, cheeks, and lips aren't moving as you tongue. You don't have to form a trumpet embouchure for wind patterns, just the shape you make for the sound *tooh.* Alternately, inhale as you continue to tongue; the sound *doo* works well on the inhale. This little exercise relaxes you and helps isolate the tongue stroke from the embouchure muscles.

Practicing your single-tonguing technique

Figure 14-1 is an exercise to help you develop speed and clarity in your single tonguing. The practice of starting with a sustained tone establishes the flow of wind and the stable embouchure that are so crucial for proper tonguing. The first four notes are played at a slow speed, but with a very quick, clear stroke of the tongue while maintaining the flow of windy tone that you've established. The metronome marking is set at 60 to the quarter note, one quarter note per second. The tone should remain steady, with no change in quality. The only difference is the sound of *t* at the start of each quarter note. Listen to the CD to get the idea. The first six measures are recorded.

After you've practiced Figure 14-1 several times and you're satisfied with the smoothness and clarity of the articulation, you can start to move faster. Increase the metronome speed by one increment at a time. When you can tongue quarter notes at a setting of about 120 beats, or two quarter notes per second for four measures in a row, you're ready to move to a more advanced exercise.

TRACK 98

Figure 14-1: Setting up the basic legato.

In the exercise in Figure 14-2, you start with a whole note, then quarter notes, and then add eighths and sixteenths, always maintaining the consistent steady tone. The CD demonstrates the consistent line of tongued notes on the first line of the exercise.

I strongly recommend playing each of the tonguing warm-ups in Figures 14-1 and 14-2 on the mouthpiece before playing them on the trumpet.

TRACK 99

Figure 14-2: Speeding up the single tongue.

The tongue should be the only thing moving when you articulate. The wind flow continues unchanged and the embouchure remains still. Think of the tongue as bouncing on the wind, much like a rope trailing a speeding boat bounces on the waves. It's the momentum of the boat that bounces the rope, and in articulation it's the wind that energizes the tongue. (I like that image — I heard it from Fred Mills, the late, great trumpeter of the Canadian Brass.)

Changing notes while single-tonguing

The challenge now is to change notes while tonguing. The trick is to get really good at tonguing on one note, so you hardly have to think about it. Adding the coordination necessary to change notes at the same time becomes possible when you've established your single tonguing.

Overtone connections

The exercise in Figure 14-3 develops your tonguing while playing *overtone connections* (connections between notes with the same fingering). Practice these drills without the tongue, as overtone slurs, before playing them with the single tongue. The CD contains the first phrase, demonstrating the idea of horizontal flow of sound, which is fueled by a consistent exhale.

I tell my students to "tongue while slurring," which seems contradictory but really isn't. You have to play as if slurring, with a connected, windy sound, while adding the tapping of the tongue.

Projecting your sound

Projection is a very important part of trumpet technique. A projected sound makes articulation much easier. You need to project your sound without necessarily playing loudly.

It helps to look at an object across the room, or out the window, and imagine that your sound is headed there on a straight line. (Actually, that's what really is happening, so imagining it should be fairly easy.)

A good demonstration of this is to find a nice quiet spot outdoors (preferably not near a library or other quiet area — people just have no sense of humor about these things, trust me), and aim your sound at a wall or grove of trees that will give you an echo. You'll hear your sound bouncing back to you, and your tonguing will be much smoother as a result.

Figure 14-3: Tonguing overtone connections.

Valve connections

In Chapter 8, I introduce the coordination of tonguing while using the valves to change notes. Now your job is to increase the speed of these note changes while playing a smooth line of music.

Once again, a scale study (shown in Figure 14-4) serves our purposes very well. Begin by slurring the notes, creating a smooth line, and don't play the exercise too quickly at the start. The idea is to start with what you can do well and work your way up to greater challenges (in this case, increased speed). You have to bang down the valves very quickly as you keep the exhale going. The slurred notes at the start of several of the measures will help you get the wind flowing smoothly. And, as always, hear the music you want to play in as much rich detail as possible.

The CD gives you the concept of smooth articulation, performing the first section in F major. Listen to it several times, and sing along. You can also do a wind pattern, playing some air trumpet while moving the valves and hearing the musical line. If you can play tongued eighth notes for a few measures at about 120 beats per minute (120 to the quarter note on the metronome), you're making good progress.

TRACK 101

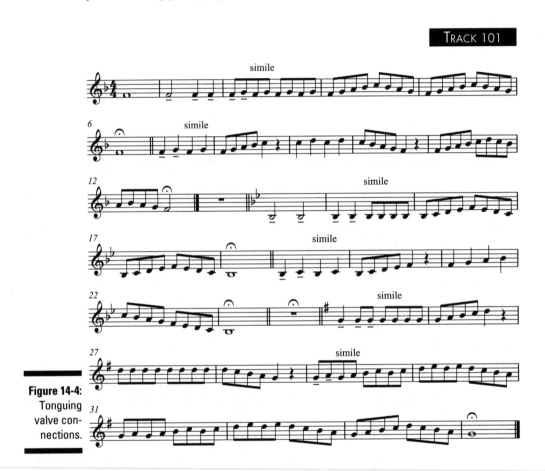

Figure 14-4:
Tonguing
valve con-
nections.

Etudes for speeding up the single tongue

Drills are necessary to set up any new technique, but you need to apply the skills you're developing. In order to be able to use your new techniques in a musical context, you need to play music that has many different kinds of patterns, as well as music involving faster tonguing.

Figure 14-5 consists of two short etudes that will help you learn to apply the principles of rapid tonguing. Listen to the CD for guidance. The first section of each etude is recorded.

Figure 14-5: Etudes for speeding up the single tongue.

Taking It Up a Notch: Double Tonguing

Because trumpeters and other wind players have to keep up with pianists, whose fingers fly on the keyboard, special techniques are required. A comparison with percussion technique is a helpful guide: Try tapping one hand on your desk — you can use a pencil if you like. See how quickly you can tap with just one hand? Now, using both hands, tap the same pattern at the same tempo that you achieved with just one. It's a lot easier, isn't it? Now increase the speed using both hands. You probably can tap about twice as fast using both hands.

Most of us have only one tongue, but we can use the front, or the tip, of the tongue, where we say *too,* and the middle part, where we say *koo.* Use the vowel *oo,* and slowly say *too-koo-too-koo-too-koo* until you're bored — or someone asks you to stop. (Practicing or even *talking* about single, double, and triple tonguing separates trumpeters from most of the rest of the population. You just have to get used to it.)

Perpetual motion: Rafael Mendez's famous recording

The famous trumpet virtuoso Rafael Mendez was a household name for many years, particularly in the United States. He had amazing technique and dramatic flare in performance. His most famous recording, one that just about drove me insane when I first heard it, is called *Moto Perpetuo.* It's a performance of Niccolò Paganini's composition, originally written for violin, and consisting of an unbroken flow of sixteenth notes at a very rapid tempo.

Mendez double-tongues all the notes, never missing a single note for over four minutes! The brilliant articulation and intense concentration required to play this piece boggles the mind. It's a virtuoso feat on the violin, but at least a violinist can breathe during the performance.

Mendez and subsequent trumpeters, such as Wynton Marsalis and Sergei Nakariakov, solved the problem by employing a technique called *circular breathing.* Using this technique, the player inhales through the nose while simultaneously forcing air out through the lips by compressing the cheeks.

Mendez's recording is found on the Internet at `http://en.kendincos.net/video-vvprrdff-moto-perpetuo-performed-by-rafael-mendez.html`. If you feel like being driven crazy, I recommend that you listen to it as a great example of double tonguing.

Double-tonguing on the wind alone

After you've experimented with the to-and-fro movement of the tongue — and it does take some practice — try some extended patterns with just wind and tongue. You can alternate *d* and *g* as another, smoother, method, as in *doo-goo-doo-goo-doo-goo*. Start slowly and maintain the consistent exhale. Emphasize the vowel *oo* rather than the consonant. Just as in single tonguing, the wind is the most important factor and the tongue taps the flow without interrupting it.

You can aim toward your palm as a way of making sure that the wind is always blowing, or hold a sheet of paper close to your mouth and blow toward it as you practice the double-tonguing pattern. Try to maintain about a 45-degree angle to the floor. The more preparation you do without the mouthpiece or the trumpet for double tonguing, the better.

Figure 14-6 is series of patterns that you can practice without a mouthpiece or trumpet. Keep a consistent tempo — I recommend using a metronome. Start with a speed that you can easily manage before increasing tempo gradually. Notice that in the first pattern, measure 2 is tongued in the normal way with a single tongue, measure 3 is a series of *koo* attacks, and measure 4 combines the *too* and the *koo*. All the tongue strokes should sound the same, or very close.

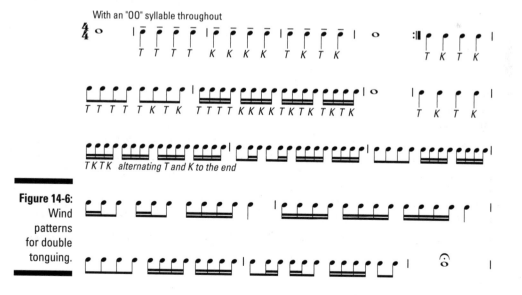

Figure 14-6:
Wind patterns for double tonguing.

Double-tonguing on the mouthpiece

The next step is to double-tongue on the mouthpiece. (My approach in all technical challenges is to establish the flow of wind, then play the mouthpiece, and finally play the trumpet.) Home-base G is a good starting point. Figure 14-7 is a setup for your double tonguing. Notice that you start with a long tone, establishing the flow of wind, then single-tonguing, four *koo* attacks, and finally double-tonguing. Listening to the CD will give you the pitch of G, as well as the concept of a flowing sound, lightly tapped by the tongue.

There should be no breaks in the tone and no changes in the intonation. Think of it as two independent parallel systems: a steady flow of wind and a tapping mechanism.

TRACK 103

Figure 14-7:
A double-
tonguing
exercise on
the mouth-
piece.

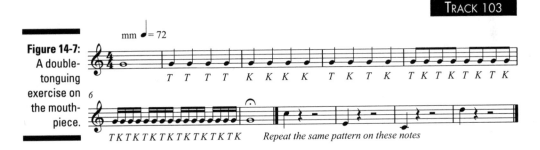

Double-tonguing on the trumpet

So, by small steps, you arrive at actually playing a double-tongued passage on the trumpet. Your patience in going through the wind pattern and mouthpiece drill (see the previous sections) is rewarded now.

In the exercise in Figure 14-8, as you start on home-base G, listen for a clear, unforced tone. Hold for four slow counts as written, and then play four quarter notes with the single tongue, followed in the next bar by four quarter notes with the *koo* syllable. From bar 4 on, the exercise is played with the double tongue. All the tongued syllables should match in sound — both the consonant (tongue stroke) and the vowel (tone). Repeat the exercise many times, until you feel comfortable with the double-tongue technique. The CD provides you with a model for playing. Listen for the consistent tone and intonation, and for the matching of tongued syllables.

TRACK 104

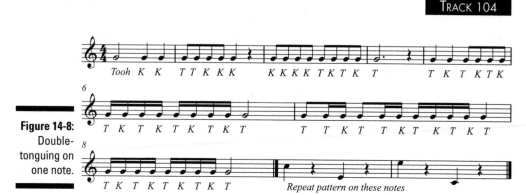

Figure 14-8:
Double-
tonguing on
one note.

Wind is the most important part of all types of tonguing.

Coordinating note changes and double tonguing

Eventually, you'll be required in any music that you encounter to play with all your articulations, so you have to practice the various ways in which you change notes using the double tongue. When changing notes, the principles remain the same: steady wind; firm embouchure; and a quick, precise tongue stroke. In this section, I give you two exercises in which double tonguing is used in overtone connections and valve connections.

Overtone connections

In the exercise in Figure 14-9, starting on home-base G connects you to a good, relaxed sound quality. When you change to the low C, remember to keep your embouchure firm. It's very easy to relax your embouchure and let the low C fall out, but the tone quality and the intonation aren't good, and your ability to move back up to the middle or high register is severely impaired. So, keep a firm embouchure.

The CD reminds you to keep a horizontal flow of sound, G and C connecting smoothly. Measures 17 through 20 of the exercise are recorded. Play the slurs with lots of wind and then blow exactly the same way when you double-tongue. Make sure that your sound is clear and consistent — no technical feat is interesting unless the sound is good. Repeat the exercise with all the seven valve combinations.

TRACK 105

Figure 14-9: Double-tonguing on overtone connections.

Valve connections

The studies in Figure 14-10 help give you what I call *fluency* (the ability to change notes smoothly and easily). Many technical skills come together in a study like this: proper breathing, firm embouchure, quick fingers on the valves, and coordination between the valves and the tongue. Listening to the CD excerpt will help you blow consistently and move the fingers very rapidly on the valves as you double-tongue. Start by slurring the patterns, except for the repeated note figures that you should tongue. When you're confident that the articulation is smooth and clear, add first the single and then the double tongue.

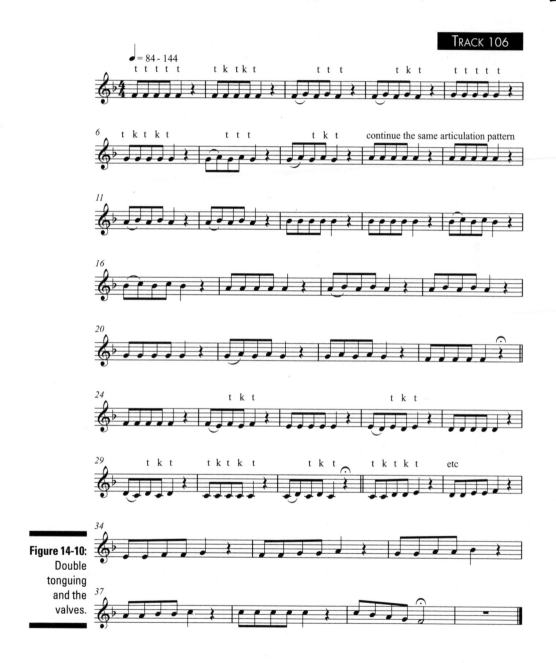

Figure 14-10:
Double
tonguing
and the
valves.

Often, players have the tendency to allow the embouchure to move each time the tongue does, sort of "chewing" the notes. This slows your technique and impairs the smoothness of the musical line. Look at yourself in the mirror while reviewing some repeated note drills such as the ones in Figure 14-2 and Figure 14-8 to make sure you're maintaining a stable embouchure.

Practicing Single and Double Tonguing with Etudes

Musicians have to be versatile, because the language of music can take unexpected turns. Just as they do in speech, people change the subject in music. Being able to change as the "conversation" changes is a very important part of musical communication — without variety, people lose interest in what's being played or sung. Employing single and double tonguing in a piece of music is standard compositional practice. The principles don't change: smooth, consistent wind; firm embouchure; and clear, quick tongue stroke.

Figure 14-11 shows two etudes with both single- and double-tonguing patterns. Listen carefully on the CD for the unbroken sound and the clear articulation, as the first sections of each etude are performed. Coordinating the fingers on the valves with the *t* or *k* syllables requires slow, careful practice. Each of the steps in improving your articulation technique must be grasped before you can profitably move on. These etudes should be practiced with the single tongue first, at a slow tempo. Gradually increase the speed as you attain clarity in the articulation and valve coordination.

You can never go wrong by practicing wind patterns. These etudes would be great practice that way. Hear the music, maybe even playing your "air trumpet" along with the CD, so that your wind and tongue are guided by your inner trumpet.

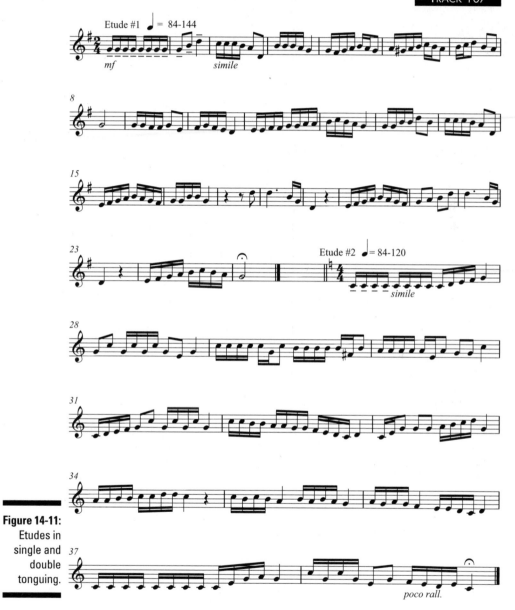

Figure 14-11:
Etudes in single and double tonguing.

More Tongue Twisting: Triple Tonguing

Yes, trumpet players do have something called triple tonguing. Triple tonguing is accomplished by using the two syllables *too* and *koo*, or *doo* and *goo*, in different combinations. You need triple tonguing to play fast triplet rhythms. Figure 14-12 is an example of some triplet figures.

Figure 14-12:
Triplet
rhythms.

pear a - pple pine-a - pple

Triplets occur very frequently in music. A *triplet* is made up of three notes equaling the time value of two of the same kind of notes. Here's how they look: A bracket appears over or under the three notes with a 3 above or below it. In Figure 14-12, you see a measure of 3/4 time, with a home-base G quarter note, then two eighth notes, then three triplets. All those figures have the same time value of one beat. The next example is a half note in 2/4 time, followed in the next measure by two quarter notes, then in the next by three quarter-note triplets.

For an easy verbal reference for the rhythm in these examples, say the words *pear, apple, pineapple* (quarter note, two eighth notes, triplet eighth notes in the first example; half note, two quarter notes, and triplet quarter notes in the second example).

The most common pattern is *too-too-koo.* Try saying these syllables slowly, noticing the to-and-fro motion of the front and middle of the tongue. I suggest developing this technique before considering the other alternatives, which you can read about in the next paragraph.

Trumpeters use three different combinations of the two syllables to triple-tongue. Many players use the pattern *too-too-koo.* Other players use *too-koo-too,* and a few players use something called *double-triple tonguing,* in which the double-tongue pattern is repeated, as in **too**-koo-too-**koo**-too-koo-**too**-koo-too-**koo**-too-koo, where the syllables in bold are stressed to establish the triplet rhythm. Eventually you can practice all these combinations — they're all useful in playing different kinds of musical figures and it's good to have them at your disposal.

Just the syllables

Mastering these combinations of syllables takes time. Here are some practice suggestions:

- ✔ Set your metronome to about 72 to the quarter note, and do a triple-tonguing wind pattern with the rhythms.

- ✔ Try the practice rhythms in Figure 14-13. Spend as much time as you need to become fluent with these syllables before you embark on the next step, which is the mouthpiece.

Figure 14-13: Wind patterns for triple tonguing.

Triple tonguing on the mouthpiece

Playing on the mouthpiece is an excellent way of improving just about everything to do with trumpet playing. When you play the mouthpiece, you need more wind than you do when you're on the trumpet, and you need to be accurate about playing the correct notes. For those reasons, your technique is stretched and improved. Triple tonguing is no exception to the rule of mouthpiece benefit.

TRACK 108

In this exercise, you set the metronome to about 72 to the quarter note, and repeat what you did in Figure 14-13, except with the mouthpiece. The CD demonstrates triple tonguing using excerpts from these patterns. Listen for the consistent tone and pitch, and the clear, but not too invasive, strokes of the tongue. Match the sound as well as you can.

Every gain made on the mouthpiece is worth at least double on the trumpet, so it's worth the effort. Start with a clear, unforced sound on the sustained note, and continue the same kind of wind when you add the tongue.

Adding the mouthpiece to the wind and tongue is a big leap, much more demanding than moving from mouthpiece to trumpet. Take your time with the mouthpiece exercises and make sure that your pitch stays consistent and that there is a steady tone that is punctuated by the *too-too-koo* or *doo-doo-goo* syllables. These patterns are an excellent opportunity to become comfortable with all three of the triple-tonguing patterns. Try *too-too-koo* first, then *too-koo-too*, and then **too**-*koo*-*too*-**koo**-*too*-*koo* — discover which one suits you best as your default pattern. I think it makes sense to have the flexibility of choosing the most appropriate syllables for each piece that you play.

Triple tonguing on the trumpet

The patience you've displayed will stand you in good stead now as you take up the trumpet and enter the world of triple tonguing. The syllables are clear and fluent and the continuity of tone on the mouthpiece is well established, so moving to the trumpet will seem easy.

Home-base G is a great place to start and the exercise in Figure 14-14 moves up and down from that central place. Listen to the CD for the tone and clarity of the performance. Start as slowly as needed — you might consider around 72 to the quarter note. Only move to a faster tempo when you're satisfied that your triple tonguing is consistent, clear, and not too difficult.

Don't be a masochist — if it's hard to do, you might not be getting it yet. Take your time. If it's easy to do and sounds good, congratulations and move on.

TRACK 109

Figure 14-14:
Triple-
tonguing
exercises
on the
trumpet.

Repeat the patterns in Figure 14-13 and Figure 14-14 in all the registers that you're comfortable playing. The first exercise in Figure 14-14 gives you an example of playing the rhythms on different notes. Make sure that you rest an equal amount of time as you play. The lips and the tongue get physically tired, and you need the time to recover.

To work on the technique of changing notes while triple-tonguing, try the exercise in Figure 14-15. Go slowly at first, but keep a steady tempo, with the help of the metronome. Don't forget to blow a steady stream of wind as you move the tongue and the valves. The CD demonstrates the first 12 measures of the exercise and gives you excellent nonverbal instruction — the more that you listen, the better your chances are of developing good technique.

TRACK 110

Figure 14-15: Changing notes while triple-tonguing.

Slurring and Multiple Tonguing

Combining slurred figures with multiple tonguing is beneficial in at least two ways:

- All the various forms of music that you'll be playing require this kind of versatility.
- Slurs help maintain the flow of wind, so combining them with tonguing helps the smoothness of your articulation.

Plus, it's just a pleasant type of playing — the notes seem to roll out freely, with lots of wind fueling them. The exercises in this section give you practice in the various forms of single, double, and triple tonguing, combined with slurs.

As a warm-up, practice these tonguing patterns just with wind. They all involve a longer note followed by double or triple tonguing, to set up the slur and tongue coordination. Holding your hand a few inches in front of your face and feeling the steady breath of wind, play the patterns in Figure 14-16. You also can hold a sheet of paper close in front of your mouth as you blow. Keep the page as close to a 45-degree angle to the floor as you can. Practice these patterns on the mouthpiece, too, getting your pitch from a keyboard or by playing the note first on the trumpet. Playing them on the trumpet also sets you up for successful performances of the exercises that follow.

Figure 14-16: Wind patterns for slurs and tonguing combined.

The most common problem that beginners encounter with slurring and tonguing combined is the tendency to shorten the last note under the slur. Carefully play the musical figures all slurred, and then when you add the tongue, just add the sound of *t,* but don't allow a space between the notes. You want one unbroken stream of sound.

Scale practice in double tonguing

Remember that the tongue bounces off the wind, like the rope of the end of the speedboat off the waves. The stroke of the tongue shouldn't be heavy and needs to be very concise. Think of a little jeweler's hammer, tapping with great precision.

Figure 14-17 gives you the opportunity to play several scale exercises with different examples of slurring and tonguing combined. The flow of wind in the two slurred notes gives you momentum as you tongue the rest of the figure. Listen to the CD performance of the first section of the exercise to strengthen your own sound concept and to give your tonguing a focused goal.

Play these exercises slowly. I suggest playing them with single tongue first, and then, at the same tempo, playing them with the double tongue. Being able to play passages in the in-between tempos with single and multiple tonguing gives you more versatility in adjusting to tempo changes in real performance situations. Notice the marking *D.C. al Fine* in Figure 14-17. This instruction means to return to the beginning (or the "top") and play to the *Fine* and fermata marking.

Composers are human, so forgive them for being a bit lazy from time to time. Many compositions are in ABA form; it's like a sandwich — bread, sardines, bread. To save time, ink, and paper, a system is used as a shortcut. The first section (bread) is followed by a contrasting middle part (sardines), and then you're instructed to go back to the beginning (bread again). The musical term is *Da Capo* (DC) and it means "from the top" or "from the start of the piece." Usually, you're told to go to the beginning and then stop where the music says *fine* (end). So when you see *Da Capo al Fine* in this etude, you'll know that I'm being lazy and asking you to repeat the A section to complete the form.

TRACK 111

Figure 14-17: Exercises in the slur and double tongue.

A tongue-twister etude

In this section, you play an etude combining many of the articulation techniques you develop throughout this chapter.

An etude differs from an exercise in that an exercise focuses on one specific aspect of technique, such as the slur and double tongue, whereas an etude is a musical composition with one or more technical challenges. An etude is generally a little bit longer and more demanding from an endurance standpoint.

TRACK 112

Tongue-Twister Etude

Listen to the CD several times, practicing the tonguing and fingering in a wind pattern. If you can master the fingerings, rhythms, and coordination of tongue and valves before you ever pick up your trumpet, you've paved the way for success.

Play the first sustained note with a crescendo as marked to get momentum headed toward the sixteenth and eighth notes that follow. I've marked a *tenuto* line over the second note of the slurs to remind you not to leave a gap there. In measure 11, the downward arpeggios need a strong horizontal approach. Blow straight out and connect the notes. The contrasting B section can be played more slowly, and a bit softer, in a legato articulation. *Legato* means well connected, and the *tenuto* lines over the notes reinforce that approach. When you return to the A section, you should go back to the original tempo and marcato style. You're invited to slow down *(Rall.)* at the *Fine.* Adhering closely to the styles indicated by the composer is a very good habit to develop.

Chromatic scales in triple tonguing

The chromatic scales in the next etude involve all seven of the valve combinations. Practice them slowly, with quick strokes of the fingers on the valves, as you maintain a steady flow of wind. Wind patterns are an excellent idea for practice here, as you blow a stream of wind at the same time as practicing the valve changes. Make sure to do this in rhythm, though slowly, and let yourself be guided by an inner sound performance as you play, blowing out with a steady stream of wind.

Triple-Threat Chromatic Etude

The performance of this etude on the CD demonstrates the continuity of sound and tongue/finger coordination required for clear articulation. The inclusion of dynamics not only helps create a musical line but also enhances the technique by supporting the line with increased wind. There are many examples of slurs to add smoothness and variety to the etude.

Be patient — there are a lot of notes, and accidentals in this etude. Go slowly and always make a good sound. I hope the last two bars give you a chuckle, after all that hard work.

Chapter 15

The Different Characters of the Trumpet

Sometimes musicians talk about "musicality" and "expressiveness" as opposed to "technique." I've heard trumpeters say, "He's a more musical player than a technical one," or "Her technique is more impressive then her musicality." I think that the best players are those with an integrated concept of music, without a split between technique and musicality. A trumpeter who, from the very start, learns the technique of playing in a musical context develops with the inspiration of music guiding the way. This chapter gives you some ideas about how to play musically.

Practically speaking, if you're learning to be a musician, then you need to learn your technique by expressing music. Every skill — even a somewhat arcane technique such as triple tonguing — can be played in a musical way, with an expressive goal. By imbuing your practicing with musical values such as contrasting dynamics, a variety of articulations, and different characters of sound, you're learning to be a musician who plays the trumpet, and the supposed split between technique and musicality ceases to exist. And the good news is that with that approach, practicing is a lot more fun!

The Art of Phrasing

The *art of phrasing* is the ability to place notes in a coherent sequence, or phrase, so that the listener's attention is maintained. Several principles derived from speaking and singing can help you learn to phrase and should be part of your daily practice:

✓ **Strive to connect the notes without gaps.** In order for verbal communication to be effective, the words must be joined together in a coherent sentence or phrase; disjointed words cause difficulty in understanding. In music, effective communication also needs a coherent line. In most cases, that involves connecting the notes without gaps between them (legato style), using a flowing stream of wind supplied by a deep, relaxed inhale. Of course, sometimes a very hard and clipped tone is used, for emphasis.

Smooth, full breaths in and out are the key to smooth, connected phrasing.

✓ **Strive for expressive variation.** In speech there are highs and lows in intensity and tone of voice. Without this expressive variation, speech doesn't sound human — think of the kind of computerized voices you hear in automated telephone systems. Trumpet playing shares this need for expressive variation. A good supply of air and the ability to blow freely are crucial.

✓ **Vary the pace of your playing.** A good speaker varies the pace, avoiding a monotonous series of words. As a trumpeter, you should play phrases with some tempo variation. Ends of phrases in particular can be slowed down, increasing coherence and also giving you time to take a relaxed breath.

✓ **Maximize the flowing line.** Tongue and slur smoothly, with the flowing line as the most important part of the sound. The tongue adds clarity and precision, as well as emphasis, but it should never disrupt the flowing melodic line.

A certain *je ne sais quoi:* Musicality

Applying the basic principles in the "Art of Phrasing" section will result in a more expressive performance, giving a working answer to the question "What does musical mean?" But there's a certain *je ne sais quoi* that's part of a musical performance when the player calls on her reserve of feeling. When a musician is expressive in this way, the listener can be receptive to subtle communication that can't always be expressed in words. A musical performance is the result.

Lyrical Style: Smooth and Mellow

Lyrical playing, also known as *cantabile,* is a large part of any musician's expressive and technical vocabulary. Lullabies, love songs, folk songs reminiscent of the old country — these are the songs that you can play with a smooth flow and an emphasis on beauty of tone and subtle dynamic changes. The cornet soloists who were so popular at the turn of the 20th century, and who are an important part of the heritage of the modern trumpeter, always included some romantic or otherwise lyrical solo in their concerts.

TRACK 114

The Last Rose of Summer

"The Last Rose of Summer" is a wonderful example of a lyrical piece for the cornet or trumpet. Solo and duet arrangements are found in *Arban's Complete Conservatory Method for Trumpet,* but here's a version of that tune.

Notice that the first three notes are in scale steps, and the fourth note is an upward leap followed by a change of direction back down toward the first note. Many beautiful songs have a similar melodic shape, and you can enhance the emotion inherent in the leap, and make the figure easier, by playing through the scale notes with a crescendo as you hear the top note clearly. This is a perfect example of uniting expressiveness and technical skill in a musical approach.

Here are some opportunities to put the basic principles of phrasing into practice. Each of the following etudes contains a flowing melodic line, several leaps up or down with balancing shapes returning to the starting note, an overall smooth articulation and variation in dynamic level, tempo, and choice of note length.

I've written the pieces to give you practice in shaping phrases using dynamics, so pay special attention to the crescendo and diminuendo markings. Connecting the notes using a steady stream of wind is also a central part of lyrical playing — be sure that your initial breath is full and relaxed.

Your inhale and exhale mirror each other, so a tight, strained breath in will result in an unclear and forced tone. For lyrical playing, the best model is a big sigh followed without pause by a smooth exhale.

TRACK 115

Lyrical Etude #1

The incomparable Wynton Marsalis

In trumpet, there is a long tradition of the jazz or popular player versus the classical or "legitimate" player. But the great American trumpeter Wynton Marsalis has recorded to critical acclaim in *both* the classical and the jazz idiom. He's one of the few major artists on any instrument to "cross over," embracing both styles convincingly, and his success has made many trumpeters more aware of the possibility of such versatility. Marsalis has recorded the Haydn and the Hummel concertos, baroque solos and duets with soprano, jazz standards, traditional music by Duke Ellington and other masters, and his own modern jazz compositions. Wynton Marsalis has proven that a great player doesn't need to be limited to one particular genre.

TRACK **116**

Lyrical Etude #2

Fanfare Style: Clear and Forceful

Fanfares are, almost by definition, loudly played because the goal of a fanfare is to attract attention and communicate a message. But many players fall into the trap of tonguing very hard when playing loudly, which leads to a clipped and often rough-sounding performance. The parallel with speech is instructive here: If you shout loudly to a friend far away, it's the vowel that carries, not the consonant. In exactly the same way, a trumpeter needs a flowing tone rather than hard tonguing at the start of each note.

A windy approach to marcato

Marcato is the style associated with a fanfare. It literally means "well marked." The best way to achieve this emphatic style of attack is to use the wind strongly with a clear tongue, but not a hard attack. Think *tAH* rather than *Tah*.

In Chapter 6, I introduce breath attacks as a way of starting a note without the tongue but with a clear sound. The *whoo* attack, as I call it, is very useful for establishing the optimal balance between attack and tone, consonant and vowel.

Practice starting several short notes in a row with just the wind at a *mezzo-forte* dynamic level. The sound should start right away, although the first one or two may scoop up into the pitch or begin with an airy sound. Play a few clear tones and then play a few more at a *forte* level. After you're successfully starting notes without the tongue, it's time to add the sound of *t*. Play a *whoo-whoo-too* pattern, making sure the sound is the same each time, except for the extra *t*.

As an additional practice technique, you can do wind patterns with the *whoo-whoo-too* sequence, each time feeling the same amount of breath on your hand a few inches in front of your mouth.

Figure 15-1 is a group of exercises designed to help you gain consistency in marcato tonguing. Listen to the CD carefully for the quick start to each note. Trumpeters call this playing "at the front of the note." Clarity and projection are the benefits.

Marcato tonguing doesn't mean that you should necessarily play the notes short, unless they're marked staccato as well.

TRACK 117

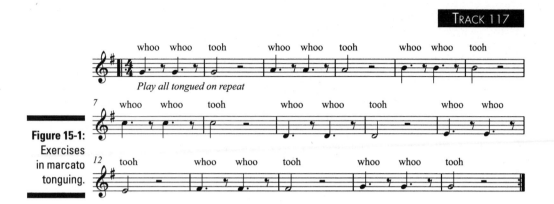

Figure 15-1: Exercises in marcato tonguing.

Calling attention to yourself: A few fanfares

There are many famous fanfares in classical symphonic music. Beethoven wrote two separate offstage trumpet calls for his opera *Fidelio;* they're known as "Leonore Call #2" and "Leonore Call #3" and are famous audition pieces. (See the "Calling Leonore" sidebar for a horror story from one of my own auditions, having to do with "Leonore.")

Calling Leonore

I don't know what happened to "Leonore Call #1." Once, while preparing for an orchestral audition, I was advised that when the panel asked for the "Leonore Call," that meant that they'd heard enough and you were finished, out of the running for the job. I walked into the hall and behind the screen (which is placed between you and the panel to achieve anonymity and remove favoritism) and was immediately asked for "Leonore." I thought, "I'm finished already?!", and in my panic and disappointment, I promptly played "Leonore Call #3" even though they had asked for "Leonore Call #2." It was downhill from there.

TRACK 118

Leonore #3

In the opera *Fidelio,* the duke (the good guy) is imprisoned in a dungeon. He's about to be killed by the other duke (the bad guy) when, at the very last second, a trumpet plays a fanfare announcing the arrival of the good duke's friends. The call is played twice and the second time can be louder, as if from closer. The good duke is spared — all is well, and all because of a trumpet. So, you see that it's not just we trumpeters who think we're important.

As you listen to the CD, notice that the style is strong, forceful, and clear; this announcement saves a life and a whole community. The music shown here is a slightly altered version, omitting the double tonguing. As you slow down toward the end of the fanfare, lengthen the sixteenth notes.

Different interpretations of this fanfare are possible. Find as many recordings as you can for comparison. You may even want to record your performance and see if you've captured the drama and urgency of the moment. Most trumpeters use double tonguing for the sixteenth notes in the original notation. (Chapter 14 gives detailed instructions on that technique.) Normal single tonguing is okay, too, but the tempo will be a little slower.

TRACK 119

Trumpet Tune

Trumpets have announced military victories, sounded retreat, and told soldiers "lights out" and "wake up." Religious ceremonies have used the trumpet to add "the voice of God" to the proceedings. The most popular current use is at weddings: The long-awaited moment when the bride and groom walk down the aisle toward the rest of their lives is one of the most exciting, and it's usually the trumpet that announces this triumph of hope! Baroque composer John Stanley's "Trumpet Tune" is listed in every wedding planner's guide, and it's a great example of an extended fanfare.

The first three repeated notes are a great opportunity to play your windy marcato style. Play full length on every note, even the dotted eighth and sixteenth figures. Most of all, play with great gusto. The joy (and possibly relief) of a wedding can be reflected in a piece like this. Listen to the CD and play along so you can create your own wedding announcement.

TRACK 120

Capriccio Italien

The famous Russian composer Tchaikovsky began his overture "Capriccio Italien" with a fanfare featuring four players in unison. This particularly grand fanfare doesn't involve fast fingering or multiple tonguing, but it is, nonetheless, brilliant and a great challenge, requiring maximum use of the wind and a concept of projection, not just loud playing.

The CD includes a solo performance of the "Capriccio Italien" opening. There are many recordings of this piece and it's definitely worth listening to some of them, not just for the opening fanfare but also for the many great examples of trumpet artistry contained throughout the composition.

A big breath is essential in order to sustain a strong, clear sound and project it to the back of the concert hall, and the windy marcato style is called for. For some extra entertainment, try playing the whole piece using first and third valves.

strong and stately, not too fast

Tales of fanfares lost

There is a rich tradition in orchestral music of offstage trumpet calls, where one player, or sometimes the whole section, stands up and goes to the wings or backstage to play a fanfare. As in the "Leonore" calls, the sound floats in from the distance. Composers from Beethoven to Verdi, Mahler to Respighi, have used the dramatic effect of sound coming seemingly out of nowhere.

There is also a parallel tradition of disasters stemming from the somewhat risky decision to let trumpeters wander around on their own for a while before having to play. In one famous story, a trumpeter at Carnegie Hall left his chair and went for a stroll before returning to the backstage area to play his solo. Unfortunately for the performance, an overzealous security guard who didn't know the piece or the player wouldn't let the trumpeter near the stage, and the solo went missing.

Another great story actually happened to me. I was playing an outdoor concert in Victoria, British Columbia. We were playing the "Overture" to *Fidelio,* with the "Leonore" calls. I left the stage and moved out into the crowd to play the solo. Right on cue, I lifted the trumpet to my lips, took a big breath, and the loudest B♭ ever heard in a performance blared out, completely drowning out my puny offering. I stopped playing and looked at my trumpet, and then at the conductor, who was staring at me in shock and disbelief. (He had told me to make sure I played it loudly enough.) Then we, and the audience, equally dumbfounded, realized that the B♭ was still sounding. It was the Cannonball ferry from Seattle, arriving at just the right moment. I was a wreck. And I never did complete the solo.

March Style: Hup, Two, Three, Four

It's hard to march and play the trumpet! I don't know how the truly adept college kids in their marching bands do it. We see them on television at half-time shows and it's astounding to me that they can play so well under those conditions. But use makes master as a wise person once said, and I can testify that I played in a theatrical production for a whole summer season that involved my leading the way as a small marching band stepped out a pattern on the stage, staying together (sort of) while playing (sort of) the march from Verdi's *Aida*. The secret, as far as I was able to discern, is to move only your legs, not your upper body, thus keeping the embouchure stable enough to play quite complicated music. It also helps to have a very firm embouchure, with highly developed cheek and jaw muscles. The arms and hands have to cushion any motion caused by the marching feet.

It's probably not the best training for a serious player. On the other hand, marching bands are a vibrant part of university and high school life. Somebody's having a good time, and I assume the trumpeters are included in the fun.

TRACK 121

Etude in March Style

This etude is in a marcato style, in a typical march form. Because people have only two feet, marches are in either two or four beats to the bar. (Try marching in 3/4 time. See what I mean?) The structure of a march is derived from the dance form of the classical era.

Listen carefully to the CD for the windy marcato style. Accents are not produced by hard tonguing, but rather by playing to the front of the note with lots of wind. Note also the contrasting articulation and dynamic level in the trio section. A steady tempo is one of the features of a march; imagine a troop of soldiers stepping to your performance of the etude, and you'll get the idea.

This march is in the British style — rather sedate compared to the brighter and faster American style. Aim for a metronome marking of about 108 to the quarter note. The piano accompaniment will provide a solid background, especially a rhythmic pad on which your tune can sit. March music should be played melodically by the trumpeter, employing marcato to be sure, but never becoming too percussive. Leave that part of the music to the percussion accompaniment. In a march, the trumpet nearly always carries the lead part, and full tone and projection are called for. "Follow the lead cornet" is a well-known military band expression, and it applies equally to trumpet.

The military trumpet

Trumpeters have served the military since the Egyptians and continue to do so in the many service bands and orchestras all over the world. In the early to mid-19th century, the cornet was invented and became the choice of most military bands. The trumpet retained its position as fanfare instrument for royalty and the military, but the bands themselves, playing marches and sometimes dance and entertainment music, preferred the cornet, with its mellow sound and nimble valves.

In the intervening years, the trumpet and cornet have become closer in sound and in usage, and the lyrical qualities of the cornet have influenced trumpet style. Because the cornet is mostly conical in design, the tone quality is rounder and somewhat more diffuse, as opposed to the trumpet's cylindrical design and distinct projected sound. The great early soloists such as Jean-Baptiste Arban specialized in the cornet and wrote many solos and etudes for that instrument. Herbert L. Clarke was the cornet soloist in the famous Sousa Band and cautioned young players to avoid the trumpet. Nowadays both instruments are played by orchestral trumpeters and band players alike.

There are remnants of a pecking order, at least in the minds of trumpeters, however: For orchestral music, the noble trumpet is preferred, and for the military band, the upstart cornet leads the way. More important, for generations, there was a distinct style difference between band and orchestral players. Heavier tonguing, including stopping the notes with the tongue, was part of the band style. Lucky for all of us, players and listeners alike, much of that style difference is gone, and orchestral style is pretty much the model for most trumpeters. The exception is the jazz soloist, whose choices concerning articulation, tone color, and variations in intonation can help create a distinct sound identity.

Part IV
The Complete Trumpeter: Knowledge and Skills for the Advancing Player

The 5th Wave   By Rich Tennant

"It's 'Dance of the Sugar Plum Fairies,' not
'Charge of the Sugar Plum Fairies.'"

In this part . . .

This part is a guide for the advancing player to continue onwards and upwards. In Chapter 16, I outline a practice routine that will strengthen your technical and musical ability.

Because a good trumpeter shouldn't rely solely on printed music, learning to play by ear is the subject of Chapter 17. Here, I also introduce you to some interesting sounds that you can make with your trumpet — sounds that don't appear in notation.

Most trumpeters like to spend time with their gear, and Chapter 18 is a guide to looking after your trumpet and mouthpiece. And just so you don't run out of gear to spend time with, Chapter 19 tells you about some accessories that are useful and fun to mess around with.

No book can tell you everything you need to know about playing the trumpet, so in Chapter 20 I talk about how and why to find a good teacher. Finally, in Chapter 21, I fill you in on the various ways of getting into the world of music making in general and trumpeting in particular.

Chapter 16

A Practice Routine for Success

The only way to maintain and improve upon your trumpet skills is to practice. But practice doesn't have to be something you dread. If it helps, say, "I'm going to play my trumpet" instead of "I have to practice." After all, you love playing the trumpet, and practice is one of the forms your trumpet-playing takes.

In this chapter, I describe a good practice routine — one that covers all the skills you're nurturing as a trumpeter.

The practice ideas in this chapter are examples of what and how to practice, but you may be wondering when you should practice. The answer: whenever it suits your life and your mental and physical rhythms. First thing in the day works best for me, but late in the evening is great if I've had a warm-up earlier in the day. What about where? You should have a space where you know you aren't bothering other people and where the sound quality is rewarding without too much echo. You'll sound too good in a bathroom or stairwell, for example. You want *some* resonance but not too much. A private space, where you can try things unselfconsciously, is a very good idea.

Warming Up

In Chapter 9, I fill you in on some good ways to warm up. The important thing to remember is that you should warm up every day as a prelude to your trumpet playing.

Your approach to the warm-up may differ according to your schedule. If you have an hour or more for a practice session, then you have time for the kind of gradual immersion into playing that I describe in Chapter 9, one that covers all of the basics. About 20 minutes is reasonable for a thorough warm-up.

On the other hand, if you have only 20 minutes to play, and you don't want to spend the whole time warming up, or if you've just arrived at a rehearsal or concert and you need to be at your best in 5 minutes, you can do an abbreviated warm-up, like the following:

1. **Take a few deep breaths.**

   It doesn't take much time, and it prepares you for a little mouthpiece playing.

2. **Buzz a short tune, or a siren sound up and down, on the mouthpiece.**

   Take a few seconds in between playing to let the lips recover from the shock of buzzing rapidly against a piece of brass.

3. **Play some quiet long tones and slurs on the trumpet.**

   I say "quiet" because your lips will be more responsive if you baby them a bit. As you get more experience playing, you'll discover what kind of warm-up material suits you best.

A warm-up is more than just a chance to get you ready to play. By warming up, you warm up your thinking, reminding yourself of the importance of the basics, of continuing to develop your tone as you receive the benefit of the long tones, slurs, scales, tonguing setups, and lyrical etudes with which you can start your trumpet playing for the day.

Starting with the Flow

The great Chicago trumpeter and teacher Vincent Cichowicz coined the term *flow study* to describe an etude that is smooth, not too fast or high, and that involves predominantly slurred articulation. The idea is to reinforce a relaxed approach with a clear attack, smooth connections, and an even tone quality.

This was, for Mr. Cichowicz, the essence of good technique. Even if you've had a good warm-up, starting your practice session with a flow study is a great idea.

TRACK 122

Flowing Along

This flow study and the corresponding CD track demonstrate the relaxed approach that is strengthened by the flow-study concept and that can be the basis of your playing. Remember to breathe! So often, trumpeters forget the most important physical necessity for playing the trumpet, which is a relaxed and easy breath. All the breathing exercises, wind patterns, mouthpiece playing, long tones, and slurs form the habit of correct breathing and blowing so that even under the stress of performance, or just fatigue, your default response is to breathe deeply and easily. That's why you warm up every day, and why you practice. You reap the rewards in every performance.

rallentando

Approaching Scales and Arpeggios Musically

After you spend time on a good warm-up and a flow study (see the previous two sections), you can begin to explore interesting areas of playing that will develop your musical and technical abilities. Many players start by playing scales, and beginning and intermediate players can add to their knowledge and skill by following their lead. The music that trumpeters play is, for the most part, constructed of scales and arpeggios. A thorough knowledge of them, in all the major and minor keys, will equip you for most of the solos, etudes, and ensemble parts that you'll encounter.

But there should be more to practicing scales and arpeggios than just learning the fingerings and coordinating them with the tongue. Making a beautiful sound and using dynamics and varied articulation to phrase in an interesting way can be part of your approach. Trying to play musically keeps your mind active and makes practicing less of a tedious repetition and more of a productive and rewarding activity. Most important, it integrates your technique and musicality, so the way that you play technically serves your musical needs.

Scales

A scale is a series of adjacent notes — ascending and descending. Scales are a big part of the language of music, and the more familiar you are with all the scales we use, the more fluent in music you'll be.

Major scales

There are 12 major scales. C major is usually the first one that trumpet players learn because there are no sharps or flats and because the octave from middle C to third-space C is well within the range of a young player. So, that's where I suggest you start. But the way I get through all 12 of the keys is interesting and requires a little explanation.

In the following scale exercises, you'll proceed through all 12 keys by way of the cycle of fifths: C major has no sharps or flats. The key with one sharp is G major, which is five alphabet steps (C-D-E-F-G), or a perfect fifth, up from C. Go up five more steps and you arrive at D major, and up five more and you get to A major. Continuing the pattern, you reach E major, B major, F♯ major, and C♯ major. This is the turning point, and now you head back to C by way of the flats.

If you look at a piano keyboard (see Chapter 4), you notice black keys in between the white ones, except between B and C and between E and F. Each black key represents either a sharp or a flat. The black key to the right of C is called C♯ (or if you think of it as left of D, it's called D♭). C♯ and D♭ use the same keys on the piano and sound the same. This dual identity is called an *enharmonic relationship*.

Go back to C♯ major. Let's call it by its enharmonic twin's name, which is D♭ major. Getting back to the cycle of fifths, if you start at D♭ and go up a fifth, five steps, you arrive at A♭. Then go up another fifth to E♭, another to B♭, one more fifth to F, and then you finally reach C again. The cycle is complete, and you've come home to where you started, at C major.

Practicing scales in this sequence is interesting and challenging and gives you familiarity with the cycle of fifths, one of the harmonic building blocks of music.

Figure 16-1 contains a scale pattern starting in the key of C, and transposed in all 12 keys. Listen on the CD for the dynamics and articulation. Only the C major pattern is recorded, but you'll get the idea for playing the whole cycle.

The range can be quite a challenge — don't play beyond your personal limits at this point. Playing the first part up to the fifth of the scale will be a great start, even if the upper part of the scale is a little high for you. You'll work more on range later in this chapter.

Approach these exercises as scale practice with musical opportunities. Remember to blow a few wind patterns before you start each one, practicing the fingerings at the same time for coordination.

Choose one or two keys for your daily practice instead of trying to play all 12 in one session. If you rotate the keys in this way, you can cover them all in a week or so.

Figure 16-1:
Major scale
pattern in
all keys.

enharmonic equivalent to C♯

Varying your practice material is a good idea. Figure 16-2 is another group of scale exercises, this time beginning on higher notes and descending. Sometimes you'll start on the octave, the third, or the fifth note of the scale. The key signature identifies the key, and the last note confirms your calculations. (The five handy rules for identifying keys are found in Chapter 4, if you need to brush up on that skill.) There is more slurring and tonguing combined in this group, to keep you alert, and because the solo and ensemble repertoire of the trumpet requires a variety of articulation styles.

The CD includes a performance of the first of the series in Figure 16-2. Start at a slow tempo, making sure that you're playing accurately and beautifully. Listening to the CD provides helpful aural instruction for articulation and tone quality.

TRACK 124

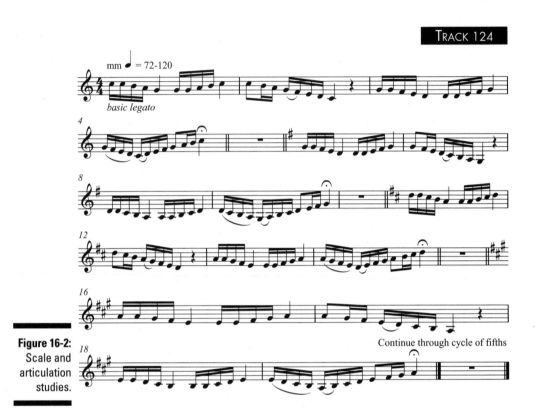

Figure 16-2:
Scale and
articulation
studies.

Continue through cycle of fifths

The two studies in Figures 16-1 and 16-2 are examples of ways to play the scales. *Arban's Complete Conservatory Method for Trumpet* (which most trumpeters refer to as "Arban's"), *Technical Studies for the Cornet* by H. L. Clarke ("the Clarke"), and many other study books offer other scale patterns. And you're always free to create your own.

TRACK 125

Etude in the Major Scales

Now it's time for an etude to put the scale patterns you've practiced into a musical context. Sections of several different scales appear in this piece. Sharps or flats on individual notes, called *accidentals,* identify the different keys. Listening to the CD will strengthen your conception of the sound and style.

An etude is a real composition, with a formal structure. This etude is in ABA form, so the melodic material at the beginning returns after a contrasting middle interlude. ABA form is one of the most common structures in music (and in other art forms, too, such as literature). The dynamic markings and articulation are part of the musical intention and should be carefully observed.

Minor scales

I suppose you've heard the one about the piano falling down a mineshaft? What do you get? A flat miner. (A♭ minor, get it?) Well, it may be a bad joke, but it's as good a way as any to dive into a whole new world of tonality.

The cliché is that sad music is written in the minor keys and happy music is written in the majors. There's a lot of truth to this particular cliché and the sad or perhaps rustic or old-fashioned sound of much of the music in minor keys adds a lot of emotional range and contrast to music's expressiveness. Before explaining very much about minor tonality I'll give you an etude to play in D minor.

TRACK 126

November Dusk

Here's an etude with a descriptive title to try to activate your imagination. This etude has some dynamic contrast and some slowing down at phrase endings. The feeling is quiet and thoughtful, perhaps melancholic. There are many lively dances and other energetic pieces in minor keys, but the slower and sadder style is very common. The CD gives you an idea of the minor sound.

The big difference between major and minor is the third note of the scale. If you use D as your reference, the third note is F♯ in D major and F♮ in D minor. There are two types of minor scales in common usage:

✔ **Harmonic minor:** The notes of the D harmonic minor scale are D, E, F♮, G, A, B♭, C♯, and D. The interval between B♭ and C♯ is called an *augmented second,* using the normal meaning of *augmented* as "increased." So, an augmented second is a larger second, still one alphabet step away but enlarged by a semitone. It's a very interesting and familiar sound in the music that you often hear.

Figure 16-3 and the accompany CD track remind you of the harmonic minor sound and give you an idea of the articulation called for, which is the basic legato. The study begins with a D minor scale. Notice that the key signature has one flat, B♭. This is the same key signature as F major, so it's said to be related to it. D minor is the relative (or related) minor of F major, and F major is the relative major of D minor. Sounds like a very intense family relationship, and, in fact, there is a lot of resemblance between the two keys. Some people think of the relative minor as a pale or pastel shade of the major "color."

TRACK 127

Figure 16-3:
D harmonic
minor study.

✔ **Melodic minor:** This scale still has the minor third but smoothes out the upper part of the scale by raising the sixth note by a semitone, thereby taking away the augmented second. Just to confuse you, that's only on the way up — coming down the scale, the seventh and then sixth degrees are lowered. Once again, this sound is a familiar one.

Figure 16-4 is the melodic minor sound in a study. This piece begins with the scale up and down. After listening carefully to the accompanying CD track, play the scale slowly to get used to the intervals. You can play the correct fingering but not quite play in tune, so get very familiar with the sounds that you want to make by listening to the CD and singing the scale.

TRACK 128

Figure 16-4:
Melodic
minor study.

The studies in Figures 16-3 and 16-4 are in D minor. Just as in the major scales, you can learn all 12 keys to increase your ability to make varied and interesting music. Figure 16-5 shows the two types of minor scales in some commonly played keys. The accompanying CD track lets you hear the A harmonic and melodic minor scales. When you feel that you're ready to tackle scales in the rest of the keys, there are several excellent sources, including *Arban's Complete Conservatory Method for Trumpet.*

TRACK 129

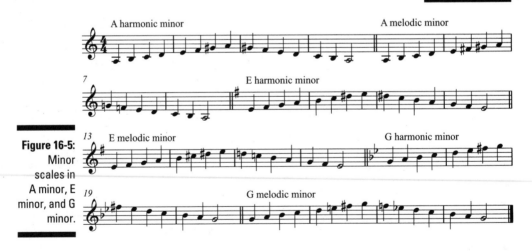

Figure 16-5:
Minor
scales in
A minor, E
minor, and G
minor.

Arpeggios

In Chapter 12, I describe arpeggios as leaps of faith, and certainly when you're starting to learn about them, there can be an element of doubt. But now you're familiar with the idea and sound of an arpeggio, and you've played them in several studies and pieces. An arpeggio creates a musical figure from the root, third, and fifth of a scale.

Major arpeggios

Two notable examples of arpeggios in tunes are the *Sesame Street* theme song, which uses the notes 5-3-1 of the major scale, and the opening to "Sir Duke" by Stevie Wonder, which is an ascending major arpeggio. Arpeggios are also a big part of technique building.

Figure 16-6 is a major arpeggio exercise (one that is taken from major scales — in this case, C, F, and G major), and the accompanying CD track is a performance of the C major section. Notice that you can start on any note of the arpeggio and that there are articulation challenges to add variety and clarity.

Figure 16-6:
Major
arpeggios.

Listen to all aspects of the music, including a general strategy of playing a crescendo as you ascend. Tone and tuning remain high priorities in this and all the music that you perform. Even in a technical study, playing with a musical idea (Is this a fanfare? A love song? A polka?) will guide you in your efforts to improve your technique, as well as elevate the exercise from a mere series of notes to be learned to a musical performance.

Minor arpeggios

As you might guess, a minor arpeggio takes its notes from the minor scale, offering the same kind of expressive opportunities as the scale. Familiarity with minor arpeggios gives you a better grasp of the vocabulary of the music you play. When you consider that scales and arpeggios — major and minor — make up a large part of the material of music, it makes sense to learn them. Smooth connections are more of a challenge when playing arpeggios as opposed to scales, because of the leaps involved. More attention must be given to flow of wind; quick valve action; and firm, stable embouchure. Hearing the notes while you play is of paramount importance, as with everything in your repertoire.

Figure 16-7 is an exercise in 3/4 time, which always lends itself to a flowing phrase. The dynamic marking is on the quiet side here, with crescendos to help the ascending lines. Inhale deeply in a relaxed way at the start, and take time to breathe as the phrases progress. The accompanying CD track demonstrates a smooth line in minor arpeggio figures.

TRACK 131

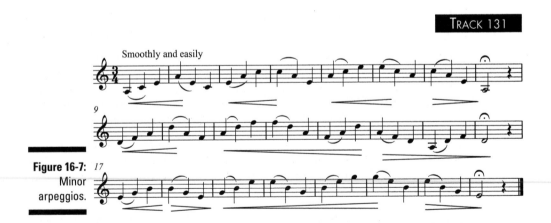

Figure 16-7: Minor arpeggios.

Arpeggios can contribute greatly to your consistency of tone through lower, middle, and upper registers. Because the pitches are an established pattern, they're predictable and available as a guide to your inner hearing. *Technical Studies for the Cornet* by H. L. Clarke and *Arban's Complete Conservatory Method for Trumpet* have very comprehensive sections on arpeggios, as well as etudes incorporating them into a musical line. The two most important factors leading to clear arpeggios are hearing the direction of the line and blowing consistently. In a good playing session, you should try to improve the arpeggios you already know, and learn a new one until all 12 keys are mastered.

Developing Smooth and Fluent Articulation

Fluent articulation is a central skill in playing well. All the basic articulations — legato, marcato, and staccato tonguing; multiple tonguing; and combining slurring and tonguing — need daily attention. In this practice session, you've warmed up, played a flow study, and played several scales and arpeggios in various styles (see the previous sections). Now's a good time to focus on tonguing.

Legato drills

It makes sense to begin with legato because smooth articulation promotes the flow of wind and a relaxed connection of notes into lines of music. The tongue is a muscle after all, and it needs to be relaxed to work efficiently. Playing the trumpet places a greater demand on the action of the tongue than speaking does, so you have to develop strength and coordination.

A steady wind supply is essential. Imagine a golden ribbon connecting all the notes in a phrase. That's how your wind supply can function. A wind pattern, just blowing and tonguing through the phrase with wind only, is a wonderful reinforcement of the good use of air. Pressing down the valves at the same time helps with coordination. So, playing a little air trumpet can really help.

A little singing never hurt either. Many people think that they can't sing, and quite a few of them are right about that, but it's not a performance for anyone but you, and singing an etude, exercise, or solo activates your musical imagination and is great preparation for playing the trumpet. Plus, it establishes a healthy breathing approach.

Figure 16-8 is a series of exercises in legato style. The accompanying CD track lets you hear the smooth connection of the last note of a slur to the next tongued note on the first section of the exercise, in D major. I remember being told not to shorten the last note of a slur, and I believed my teacher, but I didn't really get it until I heard it demonstrated. I add an *h* to the end of the tonguing syllable *(tooh)* to reinforce the wind flow all through the note, including at the end. Enjoy the slurs and let the flow of air generated through the slurred passages fuel the breezy tonguing technique.

Figure 16-8: Exercises in legato style.

For more work in this aspect of trumpet playing, try *Technical Studies for the Cornet* by H. L. Clarke. It contains many scale and arpeggio exercises that lend themselves to legato articulation practice.

Short and sweet: Staccato tonguing

Staccato literally means "half the value of the note." So, in theory, a quarter note with a staccato dot over or under it should sound like an eighth. But there's a little more to it than that.

I teach two kinds of staccato, and the easiest way to describe them is *fast staccato* and *slow staccato.* In slow staccato, there's a space between the notes, so the meaning of staccato as half the value of the written note applies. My definition of fast staccato comes from Vincent Cichowicz and means playing in a staccato style without really playing very short. It's a trick: Mr. Cichowicz called it "the illusion of staccato" — you don't really shorten the notes, but you tongue very clearly and blow a steady stream of wind. The effect is staccato, but there's no attempt to shorten each note, which would result in a choppy style with poor air flow and a diminished sense of the line.

Slow staccato

I call this style "jolly staccato" because the image of a rather large, well-known man in a red suit saying, "Ho, ho, ho" comes to my mind. There's a lot of wind flow and no sense of cutting off the end of each "ho." (It's not supposed to sound like *hot.*) Avoid breathing in between each "ho." Try being Santa Claus for a second and laugh a few jolly staccatos, and you'll get the feel of it. Then do it with a wind pattern, pretending to blow out some candles. Again, there's a free and quick release of the air. Now play the same thing on the mouthpiece, on a G, using just wind, without tonguing. Next add the trumpet, again on a G. Finally, repeat all these steps with the tongue, making sure that the quick, windy release of the air stays consistent.

After the setup in the preceding paragraph, it's time to play some exercises that establish the habit of slow staccato (see Figure 16-9). The accompanying CD track contains the first part in C major and demonstrates the free release of air and unforced tone that should be a feature of your articulation. Each line starts with a sustained note, either a half note or a full-length quarter. Play the exercises first on the mouthpiece, and then on the trumpet. Play each exercise with breath attack first, and then add the tap of the tongue. Make sure that you don't stop the notes with the tongue! Listen carefully for the sound and pitch at the very beginning of each note, avoiding a scoop into the center of the pitch.

TRACK 133

Breath Attacks

whoo whoo   simile

10   Add the tongue

tooh tooh   simile

19   First time breath attacks, add tongue on repeat

28   simile

37   simile

Figure 16-9:
Jolly
staccato
exercises.

46   simile

A very good practice method is to play a scale study like the one in Figure 16-8, or #37 in *Technical Studies for the Cornet* by H. L. Clarke, very slowly, not legato, but this time with each note a separate "jolly" staccato. First, use a breath attack and then repeat with the tongue. After you're playing a clear staccato, play the study a bit faster. Then, after a little rest, play faster still. At some point, you'll find that the puffs of wind required for slow staccato aren't comfortable anymore. At that point, you can start thinking about the illusion of staccato, which is the topic of the next section.

Speeding things up: The illusion of staccato

Mr. Cichowicz taught that even staccato notes need to be part of a musical line, connected by wind. It's the clarity of the attack and the musical flow of the line that make the best musical statement. A scale study is again a very good practice tool.

Figure 16-10 is an example of a scale study in F major. Start this exercise slowly and slurred, emphasizing the windy connection of notes in a single line and quick, precise valve action. Slurring some of the figures moves you toward the smooth "illusion of staccato," with a smooth line and clear *tah*. F major is a good starting key because it isn't high and the fingerings are comfortable. The F major section is recorded. The study is also presented in the keys of C, for low-register practice, and B♭ above, for some higher-range work. For additional practice, you can write the exercise in any key or play without music. This is a good example of expanding your technique to include as many of the keys as possible.

TRACK 134

Figure 16-10:
The illusion of staccato in F major.

Technical Studies for the Cornet by H. L. Clarke and *Arban's Complete Conservatory Method for Trumpet* contain a wealth of material for articulation practice. All the players I know have a library of different practice materials and the Clarke and Arban's are always included. Each book has a slightly different approach, so your technique is further expanded and you're challenged and energized by new repertoire.

TRACK 135

Etude in Staccato Style

Here's an etude with slow and fast staccato figures in a musical context. Apply your technical work in a musical setting, varying your session with drills, etudes, and solos. Listening to the accompanying CD track will nurture the little trumpet in your head before you play the etude. All the repeated notes and groups of eighth notes should be played full length, with a clear tap of the tongue to create the illusion of staccato, while the eighths with rests following them are examples of the slow, "jolly" staccato described earlier.

Be sure to take time to rest your chops and your mind during a practice session. If you play too much with insufficient rest, you tire your lips and embouchure muscles, making it harder to play well. Some players then continue to practice, trying even harder. This downward cycle can result in frustration and even injury to the lip nerves and muscles. A good rule of thumb is to rest as much as you play. Several shorter sessions a day is often more productive than one longer one.

Scales are a great resource for articulation development. The coordination of the tongue and the fingers, together with the range and phrasing possibilities, make scales a valuable resource.

The articulation scale study in Figure 16-11 begins with the first note repeated in sixteenth notes for two beats, setting up the tonguing. This idea comes from the well-known book *Daily Drills and Technical Studies for Trumpet,* by Max Schlossberg, an excellent source of tone, range, and scale material. Playing the repeated notes with a crescendo gives you some momentum of wind flow as you ascend the scale. The pattern starts with the first five notes of the scale and then completes the whole scale ascending and descending. Only C major is recorded as a guide, but several keys are included — more can be added by writing them out or learning the pattern by ear.

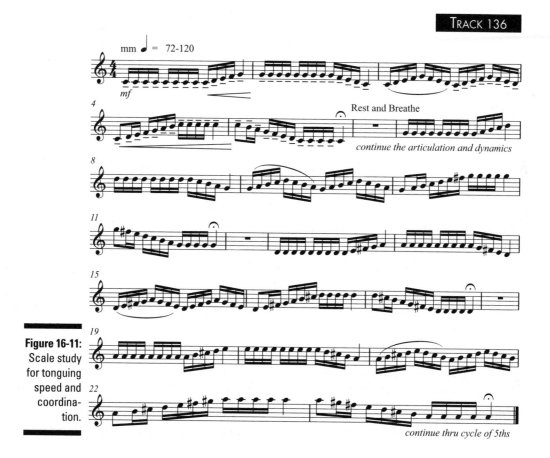

Figure 16-11: Scale study for tonguing speed and coordination.

Doubling and tripling your tonguing speed

The multiple-tonguing techniques introduced in Chapter 14 need to be part of your daily practice. The good news is that the faster, smoother, and lighter your single tonguing is, the better your multiple will be. The same principles apply to all tonguing: smooth flow of wind, light tongue, and emphasis on the vowel rather than the consonant. Again, a scale study is very suitable material for your focused practicing.

Set up the double and triple tonguing by saying the syllables and "winding" them with a smooth, consistent breath.

The approach of the double-tonguing study in Figure 16-12 is based on Mr. Cichowicz's teaching. After listening to it several times, practice it first with just wind and tongue, and then play it on the mouthpiece. Be sure to make a beautiful sound when playing multiple-tonguing exercises (as is the case with anything you play). I mention this because it's easy to become so intent on *too-koo-too-koo* that you may neglect tone and tuning. Follow the metronome marking, moving faster only when you play a good sound with clear, consistent articulation.

Figure 16-12: Scale study for double tonguing.

Now it's time for triple tonguing (see Figure 16-13). The same setup should be done, with voice and then wind and tongue alone. Triple tonguing is a little more challenging than double at first, so make sure that your syllables are clear and in the right order. If you haven't mastered the syllables without the trumpet, there's no point in going further until the coordination is developed.

Practice vocally and then with just wind and tongue. Choose the pattern that suits you best of the ones that I presented in Chapter 14. *Too-too-koo* is the most common, followed by *too-koo-too,* and last by double-triple tonguing, ***too-koo-too-koo*-*too-koo*** (with the emphasis on the syllable in bold). After you've mastered the vocal syllables and practiced some wind patterns, the mouthpiece is next, and finally a trumpet performance.

The corresponding CD track demonstrates the triple-tonguing idea. Again start slowly and when you're playing the study smoothly and clearly, begin to increase the speed. For further practice material, *Technical Studies for the Cornet* by H. L. Clarke and *Arban's Complete Conservatory Method for Trumpet* are good sources, among many others.

Figure 16-13: Tripling your fun.

Slur and tongue combinations

A good practice routine should include all the types of articulation that you'll encounter in the music that you play. Composers use combinations of slurring and tonguing for variety, clarity, and emphasis. For the trumpeter, that means extra challenge in coordinating the fingering and articulation, while maintaining a flowing line. Combining slurs with the tongue has benefits as well: The flow of wind is enhanced by slurring, so the tonguing that follows tends to be smooth. Practicing exercises like this one with both single and double tonguing prepares you for the varying tempos you'll encounter in solo and ensemble music. Arban's has a section on slurring in combination with double tonguing, and the Clarke can be played that way, too.

Working on a lot of double and triple tonguing can be tiring, so frequent rest is recommended, for about as long as you've played since the last break. After your break, play a short lyrical or flow study such as found in Chapters 14 and 15 to remind yourself of a flowing wind supply.

Always keep wind patterns in mind, especially when practicing articulation. The tongue rides on the wind, bouncing freely but precisely. Practicing wind patterns regularly is one of the best strategies I know of. While you're "playing" the music with just wind and tongue, hear it clearly in your head, just the way you want it to sound, and do the fingerings. You'll always sound much better after an air-trumpet rendition.

As you play the exercise in Figure 16-14, keep the wind flowing consistently throughout. The crescendo markings help you with smooth connections, so follow them conscientiously. Hold the quarter notes for their full value to remind you of the constant flow of wind that is essential for any kind of articulation. Use the bar of rest as an opportunity to relax and refresh your wind supply. The corresponding CD track models the smooth style of slurring and tonguing.

TRACK 139

Figure 16-14:
Combining
slurring and
tonguing.

After playing this study, it may be time for a longer rest. Give yourself time to relax, and get the blood flowing to your lips again. Resting for half an hour at this point would make a lot of sense.

Developing the Upper and Lower Registers

After a little rest, you may like to try to expand your range. Don't overdo high-register playing — always balance the high with the low. In this section, there are some playing opportunities in both upper and lower ranges.

Connecting the upper and lower notes of the trumpet is a very important part of good technique.

Down low, go slow

Figure 16-15 features some low sustained tones and slurs between the middle and low range. A firm embouchure is required to have the necessary flexibility for all-round playing. A relaxed and slow but steady stream of wind is another requirement, and you'll find that the low notes use up air very quickly. The last and most important element in successful low-range playing is the habit of clearly hearing the sounds you want in your inner musical ear (the little trumpet in your head). This facility guides your playing better than any number of mechanical instructions. Listen to the CD several times to strengthen that inner hearing.

TRACK 140

legato style, full length notes

simile

Figure 16-15:
An exercise
connecting
the low
and middle
registers.

Moving on up

After the low-range playing in the preceding section has relaxed you and opened up the breathing, it's a good move to play some higher notes. As in the low range, a good strategy is to connect to the middle register. Your goal is to be able to move throughout the whole compass of the trumpet easily and with a consistent tone quality, and this fluency must be developed.

Mouthpiece playing is always helpful; play some tunes you know well that have a wide range. The siren sound, the glissando, can help the free release of wind and firm embouchure that you need.

After a few minutes of mouthpiece playing and a few deep breaths, some high-range exercises will serve you well. Flexibilities and upward arpeggios and scales are all part of this kind of practice. Spend more time during high-range practice. Even if you play very easily and efficiently in the high register, there is a greater demand on the lip and you need more rest.

Flexibilities for the upper register

Some wind slurs or flexibilities should be part of any trumpeter's daily routine. Some players like to start with them in a warm-up; others save them for a little later in the playing session. You'll discover what works best for you. I like to do some quiet low- and middle-range wind slurs early in the session, and then some more as I play in the higher register.

More than just embouchure strength is needed — the wind flow has to be fast yet relaxed, and able to change speeds.

There are many books of wind slurs, or lip slurs as they're often called. An excellent example is *Twenty-Seven Groups of Exercises for Cornet and Trumpet,* by Earl D. Irons.

Flexibilities can be addictive, almost hypnotic. Don't play them on automatic pilot. If you forget that wind is crucial to success, you may start forcing or moving your embouchure too much. A horizontal flow of wind and sound is your goal. I know people who watch TV or read the paper while practicing wind slurs, but I don't recommend it. You need to pay attention to play musically. As always, the little trumpet in your head is the most important one you own — hear what you want to sound like, in as much detail as your imagination can create.

Figure 16-16 demonstrates wind-slur exercises. Play each pattern down chromatically in each of the seven valve combinations: open, 2, 1, 1-2, 2-3, 1-3, and 1-2-3.

Always extend the third-valve slide out for 1-3 and 1-2-3. If you don't do this extra step, those positions are very sharp. Get into the habit of always moving the slide out for D, D♭, low G, and G♭. For 1-3 about ½ inch is usually fine, and for 1-2-3 at least 1 inch. Let your ear guide you.

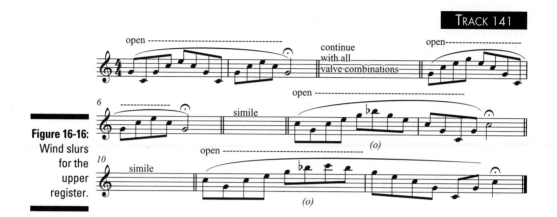

TRACK 141

Figure 16-16: Wind slurs for the upper register.

Don't play too loudly in these drills or force the sound in any way. The whole point to is to learn to play easily and fluently in this and all registers. Taking a few big sighs before you start will help you relax and establish healthy breathing.

These are suggested patterns, but there are lots of possibilities. Experiment and find the ones that work best for you.

Dashing up the steps of the scales

I like to play ascending scales with a rush of energy and wind toward the top. Blow freely and crescendo to the top note with a full tone. Make sure that you don't overblow and force the higher notes. The point of this kind of playing is to establish a good lower- or middle-range sound and ride it up an octave to a triumphant top note. Mouthpiece playing is very helpful — slide up in a glissando.

I include all the major scales in the exercise in Figure 16-17. Rest in between scales. I hope you enjoy the challenge and the rush of sound up to the top, but don't go higher than you can realistically manage. If the sound is forced and unclear, you shouldn't go any higher; instead, consolidate the notes that do sound good. The corresponding CD track with the C major scale will give you an idea of the approach I'm describing.

TRACK 142

Figure 16-17: Upward scale exercise.

Leaping up with arpeggios

Trumpeters have to play high notes in many contexts. Sometimes we approach the upper register by a scale passage; other times, an arpeggio or even a larger leap. The arpeggio range in Figure 16-18 gives you practice in leaping to the high notes. Remember that the upper register requires considerable experience, building up strength in the embouchure and efficient use of the wind. The corresponding track on the CD contains the first seven arpeggios and will help you hear the pitches and the smooth connections between all the notes. More wind is required for leaps than for scale steps, so keep blowing, but remember to start at a relaxed *mezzo forte* dynamic.

Don't try to play notes that are too difficult for you. If the sound isn't clear and relaxed, you aren't ready yet for those notes. Work in a more comfortable range, gradually moving up when you sound consistently clear and easy where you are.

TRACK 143

Figure 16-18:
Arpeggios
for range
develop-
ment.

continue up when you are ready

Rest when you are through

This exercise is based on the great lead player Arnie Chycoski's warm-up. Yes, I said "warm-up." Arnie played so comfortably in the upper register that he started with high-range two-octave arpeggios.

Pedal tones on mouthpiece and trumpet

Pedal tones are notes below the normal range of the trumpet. Low G♭ or its enharmonic equivalent, F♯, is the lowest commonly played note. Below that is the almost unusable pedal B♭, the lowest open note on the B♭ trumpet.

On other brass instruments, the pedal range is frequently used, but on trumpet it's mainly for developing embouchure strength and centering the sound. Not all players and teachers use pedal tones, but many do, and I find some pedal practice a relaxing antidote to any tension accumulated during high-register playing. Listen carefully to the corresponding CD track to get the idea of pedal playing involved in Figure 16-19. The tone sounds strange because you're basically creating a note where none exists, but when you get the hang of it, I think you'll enjoy playing in that range.

TRACK 144

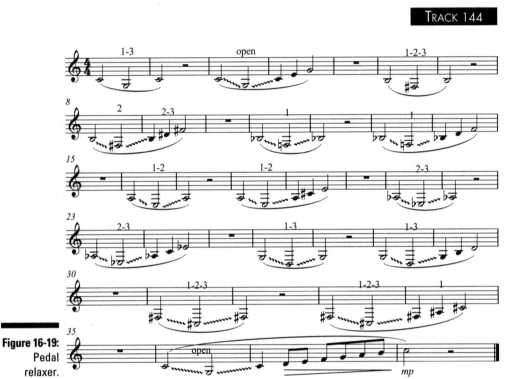

Figure 16-19:
Pedal
relaxer.

This exercise starts in the middle, slides down to the pedal-tone register, and then back up to the middle. Keep your embouchure firm — the tendency is to collapse the cheeks and lips and drop the head as you descend, but that defeats the purpose of centering the tone and strengthening the embouchure. Remember to keep the air flowing freely. As always, playing the exercise on the mouthpiece first sets you up for a successful trumpet rendition.

Etudes for Technique and Endurance

Etudes have a special place in trumpet practicing, adding as they do to the technical skills being developed, the challenge of the greater physical demands of a longer piece, and the opportunity for musical expression. There are many etude books, all with different focuses, and trumpeters are well advised to build up a library of them.

There are different ways to practice etudes:

✔ **Work on a particular section of the piece, like the opening or a difficult middle part.** This kind of practicing is necessary and should be done slowly and carefully.

✔ **Play the whole piece through, without stopping.** Pick a reasonable tempo, one that will let you meet the technical challenges successfully, even if at a slower tempo.

✔ **Do remedial work with wind patterns and mouthpiece playing.** Singing the musical phrase that you're working on can be a great help as well, making sure that your vocal version is musically expressive. Even though you may not be a singer, you can make your best attempt and your effort will be rewarded.

Play everything as a performance, even if it's much slower than called for or slurred rather than tongued. Always make it sound beautiful. You gain nothing by playing through a piece with mistakes, or stopping at every error and fixing it. This advice applies to practicing with slower, methodical section work or by playing right through without stopping. For the complete performances, it's a good idea to record yourself. In your next break, you can listen to your performance and identify the spots that need the slow, careful work.

Low-register etudes are not that common. *First Book of Practical Studies for Cornet and Trumpet,* by Robert W. Getchell (Alfred Publishing), has many very attractive and quite easy etudes in the middle and low registers. *Forty Progressive Etudes for Trumpet* and *Thirty-Two Etudes for Trumpet or Cornet,* both by Sigmund Hering (Carl Fischer), offer attractive pieces in the middle and low ranges.

Many trumpeters don't practice much in the low range — they prefer the glory of the high notes. But the better your lower register is, and the more you practice moving from low to middle, the better your higher notes will be.

Etude in the Low and Middle Registers

This etude focuses on the lower register, with occasional scales or leaps to the middle range, just to keep you honest. Often, low-register playing leads people to relax the chops too much, producing a flat, tubby sound and making it difficult to move upward fluently. Keep your embouchure firm in all registers — the less the embouchure changes, the better. Listen for a clear, centered tone that doesn't sag flat. The most straightforward way to improve on the trumpet is to keep your playing tuneful.

Next is an etude that moves around the middle and near-upper register. When trumpeters speak of the *upper register,* they usually think about the notes above the staff, from A up as high as D or E for symphonic players, and even higher for high-note specialists in jazz or baroque music.

Etude in the Middle and Upper Registers

This etude helps you move closer to the notes above the staff by playing the G, A♭, and B♭ as a flowing part of a musical line. Don't try to play too loudly as you go higher; keep the tone beautiful and unforced. Think "out" not "up" as you create a horizontal line of sound. The corresponding CD track will help you understand the concept of a centered tone.

There are many books of etudes at all levels of difficulty. I use *Second Book of Practical Studies for Cornet and Trumpet,* by Robert W. Getchell (Alfred Publishing), in teaching. In addition, the later titles in the Sigmund Hering series are of varying difficulty and reliable quality.

In Chapter 20, I talk about the benefits of having a private teacher, and one of those benefits is the guidance that a teacher offers in the selection of repertoire. Seek help in choosing musical and appropriate etudes to play. The reward is considerable, both in the pleasure of playing good music that's suitable for you and in the improvement that you'll notice.

Solos for Challenge and Fun

Playing solos written for the trumpet is another kind of enjoyable and productive playing. There are many solos, from Renaissance and baroque to contemporary pieces. Transcriptions of music written for early natural trumpets, or even for other instruments or for voice, make up a large part of the repertoire. Often a book of solos is the best choice. All the major publishers churn out solo books for all levels. Your teacher is the best guide because he's familiar with your playing needs and strengths.

TRACK 147

Prince of Denmark's March

Here is an example of a solo for the trumpet, a famous solo from the baroque era. Jeremiah Clarke wrote the "Prince of Denmark's March," commonly known as the "Trumpet Voluntary," in the latter part of the 17th century. The work was incorrectly attributed to Henry Purcell, the far more famous English composer, and it was only in the 20th century that Jeremiah Clarke was acknowledged as the true creator.

Voluntaries were written to be played on the organ, with the tune played on the *trumpet stop* (so named because it was built to imitate the trumpet timbre). Performing voluntaries on a real trumpet is, of course, a huge improvement on the original idea, and this voluntary is probably the most famous example. On the CD, you'll hear an accompanied trumpet solo.

Solos give you the chance to apply all the techniques you've been practicing. Look in music stores and online sources and talk to your teacher and other trumpeters to assemble a library of rewarding solo repertoire. And keep listening! Your CD collection should be growing, full of musical performances by a wide range of trumpeters (including the ones in Chapter 22).

Warming Down

After a strenuous practice session or ensemble rehearsal, warming down is a very good idea. The concept of warming down may sound strange after you've read about warming up, but the concept is simple and sensible: Leave your lips relaxed and buzzing easily, even if tired, and you'll play much better the next time you pick up the horn.

I play low, simple music, a little mouthpiece buzzing, some pedal tones, and some quiet wind slurs. The pedal routine that I present earlier (refer to Figure 16-19) works very well as part of a warm-down. Simple mouthpiece glissandos, starting on low C and sliding down to G and then back up are helpful as well. Wind slurs from low C up to G, proceeding through all the valve combinations, are excellent for finding the buzz.

Play softly. Your goal is to regain all the sensitivity in your lips because, during a practice session or other strenuous playing activity, fatigue sets in, causing puffiness and a lack of response. If you warm down for just a few minutes, you'll find that your lips recover for the next session.

Chapter 17

Becoming More Versatile

*O*ne of the wonderful things about playing a musical instrument is that it gives you the opportunity to make music with other people. In this chapter, I give you some tips on how to become a versatile player, able to perform with a keyboard accompaniment or to jam with other musicians without music.

I throw in some other fun stuff, too, such as the ever-popular horse whinny. Seriously, people are always asking trumpeters to make a sound like a horse. Why? Blame it on Leroy Anderson and "Sleigh Ride," I guess, but it would be nice to be asked to play something more dignified, like the theme from *Rocky*. But before we start horsing around, I introduce you to the importance and rewards of playing by ear.

Playing by Ear

A surprising number of musicians need to read a sheet of written music in order to play. Ask them to play "Happy Birthday" in F, and they just can't do it. Throughout this book, I preach the importance of listening to your musical imagination. Musicians who can listen to sounds — either imagined or real — and reproduce them on their instruments have pipelines to musical expression that can enrich their whole way of playing.

What do you learn from playing by ear? You make a very direct connection between your musical ear and the fingerings and embouchure adjustments needed to make the sounds that you hear. You get to know your instrument very well, learning to predict what sounds will be created by the various adjustments that you make as you play. This connection, oddly enough, makes you a better reader of music, because that same direct link between what you hear and what you play speeds up the transfer of written notes to sounds.

The following song lets you try your hand at playing by ear.

TRACK 148

Basin Street Blues

When I first started playing the trumpet in the ninth grade, the first piece I learned was "Basin Street Blues" and I picked it up by ear from a Louis Armstrong recording. I'm dating myself, but I listened to a portable record player, and I must've dropped that needle onto the old 45 record a hundred times as I tried to figure out the notes. I knew no fingerings and had only learned one note in school, home-base G, before being allowed to bring my trumpet home. I had so much fun! And gradually "Basin Street Blues," complete with Louis Armstrong's vibrato and tonguing style, began to emerge from the noise, until my parents actually recognized what I was trying to play. Eventually, I could play the whole piece, and I still play it from time to time, and enjoy it.

To practice playing by ear, listen to the accompanying CD track a few times and try to learn it well. Sing along at first, and then begin to play along with your trumpet. You'll need to test some notes, maybe stopping the CD many times along the way. At least it's easier than dropping the needle on a vinyl recording, trying to find the same spot.

I'll give you a hint: The first note is an open note, no valves. Now here's a challenge: Try not to look at the music until you've played it by ear. The notation is a guide, as is all written music. But there is so much more to performing in the medium of sound than simply reading written notes — and in that "so much more" is your musical personality, your statement on the trumpet. Another musical shortcut is introduced here: You'll see "first ending" at the end of the first time through, then "second ending," which you play at the end of your second time through.

Don't worry about copying — we all learn by copying others, and your own personality emerges as you do it. After the performance with trumpet and piano, the click track will keep you connected to the accompaniment. Have fun!

Playing by ear can help you get to know your trumpet better, but why is that important? Well, think of your voice. Before you could even talk, you learned to be expressive with your voice. Your voice can sound happy or sad, angry or contented, humble or smug, terrified or relaxed — because you've been using your voice to express yourself your whole life. Imagine how limited your vocal range would be if you'd only ever used your voice for reading the phonebook.

By playing your trumpet by ear, without reading music, you can explore a wider range of timbre, attack, and articulation nourished by your imagination. More practically, you learn how different combinations of fingerings sound, speeding up the communication between your performance and the little trumpet in your head. You become one with your trumpet so that it truly is an instrument of expression for you.

How can you improve this part of your trumpeting? Continue to play a variety of songs by ear, starting with "Basin Street Blues," earlier. "Happy Birthday" is a great choice. You're at your niece's fifth birthday party and you just happen to have your trumpet handy, so you give her the gift of "Happy Birthday." You can do this because you learned the song or because you've been doing enough playing by ear to be able to "fake" it.

Musicians use the term *faking* to describe playing without music, as if music must be written down to really count. I hope you come to recognize that sometimes "faking" actually means knowing something so well that you don't *need* a written guide.

You know a wide variety of songs, and being able to play them on the trumpet can be a lot of fun. But if you're like me, you forget all those songs when the chance to play them arises. If that sounds familiar, try making a list of all the songs you can remember — add to the list as more lovely tunes float up to the surface. Then play them on the mouthpiece as warm-up repertoire or just entertainment; then move on to playing them on the trumpet. How many tunes you play, and how simple or complicated they are, is your call. You're learning to play the trumpet in a way that's unique to you, which means you'll get more out of it than you would otherwise.

Improvising your way to fun

Did you know that composers such as Mozart and Beethoven improvised, just like jazz musicians do, inventing new tunes as they went along? There were even contests, in which two players would improvise on a theme and one was deemed to be the best.

Improvising can take many forms, from simple doodling to the church organist filling in for a few minutes while the bride decides if she *really* wants to get married, to an art form such as jazz. Included in this continuum can be the efforts of trumpet players inventing a new warm-up pattern or just playing some sounds in a way that pleases them.

I think we sometimes forget that we "play" music — we get so serious that all signs of playfulness disappear. An occasional free-form warm-up, can be very productive, and time spent inventing tunes can not only help your inner musical hearing, but better acquaint you with your trumpet. What better way to be a trumpeter?

Decorating Your Playing with Ornamentation and Special Effects

Musicians love to play, and literally that can mean playing in the sense of having fun, experimenting and adding things because you like the way they sound. Now I should caution that when you're reading music, especially in an ensemble, you have to play what's written, in every detail. But it's sometimes playtime, and you can decorate. The performance tradition for hundreds of years has included decorating any repeated section in a solo. Ends of phrases, called *cadences,* are also decorated quite often. There are rules in all styles, some formal and others more informal, but generally there is a fair amount of leeway for individual expression. Listening to a lot of music gives you insight into what works in a given style. So, listen and experiment, and see what happens!

Ornamentation: Gold stars on your musical Christmas tree

Just as people decorate Christmas trees with ornaments, you can "decorate" your music with ornamentation. Here are some examples of ornamentation (all shown in Figure 17-1):

- **Trills:** The trill is the most commonly used ornament. The technique is achieved by using the valves to alternate between two adjacent notes. The most common place for a trill is on the note above the *penultimate* (second to last) note in a phrase. A good example is in the "Prince of Denmark's March" in Chapter 16.

- **Mordents:** Playing a quick extra note one step above or below the written note is called a mordent. It's a simple "flip" to the adjacent note above and back and occurs very often in jazz as well as classical styles.

- **Turns:** In a turn, you surround the written note by playing first the note you see, then the note above, the written note again, the note below, and back to the written note. That description sounds complicated, but it's a simple and elegant ornament, a version of which is often used by jazz singers and instrumentalists as well as classical musicians.

TRACK 149

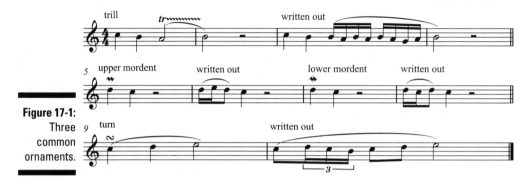

Figure 17-1:
Three
common
ornaments.

The important thing about ornaments is that they have to be an integral part of the line. Without the Christmas tree, the ornaments lying around on the floor aren't very interesting; likewise, without a strong musical line, ornamentation is only a distraction.

Figure 17-2 and the accompanying CD track demonstrate a trill. Figure 17-2 is an excerpt from the solo from "Prince of Denmark's March," transposed to F major and B♭ major; it includes trill symbols, plus written-out versions of the ornament. The version I've written is called a *measured trill,* played as written. An alternate fingering for the trill from G to A, used by many players, is open to third valve.

There are many options for the exact rendition of a trill. Listen to great musicians and they'll guide your own choices.

Different combinations of valves can present challenges to producing a smooth trill. G to A in the staff is quite easy, but C to D requires a faster flow of wind and a firm embouchure capable of easily playing a D. It also helps a lot to hear the D clearly. Figure 17-3 is an exercise to help you with various trills especially C to D . It's based on the #4 from *Technical Studies for the Cornet* by H. L. Clarke — an excellent source of practice material for the trill, along with *Arban's Complete Conservatory Method for Trumpet.*

Figure 17-2:
Excerpt from "Prince of Denmark's March" with trills.

Figure 17-3:
Exercise for trills in F.

Special effects: Doo-wahs, horse whinnies, and more

Many composers and performers take advantage of the palette of sounds available to the trumpeter. In this section, I introduce you to a few of those sounds, telling you how to produce them and where they can be used.

There's a time and a place for sounds on the trumpet that aren't necessarily part of your scales and arpeggios. You'll annoy your conductor if you make barnyard noises in rehearsal when she's trying to communicate with you.

Doo-wah

Bathroom plungers — usually altered to make them less reminiscent of their original function (the first step is to remove the handle) — have appeared on bandstands from New Orleans to New York. Early trumpeters like King Oliver and Louis Armstrong used the plunger to "talk" with a "wah-wah" effect. The great Duke Ellington soloists Bubber Miley and Cootie Williams were artists in this effect, adding a growling sound. The big bands used the plungers as devices for the whole section — the visual effect of four or five men manipulating plungers at the same time *while* playing the trumpet was part of the appeal. It was a simpler time.

Some players have rejected the bathroom plunger for expensive specialty mutes, which inevitably look a lot like bathroom plungers. I still use the good old hardware-store model, and it works fine. The trick is not to hold the plunger too close to the bell — about half an inch away works well for the closed position.

Figure 17-4 and the accompanying CD track demonstrate the sounds created by the plunger — both the growling solo "talking" and the big-band "doo-wah" effect. The plus sign over the note indicates the closed position and the letter *o* means open. Play around and see what works for you.

TRACK 152

Figure 17-4:
Plumbing
the depths
of the
doo-wah
effect.

Figure 17-5 shows a derby hat mute and a plunger mute, used by all the big bands in the swing era, and still used today.

The hat

Another big-band device that came from an everyday object was the hat. Fedoras, also called felt hats, were popular for men (think of Frank Sinatra) and trumpet players started taking off their hats and holding them in front of their bells for a softer timbre. Eventually, expensive hat mutes were created; they looked a lot like the fedoras except they were made of a hard fiber and didn't feel as comfortable on your head as the original. They also look really funny when worn.

A great orchestral example of the use of the hat is the trumpet solo in George Gershwin's *An American in Paris*. It's a very expressive bluesy part, and the hat sound adds to its effectiveness. Figure 17-6 is a short transposed excerpt of that famous solo.

Figure 17-6:
Trumpet
solo from *An*
American
in Paris
by George
Gershwin.

Jungle sounds

The term *jungle effect* was used to describe Duke Ellington's penchant for growls and plungers in the music that he wrote for the Cotton Club reviews. The growl is usually produced by *flutter-tonguing*, a technique used not just in early or big-band jazz but also in contemporary solo and chamber music. Listening to some old Duke Ellington recordings such as "East St. Louis Toodle-oo" will let you hear its expressive potential.

Here's how you do it: While producing a tone by buzzing normally, you roll your *r*'s, causing a pulsating of the air supply and a satisfyingly rough tone quality. Practice without the trumpet first.

Some people roll their *r*'s easily and others have a lot of trouble with it. An alternate method is a kind of glottal vibration between the tongue and the roof of the mouth. If you can't do either method, and you really want to, a speech therapist may be able to help you.

Making the trumpet talk: Doits, falls, rips, scoops, bends, shakes, and the horse whinny

The New Orleans and big-band jazz styles brought into common usage many sounds that formerly were heard only as yet another way for trumpeters to cause trouble at the back of the band or orchestra. The unifying feature of these effects is that the trumpet seems to "talk." The growl and plunger technique described earlier are examples of that vocal imitation, but there are many other ways to broaden the expressive palette.

The famous jazz artist Miles Davis used the half-valve sound and bends as a way of personalizing his trumpeting. A well-known example is recording he made with Gil Evans based on George Gershwin's *Porgy and Bess* in which Davis imitates the sound of a fruit peddler hawking his wares. It is a truly amazing solo, well worth searching out.

Here are some of the sounds trumpeters have experimented with:

- **Doits:** A *doit* is an upward, half-valve glissando at the end of a note. The Count Basie band popularized this ornament, and it became a standard swing figure, as well as a solo effect. Half-valve technique is accomplished by holding the valves partway down while playing a note or, often, changing from one note to another. The sound and pitch vary from very closed and indeterminate to a vaguely tuned note, depending on how far the valve is depressed. The whole trumpet section doing the doit together is a very effective part of the big-band palette of sounds.

  In the doit, you gradually push down the valves while you aim for a higher note by hearing the sound you want, blowing faster wind, and arching the middle of the tongue as if you were saying *ee.*

- **Falls:** The *fall,* similar to the doit, occurs at the end of a note, but it goes in the opposite direction to that of a doit. In a big-band chart, you'll often see a downward curved line after a note. It might specify "long fall" or "short fall"; or it may be up to your judgment or the leader's command. If the whole section is playing any ornament together, the lead player decides, and the section players follow.

  If the curved line is smooth, some half-valving carries the pitch down. But sometimes a fall will be indicated by a squiggly diagonal line; in that case, the valves are rapidly raised and lowered as the embouchure and air help you aim the pitch lower.

- **Rips:** The *rip* is a combination of rapid valve motion, exactly as in the fall, only going up, not down. As the valves move, the player bends up into the pitch using wind speed and embouchure firmness. This maneuver isn't easy to describe — players find the way that works for them and, in the process, create an individual sound. What is absolutely necessary is a strong inner hearing of the desired pitch.

  The most famous player to make ripping up to a note a signature effect was Louis Armstrong. For Armstrong, the rip expressed exuberance, energy, and confidence and was one of his most recognizable techniques.

- **Scoops:** A *scoop* is a variation on the rip, in that it's an upward slide into the note. It comes from singing, a glissando that intensifies by delaying the destination. A small amount of half-valving gives you the indeterminacy of pitch to ease your way up into the note. What is often called "lipping" the note into tune is also part of the technique.

✔ **Bends:** Bending the tone is directly related to singing — and singing the sound you want before trying it on the trumpet can be very helpful. You can *bend* the tone in a variety of ways:

- Hold your embouchure very firm while opening the oral cavity, making the shape for the word *yaw*. This is probably the best way because it actually strengthens your embouchure and centers the tone.

- Start your tone normally, except for the valves, which can be in the half-valve position. Again, the embouchure needs to be firm.

- Relax the corners of the mouth, letting the tone sag.

Most players use a combination of techniques. There are no rules, so do what you need to do in order to make the sounds that you want.

Bends and other effects are not core trumpet technique. Firm embouchure and straight, clear tone are your constant goals, with occasional extra sounds for variety and expression.

✔ **Shakes:** The *shake,* another ornament made by popular by Louis Armstrong, is a type of trill. Whereas in a trill, the player moves between two adjacent notes using the valves, the shake doesn't use valves and usually has a wider interval between the two alternating notes. Armstrong used the shake extensively, expressing energy and enthusiasm as well as great playing skill.

The first thing you need is a very strong sound and a feeling that you could easily play a higher note. Then you either move the lips closer and farther apart very quickly to move up to the next harmonic in the series, or actually shake the trumpet (not too hard!), moving it in and out against your lips while continuing to blow strongly. Big-band and other jazz trumpeters employ shakes often, but they also occur in baroque music when played on a natural trumpet, without valves. The higher you are, the easier shakes are to produce, because the overtones are closer together and easier to move from one to another.

✔ **The horse whinny:** It's embarrassing, but sometimes trumpeters are actually called upon to sound like a horse. The most famous example of a horse whinny is in Leroy Anderson's "Sleigh Ride." The horse whinny works best around the top of the staff — E or G. The valves are depressed halfway, the shake technique is applied, very slightly moving the trumpet in and out (not hard) against the lips, and an ascending and then descending glissando is played with a combination of embouchure and wind.

Figure 17-7 and the accompanying CD track demonstrate doits, falls, rips, scoops, bends, shakes, and the horse whinny. You can indulge in some experimentation here. There's no strictly right or wrong technique, although the tips that I give here work well — just try to imitate the sounds on the CD and have some fun!

TRACK 154

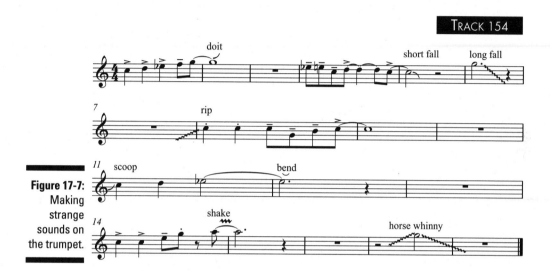

Figure 17-7: Making strange sounds on the trumpet.

Some other weird noises

Contemporary composers have discovered, probably from listening to badly behaved trumpet sections at rehearsals, that trumpets can make other sounds — sounds that don't try to sound like a voice or even a trumpet. You may come across a marking in an ensemble piece that reads "Blow air through instrument." This isn't good advice on how to produce good tone; instead, it's an extra-musical effect. Blowing just air, no vibration of the lips, can sound like wind blowing and be effective in music that's trying to describe a scene (a storm, for example). You can crescendo and diminuendo, and for an extra variation try moving the valves rapidly as you blow. Of course, practicing this sound effect is suspiciously like a breathing exercise, so I encourage it as a way to get a good flow of wind through the trumpet.

Another, less helpful, effect is to hit the mouthpiece with the palm of your hand. It makes a satisfying pop just loud enough to thoroughly annoy the teacher at the front of the ensemble. ***Warning:*** If you try this, don't hit the mouthpiece too hard, because you may get it stuck in the mouthpiece receiver and cause many complications.

Finally, some composers may ask you in the part to "Loosen valve casing tops and move valves quickly." This creates quite a din, especially when tuba players do it.

I've been required to make all these effects — not often, but it is helpful to know that it could happen. In the meantime, spare your conductor or teacher and only practice these effects at home.

Enriching Your Tone with Vibrato

Now it's time to get serious again. Every singer and all wind and string players use vibrato to give the tone intensity and richness. *Vibrato* is a slight undulation in the tone and can be very wide (so that the pitch obviously goes sharper and flatter) or very subtle (so that the tone seems to shimmer).

Some instruments need to be told *not* to use vibrato if the music calls for a straight tone, because vibrato is part of the normal sound of the instrument. Stringed instruments and, to a lesser extent, woodwinds fall into this category.

For a trumpeter vibrato is a valuable expressive technique, and you can create a personal sound with it. But learning to play with a straight tone is very important. When I started to play, I listened to a lot of recordings of trumpeters who used a wide, constant vibrato, and I copied that sound. It took practice to learn to play with straight tone, so I recommend that you practice without vibrato as much as with it.

The general rule is that in an ensemble trumpet section, straight tone is usually called for, only occasionally matching the lead player's vibrato. In solo playing, it's your call.

There are three different techniques used for different effects:

✔ **Wind vibrato:** Also known as diaphragm vibrato, this technique is used by flute players and some other instrumentalists. It is far more common in Europe than in North America and is a very distinctive effect. It's used by classically trained players, rather than by jazz artists. In the wind vibrato, the stream of wind is varied by little puffs, as slightly faster wind alternates with slightly slower. Don't let the pitch go obviously up and down. Keep a beautiful, flowing tone as you experiment with this technique. Practice on an easy note, like home-base G.

Figure 17-8 starts on a G with a straight tone; then vibrato is added. Be sure to take a big breath and start with your normal straight tone, and then begin to slightly vary the speed of the wind, blowing first faster and then slower. The speed of the vibrato and the amount of change in the pitch are part of your expressive potential, so experiment.

TRACK 155

Figure 17-8:
Wind
vibrato.

✔ **Hand vibrato:** A more common type of vibrato in North America is produced by moving the right hand on the valves very slightly back and forth, toward you and away from you. This motion is slight — too much motion can destabilize the embouchure and create problems in tone production. Trumpeters have more control with this technique, as the slight motion of the hand can be observed objectively and the speed manipulated easily. While playing a G in the staff, rest the fingers lightly on the valves, with the thumb in its position under the leadpipe.

Figure 17-9 and the accompanying CD track begin with a straight tone and then gradually add vibrato. Make sure that you only slightly move the hand back and forth. If you hear that your pitch is obviously going sharper and flatter, you're overdoing it. In Figure 17-9, the next note is an F♯. With the valve down, the motion is slightly different. Practice the exercise in Figure 17-9 to get experience using vibrato with different fingerings.

✔ **Lip or jaw vibrato:** The third method of producing vibrato uses the lips and jaw to vary the sound. If you say a very subtle *wa-wa-wa-wa,* you're forming the shapes for lip vibrato. I say "lip or jaw vibrato" because the jaw does move a little bit, but it's mostly the lips. When you open the lips *very* slightly, the pitch goes down; when you bring them closer together, the pitch goes up.

As with the other methods of producing vibrato, a very slight change is all that's needed. If your lips open too much, the note will go very flat and the sound quality will change, and if you bring the lips too close together, you'll pinch them, inhibiting the vibration.

Figure 17-10 and the accompanying CD track demonstrate the lip vibrato. Again, an easy note is the best one to start with. In the figure, the first note is a home-base G, the most reliable and comfortable note. Listen for a straight tone first and then gradual vibrato.

TRACK 156

Figure 17-9: Hand vibrato.

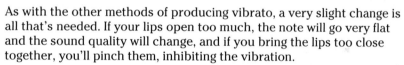

Figure 17-10:
Lip or jaw
vibrato.

You may want to record these first experiments and listen to yourself after-ward. You'll probably find that one of the three methods seems the most com-fortable for you, and you'll prefer the effect of one over the others.

The use of vibrato is an important part of playing the trumpet. Tone can be made more intense or more relaxed by varying the rate and width of your vibrato. Of the three methods, the first (wind vibrato) is the least disruptive of the embouchure. However, it isn't as widely used and has a very distinc-tive effect. The hand vibrato is the easiest to control and the easiest to teach because the motion of the hand is visible. It's very widely used in both orchestral and jazz style. The lip or jaw vibrato is the one that I use; I believe it's the most natural, but it isn't necessarily the best because it can be hard to control. The choice is yours — you can even master all three and use the one that best suits the music that you're playing.

Vibrato should be *a* feature of your tone, but not the *main* feature. Your clear, resonant sound is your trumpet voice, produced by a relaxed, consistent flow of wind and a strong inner concept of sound. Vibrato adds variety and inten-sity and can further deepen a beautiful tone, but if it's the most prominent feature of your playing, you need to go back to the straight tone.

Etude for Vibrato

This etude is a slow, lyrical piece with lots of long, sustained notes. Try the different kinds of vibrato, and if you're most comfortable with one of them, experiment with rates of vibration and width of undulation. As an ongoing activity, you may want to listen to different players specifically for their vibrato. You'll find that some sound better to you than others do, and you can develop your own technique with that to guide you. Sometimes the vibrato can start slowly and intensify toward the end of the note. Many jazz artists use this style — Chet Baker is a wonderful example. Other times it can be appropriate to have a constant, subtle vibrato. An example of that approach would be the offstage solo in Respighi's *Pines of Rome.* There is a Philadelphia Orchestra recording, conducted by Eugene Ormandy, with Gilbert Johnson playing the solo, that is a perfect use of light, shimmering vibrato.

Understanding Concert Pitch and Trumpet Pitch

One of the ways in which you can become more versatile as a trumpeter is understanding concert pitch and learning how to read it. Very often, you'll find yourself at a party or get-together, and someone will have some piano or vocal music. "Let's play this piece," you all cry out, and then pandemonium erupts. The music just doesn't sound right.

Here's the situation: Trumpets come in different keys — B♭ is the most common by far. The B♭ trumpet is so called because its lowest open note is a B♭ on the piano, otherwise known as *B♭ concert*. That open note, which we trumpeters call C, is actually a B♭ concert. There are many precedents for this kind of dual identity. It's like translation — in trumpet language, the open note on the ledger line below the staff is C, and it's translated into piano language as B♭.

The practical application of this is that if you and your friend with some piano music want to read off the same score, you, the trumpeter, will have to make the translation. In music, we call this translation *transposing,* and one way to become more versatile is to be able to transpose from a concert-pitch part. Every note you see will be up a tone from where it's written, two semitones, and you have to look at the written note, make the mental adjustment, and play the correct pitch. An F on the part becomes a G for you, a B♭ becomes a C, an E♭ becomes an F (remember it's two semitones), and so on. And this has to happen very quickly. You don't have time in a piece of music to stop and do a calculation for each note.

The good news is that, with practice, transposing up a tone and reading from a piano or vocal part becomes easy. New repertoire is available to you, new opportunities to make music with others arise, and your musical experience is richer for it.

Figure 17-11 begins with some whole notes in concert pitch and continues with some half and quarter notes. Try your hand at playing them on the trumpet. To check if you're correct, play the notes on a piano and see if they match. The fingerings for B♭ trumpet are above the notes for the first few bars. After that, you're on your own. For additional practice get a book of easy piano solos, for beginners, and play the pieces up a tone; then graduate to more advanced music. Soon you'll be able to transpose and you won't ever cause an orchestra to grind to a confused halt.

TRACK 159

Figure 17-11: Practice with concert pitch.

Playing Other Trumpets

There are many different kinds of trumpets, including C, D, E♭, and F trumpets, as well as piccolo trumpets in A and B♭, cornets, and flugelhorns.

Trumpets are very expensive, especially the specialty models, and playing some of the higher-pitched orchestral trumpets can cause playing problems for any trumpeter, especially one who isn't advanced, with a strong breathing habit and efficient embouchure.

The higher trumpets — the D, E♭, and piccolo — tend to be tighter and harder to play with free wind production, and they have tuning problems that have to be dealt with. But a C trumpet, cornet, and flugelhorn can add to your versatility earlier in your development.

The C trumpet

There's another way to deal with reading concert pitch music (see "Understanding Concert Pitch and Trumpet Pitch," earlier in this chapter) besides transposing it up a tone for B♭ trumpet. The C trumpet is a concert-pitch instrument, because its open C actually is C concert. You see a C or any other note on a piano or vocal part and you play it as written.

The next time you're in a music store, look for a C trumpet. You'll see that it's shorter overall than the B♭ trumpet, the difference equating to one tone higher. You can see it in the main tuning slide. Figure 17-12 shows the difference between the B♭ and C trumpets. Notice also that the bell is very similar, but the tubing generally is of a smaller diameter. This means that the tone quality is very similar, but the playing characteristic of the C trumpet has more resistance, so it'll feel a little less free blowing.

The difference in pitch does take some getting used to, because you'll have the pitch of the B♭ trumpet in your ear and you may have difficulty finding the center of the sound on the C. But if you play it for a little while, playing some of the same familiar material that you know on your B♭, you'll begin to get accustomed to the difference. Orchestral players use the C trumpet for most of what they play, and if you're able to perform with an orchestra I strongly recommend that you get one and learn to play it comfortably. It's also very useful for playing with piano and reading vocal parts and hymn tunes, avoiding problems caused by music in concert pitch.

Many trumpeters — myself included — love C trumpets, but the B♭ is still the first choice for most of the playing you'll do, and it's the best instrument to warm up with and to use for much of your practicing.

Learn to transpose up a tone, whether you have a C trumpet or not. Transposing is very useful and adds to your versatility because you can choose the trumpet that sounds the best for the music.

Figure 17-12: The B♭ trumpet (top) and the C trumpet (bottom).

The cornet

The cornet is a delightful instrument to play. It's pitched in B♭ like the B♭ trumpet, so the entire trumpet repertoire is available to play on the cornet without transposition. There are C and E♭ cornets, but they're specialty instruments, played mostly by professionals. The cornet is lighter, or at least feels lighter, than a trumpet, because the center of balance is where the hands are placed on the valve casing. (See Figure 17-13 to compare the trumpet and the cornet.)

Many teachers prefer to start their young students on the cornet, partly because of the difference in perception of weight and partly because producing a sound on the cornet is somewhat easier than on the trumpet.

The conical bore (see Chapter 2) tends to produce a mellower, warmer tone, and less wind flow is required. If you're asked to play for a wedding — say, in a small chapel or someone's living room — the cornet is less obtrusive. Some community brass bands require a cornet rather than a trumpet, so it's a handy extra instrument to have. And there are very seriously good cornet soloists, who play for amateur and professional brass bands, whose melodic approach is well worth emulating. The great Herbert L. Clarke, whose *Technical Studies for the Cornet* is used by brass players of all instruments, was a virtuoso who redefined technique for cornetists and trumpeters; and Philip Smith, the principal trumpet of the New York Philharmonic, is also a wonderful cornet soloist.

Figure 17-13:
The cornet (top) and the trumpet (bottom).

The flugelhorn

I love to play the flugelhorn. The tone is even more mellow and warmer than the cornet, and somewhat lighter. The left-hand grip on the flugelhorn has a larger reach than the trumpet or cornet (see Figure 17-14), so a young student may have some trouble holding it. The flugelhorn is played in brass bands, in some wind-ensemble pieces, and in chamber music. It's also widely used in jazz, for ensemble playing in big band, or for soloing. Clarke Terry, Chuck Mangione, and

Guido Basso are three of the most prominent practitioners of the flugelhorn. The tone, flexibility, and easy response of the flugelhorn make it a very nice addition to your collection and will help you broaden your musical experience.

Figure 17-14:
The flugel-horn (top) and the trumpet (bottom).

Sight-Reading

Versatility as a trumpet player is greatly enhanced if you can sit down and read a part at sight with accuracy and musicality. If you've taken the time to understand transposition (see "Understanding Concert Pitch and Trumpet Pitch," earlier in this chapter), sight-reading won't be too great a challenge, because most of the music you play is specifically written for the B♭ trumpet. But you have to read more than the notes, with correct fingerings and rhythms. With practice, you can play the part musically, with dynamics, nuances of phrasing, and consistently beautiful tone quality. All this comes with patience and experience.

How can you practice sight-reading? Well, like anything else on the trumpet, start slowly, within your level of ability, to read new music once through, without stopping to correct anything and striving to make it a musical performance. Record yourself, and then listen back, reading the music as you do, making a mental note of any problems that you encountered. Play with a metronome and stay exactly in time, making sure that the tempo you set is slow enough that you can keep up. You may notice some repeated errors, such as not holding a dotted half note for three counts, or forgetting that F♯ is second valve. After studying those problem areas and playing them a few times, play the whole piece again at the same tempo. The second time will be much better, and you'll have taken a step toward becoming a good sight-reader.

Finding appropriate material for sight-reading is important. Music such as easy piano pieces also can be played as if they were written for B♭ trumpet, without transposing. Then when you've sight-read them successfully, you can transpose them up a tone, further enhancing your versatility.

TRACK 160

Sight-Reading Etude

This little etude is typical of the kind of material that you can use to improve your sight-reading. Listen to the CD track *after* you've sight-read the music, as a way of checking how accurately you read the music.

Chapter 18

Valves, Slides, and Leadpipes: The Greasy Side of Trumpet Playing

In This Chapter

▶ Keeping the valves moving

▶ Greasing the slides

▶ Polishing your act

▶ Getting into the trumpet, literally

▶ Looking after your mouthpiece

"**I**t's a poor workman who blames his tools," as the old saying goes. Playing a trumpet isn't easy even in the best scenario, but it's even harder if the valves are slow or sticking, if the main tuning slide is stuck, if the third valve slide won't move easily, if something is lodged in the bell section, or if the leadpipe is obstructed.

This chapter gives you all the information you need to keep your trumpet in good working order. And when your trumpet is in good working order, you're giving yourself the chance to play well. What more could you ask for?

 This chapter is about the regular, routine maintenance that you need to do for your trumpet on your own. But every so often, you should also take your trumpet to a repair shop for a cleansing chemical bath. This bath removes the accumulated mineral residue from your saliva. If you keep up with your regular maintenance, you should only have to take your trumpet in for a chemical bath every few years.

Why Maintenance Matters

The last thing you want to spend your time on, if you're like most people, is cleaning and maintaining your trumpet. You'd rather be playing it — and I don't blame you. But in order for your playing to be profitable, you need an instrument that's reasonably clean and free of dents. Here are the main parts of the trumpet that you need to devote attention to, along with the reasons why:

✔ **The leadpipe:** The leadpipe is the first part of the trumpet with which your song and wind interact. A combination of calcium (from your saliva), dirt and grease (from the atmosphere), and food (from your recent meals) collects on the inside of the tubing in the leadpipe. As you can imagine, all this stuff in the leadpipe affects the intonation because it interferes with the nodal points of the sound waves that create your tone. Plus, a dirty leadpipe changes the initial point of resistance, which makes the trumpet feel stuffy or tight as you blow into it. Finally, a buildup of calcium inside the pipe causes *red rot,* a condition that actually can eat through the pipe.

✔ **The main tuning slide:** Connecting as it does to the leadpipe, the main tuning slide is prey to the same buildup of harmful materials, with the same consequences. Add to that the tendency of slides to suffer dents, and you have further disruption of the blowing characteristics of the instrument. The slide can become stuck because of calcium residue and improper lubrication, and then you won't be able to tune with other instruments. If you try to play in tune, you'll be forced to play out of center, either pinching up or sagging flat.

✔ **The water key:** The water key can cause trouble if the spring is too tight or too loose. Tone and response can suffer as a result. A repair technician is often required to get this just right, but springs are obtainable at music stores and it's not a difficult fix.

If the cork doesn't seal, you could have a leak with a harmful effect on the sound and tuning. The cork can wear out (or even dry up and fall out), so it may have to be replaced. You can do this yourself, or take it in for a simple repair.

I've seen many trumpets, some of them mine, with an elastic band holding the water key closed; this quick fix is okay in an emergency, but it can affect the way the horn responds.

Some trumpets have another type of water key, known as the Amado water key. (Trumpeters always call them spit valves. Less refined, but it keeps us in touch with the common folk.) The Amado key has a sliding cylinder, which opens or closes the valve. If you have an Amado water key, put some valve oil into the little hole on the side opposite the moving cylinder twice a month. Amado keys work well, but if left without lubricant, they can become seized.

✔ **The valves:** The same stuff that collects in a leadpipe can reach the valves, causing them to move slowly or get stuck entirely. Sometimes the valves can rotate in the casing, so that the ports aren't perfectly aligned; this causes an inadvertent half-valve effect or, in the case of complete misalignment, a completely blocked trumpet. Figure 18-1 is a photograph of a valve, with the ports clearly shown.

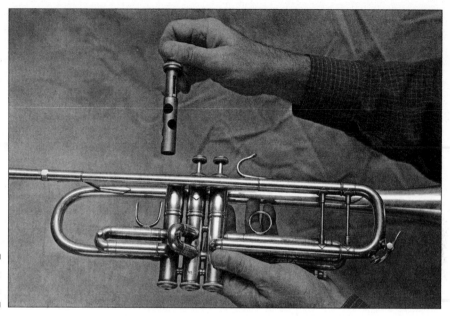

Figure 18-1:
A valve.

Another serious valve problem occurs if the casing is dented by careless usage or storage, causing a valve to stick. I know about that one, from bitter experience. After dropping a valve on the casing, denting both, and trying to fix the problem myself, I had to send the trumpet to the manufacturer for an expensive refit. ***Remember:*** Don't try to fix badly stuck valves or slides yourself.

✔ **The bell:** The bell is easily dented, and a dented bell can cause your trumpet to play out of tune, with a stuffy sound. Music teachers have tried to straighten bells with drumsticks, with total confidence and complete incompetence, causing far worse problems. So, don't try to fix a dent yourself, and don't let any well-intentioned people try to fix it for you. Instead, take it to an instrument technician to have it repaired.

Valuing Your Valves

Valves can be your best friend or your worst enemy. There's something about picking up a trumpet with slow, sticky valves — not only does it just feel wrong, but it makes playing less than fun. And the opposite is true: Quick valves inspire you to play brilliantly!

In this section, I tell you what you need to know to keep your valves moving quickly.

The way that you push the valve down will affect the wear and the response. Many players push down on an angle, because they haven't read this book, and they don't have the correct right-hand position. The pads of the fingers, just down from the tips, make contact with the button, and the action is straight down. This not only improves the working and the longevity of the valves, but also develops very good finger technique.

If you plan to leave your trumpet untouched for a few weeks, some technicians recommend that you remove the valves and keep them in a safe place until you return.

Oiling the valves

The first step is to start with good-quality valve oil. Many instrument makers and music stores sell oil that's very thin and practically useless. Pay a little more for professional oil, and your valves will last much longer. The motion of the valves causes wear; eventually, valves will wear down to the point where air leaks around them and the trumpet doesn't respond properly. Good oil can prevent or at least delay that. I recommend Hetman Synthetic Classic Piston Lubricant, Al Cass Fast Valve Oil, and Holton Valve Oil.

To oil the valves, you shouldn't need to remove them completely. Here's the way that I do it:

1. **Hold the trumpet in your left hand as if you were going to play it.**

2. **Unscrew the top retaining cap — not the finger button, but the cap that holds the valve in place in the casing.**

3. **Slide the valve straight up to about two-thirds of the way out, still safely in the casing.**

4. **Put several drops on the valve, but not on the spring section, and push it back into the casing, making sure that the valve guide clicks into the slot.**

5. **Tighten the cap, but not too hard.**

   Sometimes caps get stuck because of overtightening. Also, it's possible to damage the casing if you tighten the cap when it isn't threaded properly. If there is any resistance to tightening the cap, make sure it isn't cross-threaded before tightening any more.

6. **Proceed with the other two valves, one at a time.**

Don't work on the valves while standing on a cement floor. A thick carpet is the best surface to be standing on, just in case there's an earthquake, or your dog jostles you, or you hear that you've won the lottery and you drop your instrument. The best plan is to sit with your trumpet lying across your lap.

Don't oil your valves too often — every couple of days is usually enough, unless you're playing a lot, and then daily oiling might be required. If you oil your valves too often, they'll get very sluggish and the oil will mix with collected grime. If you oil them and there's not much improvement, check the bottom cap. Sludge tends to collect there and mix with the oil. Clean the bottom cap with a cloth, and that may be all that's necessary. If that doesn't do the trick, then it's time for an oil change (see the next section).

Changing the oil

Every month or two, depending on how much you play and the acid content of your saliva, give your valves an oil change, removing the valves completely from the casing. I usually sit with a cloth on my lap (as shown in Figure 18-2), because it does tend to get a bit oily. (Of course, I could wear my gig suit — any extra grime wouldn't be noticed.)

Here's how to change the oil:

1. **Remove each valve completely and place it on an old towel.**

2. **Remove the bottom retaining cap, wiping any residue from it.**

3. **Take a lint-free cloth and swab out the casing.**

    Some people use a chopstick to push the cloth through, but I just push and rotate the cloth. Just make sure you don't use too thick a cloth and force it into the casing because it could get stuck.

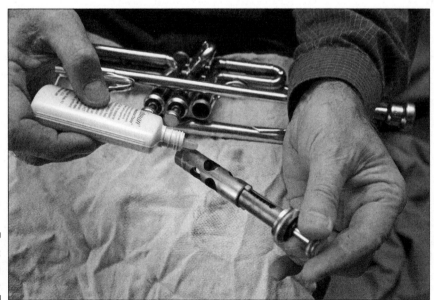

Figure 18-2:
Changing
the oil.

4. **After the casing is clean, wipe the valve, checking both the casing and the valve for lint, and checking the valve ports, which are the tunnels through the pistons, where there may be some residue.**

5. **Put about five drops of oil on the valve and carefully insert it into the casing, lined up so that the valve guide and the slot connect.**

6. **Remember to avoid rotating the valve in the casing any more than is necessary to line up the ports.**

Caring for Your Slide

Your trumpet has four slides, two that are supposed to remain in one position while you play and two that need to move smoothly. In this section, I tell you how to care for all four of them.

The main tuning slide

The main tuning slide needs to be adjustable for tuning purposes. Various factors cause the trumpet to need to have adjustable tuning. The tubing is cut so that the instrument will sound an A concert at a frequency of 440 hertz (Hz), with a little room for adjustment in or out for flatter or sharper. The slide has to be firmly in place so it can't move while you're playing, but it must move easily enough for minute adjustment.

The secret of maintaining this balance is to wipe the slide free of extra grease about once a month, and reapply a small amount of high-quality slide lubricant. I've used anhydrous lanolin for 30 years, ever since I bought a small jar of it at a pharmacy — I'm still using the same jar, so that should give you an idea of how little of the stuff you actually need. Hetman, Yamaha, and other companies produce excellent slide grease, too.

When you aren't playing, it's a good idea to move the slide all the way in, so that calcium doesn't form and cause the slide to get stuck. Sometimes the slides aren't fitted properly when they're made. If the slide is too tight or loose, the playing characteristics of the trumpet are impaired. A technician has to make the necessary adjustment — no spikes or chopsticks wielded by family or friends, please.

The small crook on the second valve

The other stationary slide is the small crook on the second valve. This slide is cut to the exact length to lower the tone a minor second when the valve is depressed. A brass technician may need to remove it for maintenance purposes (if it gets dented, for instance), but it's unlikely that you'll ever need to remove this slide yourself. I've owned trumpets for years and never touched the second crook. Some people like to take things apart, but I advise you to avoid it.

If you put the trumpet down on a flat surface, always have the second crook up, so it won't be in danger of being dented. Beyond that, you can forget about the second slide.

The third valve slide

The third valve slide needs to be almost as movable as a valve. Many trumpet players neglect the third slide and play out of tune on low D and D♭ as a result. I tell my students that the fingering for D is not first and third, but first and third *and* the third slide extended about half an inch (see Figure 18-3). If you don't have a freely moving slide, you'll have to struggle to extend it, causing disruption of your tone. If it won't move at all, you'll have to play it flat, using a widening of the lips, with a resulting poor tone, or you'll simply play very sharp.

The best lubricant is something called key and rotor oil. Players of rotary valve instruments — mainly French horn, but also some tubas, euphoniums, and some trumpets — use it. Superslick, Hetman, and Yamaha make the best products I've seen.

Figure 18-3:
Proper hand position on an extended third valve slide.

The third slide usually needs lubricating twice a week, but this can vary between individual players and the climate where they live. If it slows down, oil it.

The first valve slide

The same oil you use on the third valve slide can lubricate the first valve slide. Professional-level trumpets and some student and intermediate models have thumb rings, or saddles, on the first valve slides. This slide can help intonation on all first- and first-and-second-valve notes, as well as help with the adjustment for the low D and D♭.

The first slide needs regular lubrication — the frequency depends on how much you're playing and how much acid you have in your saliva. Different players go through valve oil, slide grease, and rotor oil at different rates. When the action slows down, you'll know that you need to oil the slide.

Polishing Your Trumpet

Some players love a funky-looking trumpet, with tarnish on the bell and slides. I prefer a shiny trumpet myself, thank you very much. Only you know how shiny you want your trumpet to be.

Here's how to keep your trumpet looking shiny, whatever finish you have:

- **Unfinished:** If you have an unfinished trumpet — without lacquer, silver, or gold — you can use a basic brass cleaner as needed, depending on how shiny you like your trumpet to be. Unless you really love to polish brass, I recommend a finish of some kind.

- **Lacquer:** The most common finish, especially for student and intermediate trumpets, is lacquer. All you have to do to keep a lacquer finish clean is wipe it with a cloth. Pay special attention to the parts that your hands come into contact with.

- **Silver plate:** You can keep silver plate finish looking shiny with obsessive polishing before, during, and after a performance — and I know players who do that. That kind of polishing is certainly not necessary, but wiping your trumpet clean after use is always a good idea — perspiration from your hands can eat into the finish and even the brass, especially on the valve casing. Once every couple of years, clean your silver-plated trumpet with a high-quality, nonabrasive silver polish — you can buy it at jewelry stores. Don't use silver polish on your trumpet more than every other year — it does tend to wear away the finish.

- **Gold plate:** Gold plate is particularly soft and should be polished gently and not too often.

Specially treated cloths for gold and silver plate are available from music stores, and from the instrument manufacturer.

You can buy a leather or plastic guard for the valve casing that protects the finish and your hands. Some players don't like the feel of them, but they do add years to the life of the finish.

Exploring the Inner Life of Your Trumpet

I have a friend who is a brass technician and who has a tiny camera that he can push through the entire length of the instrument to check for problems. Although I don't think you have to go that far yourself, paying some attention to the inside diameter of the tubing is a good idea. Earlier in this chapter, I describe the way an accumulation of gunk in there can cause the trumpet to behave badly. Luckily, keeping it clean isn't too difficult.

Cleaning the leadpipe and slides

Regularly cleaning out the leadpipe can prevent the buildup of calcium and other deposits on the inner diameter. To clean the leadpipe and slides, you need a *snake* (a coiled wire with a brush on the end), which fits through the pipe, giving it a good scouring.

If you wait until there is a calcium deposit, you'll never remove it with a snake. A trip to the repair shop for an acid bath is the only solution.

Be sure to remove the main tuning slide — you don't want to shove the greasy stuff into the slide and, even further, into the valve casing. After you've removed the main tuning slide, swab out the pipe, as shown in Figure 18-4. After the first pass, which can yield a surprising and gratifying amount of gray sludge, moisten the brush with valve oil and pass it through again. A coating of oil on the inner sleeve can help prevent material from adhering to the surface.

After you've cleaned the leadpipe, you can pass the snake through the tuning slide, which you've completely removed. But don't continue your voyage to the interior. I speak from experience: Once, younger and less wise, I thought I would push the snake right through the entire trumpet. I did remove the valves first, but still, it was a dumb idea. The snake got stuck and I had to crawl humbly to the repair shop for a "snake-ectomy," which cost me much more self-esteem than money.

Figure 18-4:
Using
a snake
on the
leadpipe.

Some players remove all the slides and snake them, even just partway, but all that this does is push the offending material to the curved part of the slide, where you can't reach it. Most of the buildup occurs in the leadpipe, and the rest of it occurs in the tuning slide, so more snaking isn't necessary and can create problems.

Giving your trumpet a bath

Before my university graduation recital, I took all the trumpets I was using (four in all), filled a tub with water, and gave them a bath. It was very therapeutic for me and seemed to make them better to play.

Giving your trumpet a bath once a year or so is a good idea. Here's what to do:

1. **Fill a tub with warm (not hot) water, and put a little mild dishwashing detergent such as Dawn in the water.**

   You can use the bathtub (with a rubber mat to place the trumpets on), a laundry tub, or even a baby bath.

2. **Remove your valves, placing them carefully on a towel.**

   Don't immerse valves in water — they don't need it, and the felt under the retaining cap can become waterlogged and flatten out, changing the way the valve ports line up with the crooks.

3. **Carefully take the slides and the bottom valve caps out, and lay all the parts of the trumpet carefully in the tub for a good soaking.**

   Not all players take this step — some people feel that it's unnecessary and could cause damage. It's up to you, but I do it when I give my own trumpets a bath.

4. **Leave everything in the bath for half an hour or so.**

5. **Take each part out, one at a time, and rinse it off with warm water.**

6. **Run the snake through the leadpipe and tuning slide, separately, and run water through them.**

7. **Dry everything with a clean towel.**

8. **When everything is dry, reapply slide grease to the main tuning slide and rotor oil to the first and third slides and assemble the trumpet.**

9. **Wipe off the valves, oil them, and put them in carefully, in the correct casing, facing the right way.**

My trumpets never fail to sound better after a bath, an oil change, and a polish. I always enjoy the process, too. It's a good time to listen to some inspiring trumpet playing, giving your inner trumpet a sprucing up as well.

Giving more than Lip Service to Your Mouthpiece

The mouthpiece is much easier to look after than the trumpet — there are no moving parts. The cleaning kit supplied with your new trumpet or purchased at a music store will contain a mouthpiece brush, which resembles a small bottle brush (see Figure 18-5). I put a little soap and water on the bristles before I clean out the shank. The throat can be cleaned with a smaller brush that easily fits through the narrow opening. Rinse the mouthpiece and dry it off. You can do this quick cleaning often — I keep a brush in my case and clean the mouthpiece at least once a week.

If you dent the end of the mouthpiece shank, you can use a tool called a *mouthpiece reamer* (also known as a *hand mandrel*) to remove the dent, as shown in Figure 18-6.

If you push too hard into the shank with the hand mandrel, you may widen the diameter too much, so be careful, and only use a hand mandrel in emergencies. You're better off taking the mouthpiece to a repair technician and having him do it for you.

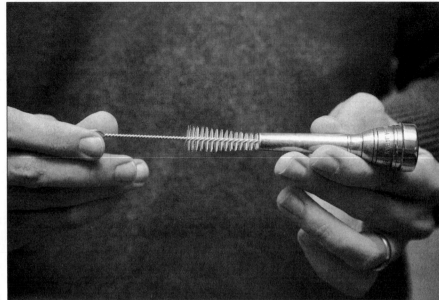

Figure 18-5:
Cleaning
your
mouthpiece.

Figure 18-6:
Using a
mouthpiece
hand
mandrel.

The most common problem encountered by trumpeters of all stages is the mouthpiece getting stuck in the receiver. Even playing with too much "right-arm embouchure," as one of my teachers called pressure against the lip, can cause a stuck mouthpiece. (Think of how your lip feels.) The trumpet can fall or you can tap too hard on the mouthpiece with your palm. If it gets stuck, unless you have the proper equipment, don't try to remove it yourself! Most music teachers (and some trumpeters) have a tool called a mouthpiece puller (shown in Figure 18-7). If used skillfully, mouthpiece pullers can remove the mouthpiece without damaging the instrument, but if you're at all hesitant, take it to the shop!

Never use pliers, vice grips, boiling water, or teams of friends (each holding a different part). Either use a mouthpiece puller or take it to a repair technician.

The silver or gold plating on your mouthpiece may, over time, wear through. If raw brass is showing on the rim, coming into contact with your lip and possibly your tongue, you could be adversely affected — poisoned, in fact — so you should get the mouthpiece re-plated.

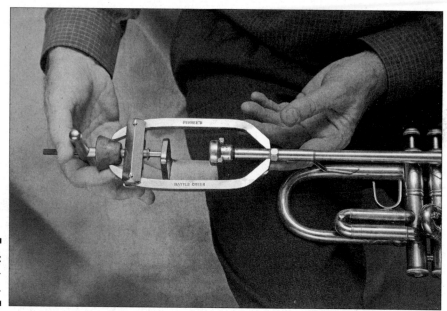

Figure 18-7:
A mouth-
piece puller.

Being Smart with Your Trumpet

If you're smart with your trumpet, you'll be able to avoid many problems and keep your instrument playing problem-free. In this section, I offer some useful tips to follow when caring for, and living with, your trumpet.

Making a case for safety

Always stow your mouthpiece and any other gear safely in your case. In most cases, there is a hole where the mouthpiece is stored — make sure this hole actually will keep the mouthpiece in place, and if you have doubts, don't keep the mouthpiece there. You can buy a mouthpiece case and keep it in your pocket or in a separate compartment in the trumpet case.

Close the case. This sounds obvious, but I've seen a trumpet tumble to the floor as the case was picked up, improperly latched. As a friend of mine said, "There's music to the repairman's ears."

Check the handle. It's the most vulnerable part of the case and often needs to be replaced long before the rest of the case wears out. If the handle breaks while you're holding it, the trumpet can easily be dented as the case hits the ground.

Make sure that the foam or other material that holds your trumpet safely in place is intact and secure. Damage can occur if the trumpet shifts in the case.

Taking care of your trumpet wherever you go

If you only ever played your trumpet in the safety of your own home, with carpeted floors and padded walls, you wouldn't have to worry too much about its safety. But most musicians like to get out and play for an audience once in a while, so you need to know how to keep your trumpet safe wherever you are.

On the job

Whether you're performing with your school band or you've got a regular gig, here's how to protect your trumpet on the job:

- ✔ **Never stand your trumpet on the bell.** It could easily topple over, and you don't want that to happen.
- ✔ **Never leave your trumpet lying on your chair or on the floor if you're not there to mind it.** During the intermission, put it in your case and close the case. Never underestimate the carelessness of other people.

✔ **Don't hit the mouthpiece with your palm, to make a cool noise, and don't let anyone else do it either.** They'll want to — trust me. Your mouthpiece could become stuck.

✔ **Use a hard case, rather than a soft gig bag (or, as it's sometimes called, a dent bag).** If you absolutely can't resist using a gig bag, be extra careful and keep your trumpet with you at all times.

On the road

Whether you're going on a short road trip to the next town over or flying cross-country with your trumpet, here's how to keep it safe while you're traveling:

✔ **If you're taking your trumpet on a road trip, take the hard case and make sure it's safely packed in the car.** A sudden stop could send the case forward and cause damage. Don't put heavy bags on top of the case.

✔ **If you're flying, use a travel case made of molded plastic, and store the case on the floor in front of you or in the overhead luggage compartment.** I once checked my trumpet with the rest of my luggage. You can imagine my horror when I looked out the window as luggage was being loaded onto the plane and witnessed my trumpet case being thrown by a baggage handler off the cart to the tarmac. With the amount of money I had to spend on repairs, I could've bought an extra seat for the trumpet case.

Chapter 19

Collecting Stuff for Your Trumpet

In This Chapter

▶ Using mutes to alter your sound

▶ Looking at different cases

▶ Buying music stands and more

▶ Adding metronomes, tuners, and lights

▶ Trying out some trumpet trinkets

You really need only a few things to play the trumpet: a trumpet, a mouthpiece, and some valve oil for starters. And the chances of becoming a better player by buying stuff are very slim, unless you also practice consistently. But shopping with a purpose is a lot of fun. All kinds of toys are available — some more gimmicky than others. This chapter gives you some ideas on how to spend your money and possibly enhance your trumpet experience.

Changing Your Tone with Mutes

There is nothing frivolous or gimmicky about mutes. Mutes — at least the basic ones — are necessary, so you can shop for them with a clear conscience. Every trumpeter needs a straight mute and a cup mute, but other mutes also are available.

The word *mute* comes from the Latin verb *muto,* meaning "to change." So, contrary to what many conductors and composers think, mutes are not primarily intended to soften the tone, but rather to change it for variety. Some mutes do make the instrument project less, but it's the palette of sound color that makes them so important.

The straight mute

The straight mute is the first mute you'll need. It's the simplest mute, and it's been around for centuries. In Figure 19-1, you see a variety of straight mutes. Basically a hollow bulb-shaped object with an open, tapered end, the straight mute has several corks around the tapered end, which fits into the bell and usually stays in place.

I say "usually" because the clank or thud of a mute hitting the stage is an all-too-familiar sound in rehearsals or even concerts. Composers have a knack for calling for mutes at very quiet places in the score, and they often give the trumpeter very little time to insert the mute before having to play again.

If the part just asks for a mute (*con sordino* in Italian, *avec sourdine* in French, and *mit dampfer* in German), then a straight mute is what the composer means.

Figure 19-1:
Several
straight
mutes.

Straight mutes can be made of plastic, fiber, or metal:

- ✔ **Plastic:** Plastic straight mutes can play quite well with a surprisingly clear and edgy timbre. The Bach Corporation makes a good one, and it's not as expensive as some of the other brands, which include Emo and Pro Tec.

- ✔ **Fiber:** Most school music rooms are stocked with mutes made of paper fiber. The most common type is called Stone Lined and has been manufactured for many years by Humes & Berg. These mutes are only slightly edgy and are quite suitable for general use or if a mellower tone is called for. A new fiber model by Trumcor is the Lyric Mute; it has a beautifully delicate, subtle tone.

- ✔ **Metal:** Metal straight mutes are very common. Tom Crown, Emo, Alessi-Vacchiano, Dennis Wick, Jo-Ral, and Trumcor are just a few of the available models. Some of the mutes are made from brass; others, from copper or even aluminum.

The tone of the straight mute is very intense and edgy. Some sound escapes from the gaps around the tapered end where it fits into the bell, but much of the distinctive tone of a mute is created by the vibrating material and the shape. The straight mute sounds metallic, even if made of fiber or plastic. But every mute has its own sound, and Impressionist works by composers such as Debussy and high-octane arrangements for Latin big bands need very different timbres.

Your musical judgment is often the deciding factor in mute choice (although it should be influenced by a desire to match with the trumpet section that you play with), so try a number of different ones to learn what the range of tone is. Over the years, I've accumulated about 15 straight mutes, but you don't have to go that far.

Unfortunately, all straight mutes make you play sharper, but some are definitely in better tune than others. (The Bach plastic mute is reasonably consistent, as is the Trumcor model.) So, adding to the problem of turning a page, and grabbing and then inserting a mute, all in one or two beats, you have to find the time to reach out to your main tuning slide and pull it out a quarter-inch or so. Then you have to remember to push the slide back to its original position when you, also hurriedly, remove the mute. Trumpeters learn to be very clever about this, placing the mute under the arm, or behind the knee for easier access.

Straight Mute Etude

Straight mute timbre does vary from mute to mute. Here's a little etude that demonstrates a mellow fiber mute and a brighter metal one. Different players produce a spectrum of tones and this is reflected in mute sounds. Your own experimentation is an important part of choosing the best mute for you.

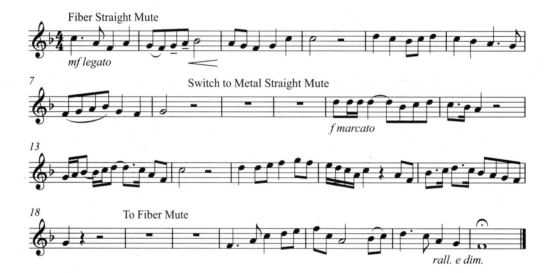

The cup mute

By adding a cup-shaped bottom to a straight mute the cup mute was born. The cup muffles the sound, and the resulting tone can be very pleasing. Big band charts often call for cup, and jazz soloists vary their timbre with it. Some orchestral music and a great deal of wind band repertoire calls for the cup mute, as well as solo and chamber music.

As with the straight mute, a variety of shapes and materials are available (see Figure 19-2). Fiber cup mutes are the most common, and Humes & Berg Stone Lined mutes are in every professional player's mute bag. Another popular fiber cup is the Ray Robinson mute, similar in design to the Humes & Berg.

The Mic-a-Mute is a variation on the cup: It has a closer-fitting bottom with a rubber edge. The Mic-a-Mute was designed for playing close to a microphone.

Dennis Wick makes a very popular adjustable cup mute. The cup can be removed entirely, creating a reasonable straight mute, or moved very close to the bell for a dark, soft sound or farther out for a more open tone. It's made of metal.

Figure 19-2:
Cup mutes.

Cup mutes tend to lower the pitch, making you sound flat, because of the muffling effect of the cup. You generally can deal with this simply by blowing faster wind and hearing a higher pitch. I rarely adjust the tuning slide when playing cup mute. The lower register, below low C, isn't as reliable for response of tuning as the middle and high range, but with careful listening and adjusting you can play in tune.

Cup Mute Etude

This etude features a dark, muffled cup mute sound, and then a more open timbre. You can use an adjustable mute, sliding the cup out for the more open sound. If you're switching mutes, you'll still have several beats of rest to accomplish the change. This etude is slow and mellow, as is much of the music for the cup.

The crazies: Wah-wah, buzz-wow, Solo-Tone, and bucket

The names sort of give them away: These mutes are a little weird. Trumpet tone is lovely, as we all know, and straight and cup mutes add variety, but some composers, arrangers, and players have felt the need to experiment with different sounds, and the results are interesting, to say the least. The big band era of the 1930s and 1940s ushered in new mutes, such as the derby, the felt hat (see Chapter 17), the Solo-Tone, and the Clear Tone.

The Harmon (or wah-wah) mute

The most common of this group is the Harmon mute, also known as the wah-wah mute. The Harmon mute is used for many effects, some serious and some on the novelty side. It looks like a little pot, open at the top and the bottom. The tapered end is lined with cork, sealing the mute to the bell, so the tone is altered more than with the straight mute or cup mute.

The Harmon mute also falls out of the bell more often. Some players lick the cork before inserting it into the bell, but this is disgusting. I recommend breathing some warm air into the bell, thus creating condensation, and then rotating it a little as you put it in, which helps make the seal between cork and brass. The mute will still fall out sometimes — my Harmon of the moment has several dents (badges of honorable service, really). A good Harmon needs a few dents before it really has that classic sound.

Protruding from the top of the Harmon mute is a metal tube with a cup-shaped funnel on the end. This is called the plunger or stem. By covering and uncovering the end with your left hand, you can create the "talking trumpet" style made popular by the Duke Ellington band (hence the name "wah-wah"). Miles Davis used the Harmon extensively, but he removed the stem for a very compressed, metallic sound that's beautifully expressive. Below low C is not really usable with a Harmon minus the plunger. Big-band arrangements often call for "Harmon no stem"; in fact, most jazz playing doesn't use it, except for the "wah-wah" effect. In the solo repertoire, the third movement of the trumpet sonata by Halsey Stevens asks for two different placements of the stem in adjacent phrases.

The Harmon is very sharp, especially minus the plunger, requiring the main tuning slide to be extended at least ¼ inch.

TRACK 163

Etude for the Harmon Mute

This etude (and the accompanying CD track) demonstrates the different sounds of the versatile Harmon mute.

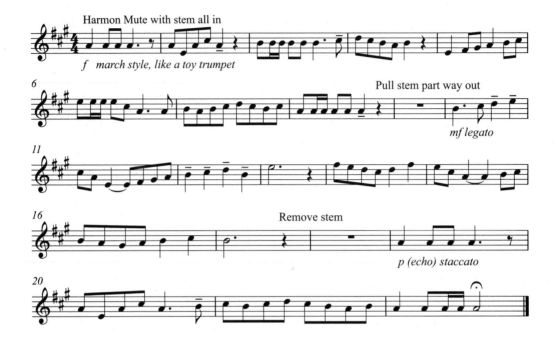

The buzz-wow, Solo-Tone, Clear Tone, and bucket mutes

The buzz-wow mute was created to imitate the sound of a kazoo. Why, you might ask? I guess the answer is the interest in novelty sound effects, which just elicits another question: Why do people have such weird taste? Inspired by placing three kazoos, held together somehow, into the trumpet bell, the buzz-wow is, thankfully, not used very much any more.

The Solo-Tone, made by Shastok, and the Clear Tone, made by Humes & Berg, are very rarely called for. I had to use one in the musical *Showboat,* and I know now why these mutes aren't in demand: They're awful to play — very stuffy, horribly out of tune, with a terrible sound. Except for that, they're wonderful mutes.

The bucket mute has been superseded by the timbre of the flugelhorn, but it was a popular mute in its day. It does have the advantage of softening the tone considerably — I bought my ancient bucket mute because I was about to be fired for playing too loud in a small dance club. It worked, but the mute is heavy and stuffy, so it's not much fun to play.

Other mutes fall into this category of interestingly named and sometimes off-the-wall mutes. The titles are the best part: There's a Whee-Zee, a Voca-Tone, a Meg-a-Mute, a Whispa Mute, the Manny Klein ssh-ssh Mute, and the ever-popular Wah-Wah-Du-All. At least we're not trombone players, who've been known to play into a megaphone mounted on a stand — and that's before the party started. Figure 19-3 shows some of the mutes mentioned here.

Figure 19-3:
A whole bunch of mutes. Left to right: Jo-Ral Bubble Mute, Manny Klein ssh-ssh Mute, pixie straight mute (for plunger playing), bucket mute, and Wah-Wah-Du-All..

The practice mute

Practice mutes are made for people who live in apartments and like to practice all night, or who are on the road and have to warm up in their hotel rooms. They're pretty awful to play because the response is very tight and stuffy, and most of them sound terrible. Some are better than others: Dennis Wick makes a reasonable model. The Trumcor Lyric Stealth Mute, the Best Brass Practice Mute, and the excellently named Bremner ssshhhhhhMute are other possibilities.

Yamaha makes a practice mute that has a built-in microphone leading to an amplifier. Called the Silent Brass, it offers the advantage of being able to hear, through headphones, a louder version of the practice mute tone. You can add reverberation, choosing different settings. It's made of plastic, and it plays quite well in tune, with not as much resistance as other practice mutes. I often use mine without the amplification — I'm not sure how much of an advantage it is to amplify the muted tone. It still doesn't sound like trumpet tone.

Practice mutes are great for emergency warm-ups backstage or on tour in a hotel room, but as regular practice aids I don't recommend them. You can't build tone and smooth connections when you sound bad and the response is tight.

Standing on Ceremony: Music Stands, Trumpet Stands, and Mute Stands

Music stands are a must if you want your practicing to achieve optimal results. You need to have good posture to breathe and blow properly, and if you're craning your head down to see the music as it's balanced on your pillow while you're half-reclining on your bed, you won't have good posture. Stands come in many designs, from the less expensive wire stand to costlier and heavier concert stands. I have a solid stand for my practice room and a wire, fold-up stand for gigs or traveling.

Trumpet stands are useful, particularly if you're changing instruments on the job. Most players have a small trumpet stand, or several of them.

A stand can tip over easily, so I recommend putting the horn in the case if you aren't there with it.

One strategy for making fast mute changes is to buy a mute rack to attach to the upright post of a heavy concert music stand. The mutes are off the floor, so they're less likely to be booted off the stage (this has happened to me) and more accessible. Some players also have small trays for valve oil, pencils, and other accessories.

Stand lights are often a necessity. Many places where you play, especially churches, can be very hard on the eyes, and finding an electrical outlet is often a challenge. Battery-powered stand lights are very useful. Mighty Bright makes the XtraFlex Duet, the Orchestra Light, and the encouragingly named Sight Reader Music Stand Light, all of which are battery powered. Lamp Craft makes the battery-powered Giglight. Giardinelli and Manhasset make good lights with power cords.

Finding the Right Case for Your Trumpet

When I was first starting to play the trumpet, the only cases available were very heavy pieces of luggage. My first triple case was so weighty that I suffered from tendonitis in my elbow from carrying it. Lighter cases began to appear, because touring players needed something lightweight and protective. Some trumpeters made their own, by taking light cases such as ones for cameras and fitting foam inserts to suit their needs. Now many cases are on the market — for one instrument, two, three, or even four — made of soft and hard materials.

When you buy your trumpet, it'll come in a case. That case will probably be fairly large and heavy, unless you negotiate a smaller, lighter model. The next step is usually a gig bag, known as a dent bag by happy and prosperous instrument-repair technicians; these sometimes are made of leather or a durable material called cordoba. Gig bags look good but are notorious for their lack of protection. A better choice for those who, like me, tend to be a little uncoordinated is a gig bag made of molded plastic or other fiber.

Double cases can be of the luggage variety or a more convenient backpack design, and the same goes for triples.

Your choice is partly dictated by cost. Cases are very expensive — you can easily spend a few hundred dollars on one. Despite the cost, most trumpeters own several — more cases than trumpets, in fact. There's always a newer, lighter, cooler model appearing.

My advice? Do as I say, not as I've done — I own eight cases, almost one per trumpet. Find something that suits your needs. If you travel a lot, you should have something small enough to go into the overhead compartment of an airplane and sturdy enough to protect your instrument. If you stay at home, and drive to engagements, you're probably fine with the model supplied by the maker of your trumpet.

Whatever case you use, what matters is that the trumpet is held firmly inside the case. You can add foam if you aren't satisfied with the security of the instrument inside.

Staying in Time and Tune

Sometimes you need help to keep from rushing or slowing down without realizing it. The metronome (see Chapter 5) gives a steady click (or even a voice on some machines) to keep your time honest. You need to have a loud enough metronome that you can hear it while you play. You can also use either a mechanical metronome with its inverted pendulum, or an electric one with a light that gives you a visual beat. Electronic tuners also are helpful. In this section, I fill you in on tuners and metronomes.

Tuners

A *tuner* is an electrical device that gives you an objective reference for good intonation. You can hear a specific note on one setting, or play a note and look at the read-out to see if you're sharp, flat, or right on.

Being able to confirm the accurate tuning of certain notes is reassuring, and I sometimes use electronic tuners in my practicing and teaching. *But you should never think that your eyes are the judge of good intonation.* Here's why:

- ✔ **You can't play music while watching the dial of a tuning device.** It's like watching your partner's feet when you're dancing — you'll always be at least a step behind.

- ✔ **Tuning goes along with good tone, so your ears have to judge not just the pitch, which a tuner can confirm, but also the quality of your tone, on which the tuner has no comment.** If you let a tuner dictate your concept of intonation, you'll be misled. Tuning is relative, not absolute, and the final arbiter of accurate intonation is how it sounds.

So how *should* you use a tuner? I recommend tuners as confirmation, rather than a guide to your playing. In other words, as you play, your ears judge the tuning and the tone together and guide the micromanagement of your tone production. This micromanagement is not necessarily conscious — ideally, you adjust automatically to the standard that you've honed in your practicing.

But, no matter how expensive an instrument you own, some notes won't be perfectly in tune. If a note is causing problems — either just not sounding right in your practicing or not matching with other players — you can turn to the tuner for help. Play the problem note, approaching it as part of a musical phrase or scale rather than taking a stab at it out of context, establish the tone and tuning to your ear's satisfaction, and then look at the tuner. I'll wager that the dial will be right in the center most of the time — but if it isn't, you've received helpful information, and your ear will have to be retrained to hear that note in tune.

One type of tuner attaches to your bell, so that you can easily see it while playing. Other devices sit on your music stand or table. These tuners are inexpensive and available at all music stores.

Metronomes

The old-style wind-up metronome that my piano teacher had has been replaced by an array of electronic alternatives. Music stores have all price ranges and sizes, from something no bigger than a credit card (not loud enough except for reference) to the impressive Dr. Beat, which features several strong tones, plus an irascible female voice (just like my piano teacher's, now that I think of it — some things never change).

Metronomes are very helpful for checking tempos. You'll develop a good sense of time with practice.

Try to set the tempo before checking the metronome. Use the metronome to confirm what your musical instinct and memory have told you. You may suspect that you aren't staying in tempo in a certain piece or passage, either because your duet partner or conductor is glaring at you, or because you sense the inconsistency yourself. In that situation, I recommend turning on a loud metronome and playing along with it. You'll discover the places where you slow down or speed up.

Using a metronome as a rhythm section in this way can help steady your tempos, but you shouldn't rely completely on this approach. You're better off also recording your playing and then listening back to discover where the problems are.

Really Cool Miscellaneous Stuff

There are so many gadgets and doodads out there for trumpeters that you'll never find them all. New toys are being invented as you read this. Music stores always have lots of them, online sources are very informative, and you can always hang out with your trumpet buddies and talk about new ways to spend your money.

Just like cleaning or shining my trumpet makes me feel like I can play better, a new device can give you a burst of confidence. There may be a quantifiable difference in the way the horn responds, and this will give you the confidence and energy to play well, but the effect won't last — other variables intrude. The best plan is to practice consistently, nurturing strong habits. Don't let anything substitute for steady playing with a song-and-wind approach.

Tricking out your trumpet

There are all kinds of fun ways to trick out your trumpet — customizing it beyond the form it was in when you brought it home from the music store. Here are some you may want to consider:

- ✔ **O-rings:** You can buy plumber's O-rings, and slide them onto the third valve slides, so that when you bring the third slide in quickly, it doesn't make an audible clank.

- ✔ **Heavy-bottom valve caps:** These inhibit vibration in the valve casing, the theory being that you get improved sound and resonance if the instrument doesn't vibrate too much. (You can also put pennies in the bottom caps and put them back on. Cheaper, but maybe a bit wacky.)

- ✔ **Weighted collars:** Dennis Wick makes a weighted collar, called the Tone Collar, that fits at the bottom of the third valve. This dampens extra vibrations and helps produce a more resonant sound.

- ✔ **Extra bracing:** You can buy extra bracing for the bell and the lead pipe.

- ✔ **A sliding bell conversion:** This enables you to change bells as the mood strikes you.

- ✔ **A different bell:** Yellow-brass tends to help produce a clear sound that projects well — your trumpet will probably come with a yellow-brass bell, unless specially ordered. If you prefer, you can buy a gold-brass bell, a silver-brass bell, or a sterling-silver bell. They all have different characteristics; gold-brass tends to be darker or warmer than yellow, for example.

- ✔ **A second bell:** I know a trumpeter who had another bell added, with a special valve to divert the air. He would put a cup mute in one bell and a straight mute on the other, making mute changes very easy indeed. He had a lot of time, a bit of money, and a sense of humor.

- ✔ **Grime gutter:** This is a plastic tray that you place under the valve section, catching the grease and water that inevitably leak out of the valves. Oh, it's not pretty, but if you wear dark clothing, you can get away without the grime gutter. Old black pants or disreputable jeans are excellent trumpet accessories.

Manipulating your mouthpiece

Mouthpieces are fun to mess around with, but I recommend that you buy two matched mouthpieces that you like, and only experiment with one of them — both for comparison and in case you really destroy the experimental model.

Here are some different mouthpiece accoutrements you may want to try:

- ✔ **Sound Sleeve:** Made by Mark Curry, the Sound Sleeve is designed to fit onto the shank of your mouthpiece, adding density and focusing the vibration for a more centered sound. Dennis Wick makes a similar product, called a Trumpet Booster. Some players like these devices for their focusing effect.

- ✔ **Vibrass:** This is a Dennis Wick product that your mouthpiece fits into. It vibrates, causing the mouthpiece to vibrate against your lips, relaxing them.

More gadgets

Here are some toys that are worth looking at, that aren't part of a trumpet or a mouthpiece:

- **The Schulman System:** The Schulman System (shown in Figure 19-4) is a brace to hold up your trumpet while you play. A neck strap and a flat base lie against your chest, holding it up, and your trumpet is cradled in playing position.

  In the spirit of full disclosure, I must admit that I own one of these. I bought it when I was suffering from extreme pain in my left bicep and shoulder. The brace takes the weight away and the left hand just needs to hold the trumpet steady. It helped me practice while my injury healed, and using it was interesting — the vibration against the chest adds another, tactile, dimension to playing the trumpet.

- **Buzzing devices:** I heartily recommend mouthpiece buzzing devices, like those shown in Figure 19-5. Several are on the market: the Buzz-Aid, the BERP (short for Buzz Extension and Resistance Piece), and the Brass Buzzer. The mouthpiece is inserted into a receiver and the whole device is placed in the trumpet's mouthpiece receiver, enabling you to hold the trumpet and use the valves while only buzzing on the mouthpiece. The increase in wind flow when using a buzzing device, coupled with the greater accuracy gained by locating the pitches, leads to a very rewarding improvement upon the return to the trumpet. You can find all three models online and in music stores.

Figure 19-4:
The
Schulman
System.

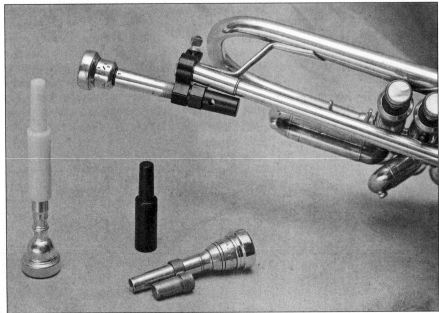

Figure 19-5:
Buzzing
devices.

✔ **Mouthpiece practice holder:** This adds the left hand grip to the buzzing device concept. Valves can be added to give you the dimension of coordinating the tongue and the fingers.

✔ **Rim/Visualizer:** This is a mouthpiece rim mounted on a metal rod. I've used it to check the position of a student's lips, but the real purpose is to use as a buzzing device. I've found that the rim helps locate a centered buzz if a player is having trouble producing a clear tone. Arnold Jacobs used these rims, but he cautioned that you should play on them only for a short time as a remedial technique to focus the buzz. A few seconds is enough and then you should return to the real sound on your trumpet. They're available at some music stores and online, in various rim sizes, so you can get the size that you're playing.

Chapter 20

Studying with a Teacher

. . . .

In This Chapter

▶ Determining whether you need a teacher

▶ Knowing what to look for in a teacher

▶ Finding your ideal teacher

▶ Getting your money's worth

. . . .

Although many trumpeters have survived without regular private teaching, most successful players have had very good instruction at some point. This chapter will help you take the step of contacting a teacher — why you need one, what to look for in a teacher, and how to make the most of the experience.

What Teachers Bring to the Table

You can learn a lot about trumpet on your own (and books like this one are excellent sources of support in this endeavor). But nothing can replace the experience of studying with a teacher.

So, do you need one, or should you go it alone? Louis Armstrong had no formal lessons, and many other fine musicians managed to learn without an instructor. But most good players have had good teaching. Look at it this way: Your odds of achieving success are improved with one-on-one instruction.

Learning on your own

The most successful students listen like mad. They have an idea of trumpet sound and style imprinted in their musical imaginations. When I was a kid, I listened to Louis Armstrong, Harry James, Bert Kaempfert's Orchestra, Al Hirt, the Tijuana Brass, Ray Anthony, and Bobby Hackett, plus all the classical recordings that we had in the house. I always noticed and listened when the trumpet was played, whether live or on a recording. So, I started learning the trumpet before I ever played one.

The importance of having an inner sound concept, a real aural imaginative grasp of trumpet sound and style, cannot be overstated. It's the main ingredient in musical and accomplished trumpet playing, and you don't need a teacher to achieve it. Louis Armstrong listened to Buddy Bolden and King Oliver and developed his style out of what he learned by incorporating all that he heard into his trumpeting. He also listened to Caruso and other opera singers on his primitive gramophone, and absorbed the sounds and life of the brass bands, orchestras, military bands, and street musicians of New Orleans, one of the richest musical centers in the United States. His example is a good one to follow, whether you have a teacher or not.

Identifying what a teacher can do for you

When you have a strong inner trumpet, you'll benefit greatly from working with a teacher. Although many technical aspects of playing, such as breathing and forming an embouchure, can develop quite naturally if guided by the little trumpet in your head, having an accomplished trumpeter by your side, making sure that you're on the right track, is helpful.

Here are some of the things that a good teacher can do for you:

- ✔ **Ensure that you form correct playing habits right from the start:** A teacher can correct your embouchure if your lips are too open or if the mouthpiece isn't centered. You can be instructed in good posture, how to hold the trumpet, and the importance of taking a big breath. You may be able to start properly without a teacher — but with a good teacher, you have a better chance of getting off on the right foot.

- ✔ **Guide your selection of repertoire, with your interests and needs always in mind:** The music that you play has a formative role in the kind of trumpeter that you become. Most teachers I know have their favorite teaching materials and share them with their students, guiding the purchase of more advanced music.

- ✔ **Play for you, modeling tone and style:** Having a goal is important in any activity, especially in trumpet. Many skills can be explained just by demonstrating.

- ✔ **Cheer you on:** One of a teacher's most valuable roles is that of cheerleader. Learning any new skill can be frustrating, and a friendly, understanding word from your teacher can go a long way toward improving your state of mind — and your playing.

- ✔ **Help you buy an instrument:** If you're interested in a good used trumpet, your teacher will be in touch with other players and teachers who know what's available in your area. If you want to buy a new trumpet, your teacher may be able to go to the store with you and try the various instruments, listening as you try them. That second set of ears — and expert ears at that — is invaluable.

What to Look for in a Teacher

The first things you should look for in a teacher are a positive attitude and good communication skills. A friendly, direct person, who speaks clearly, in terms you can understand, is what you're after. What else should you look for? Here are some qualities that I think are important in a teacher:

✔ **Someone whose playing you like:** Even if the teacher is no longer a full-time professional, he should still play with a strong, clear sound and the kind of style that you admire. It's the rare individual who can teach an instrument without playing it, but your odds of success are much better with a skillful and musical player.

✔ **Someone in your area:** Long-distance relationships are difficult, and musical ones are no exception. If you live fairly close to your teacher, you improve the odds that you'll have regular lessons, which are very helpful, especially in the early stages.

✔ **Someone with a sense of humor and perspective:** Trying to avoid someone with a strong ego when seeking a trumpet teacher is a bit like trying to stay dry when you go swimming. Quite a few trumpeters are somewhat competitive and egocentric, so it helps if those personality traits are balanced with a sense of humor. If your prospective teacher seems to be more interested in himself than in you, another person may be a better choice.

✔ **Someone who's relaxed and patient:** Most beginners need a relaxed, patient person who understands the basics and how to communicate them. Later in your career, when your basic skills are established, you may want a more intense teacher who doesn't want to get involved with technical skills but is more suited to musical guidance.

✔ **Someone who matches your learning style:** Part of your selection involves knowing your own learning style. Each of us has a different way of absorbing and incorporating information. Some people are aural learners — they respond to the stimulus of hearing the music performed, which means they need teachers who play well and are willing to demonstrate. Other people need to read and absorb information over time, on their own; they need teachers who are able to accommodate that style of learning. Still other people are visual learners; a chart, a photograph, a demonstration, even hand and arm gestures, help them the most. And many people combine these styles in different proportions. If you know yourself well enough, you can find a teacher whose style of communication best matches yours, or who shows the versatility to adapt his teaching to best reach you.

✔ **Someone who specializes in the trumpet:** Although it is possible for a musician to impart very good information and guidance in an instrument that she isn't an expert in herself, this is rare. You're better off with someone who has a thorough grasp of the trumpet and a high level of performance ability. A brass player, even though not a trumpet specialist, can be a help to a beginner since most of the principles of trumpet playing are common to the whole brass family.

✔ **Someone who has experience teaching at your level:** A principal trumpeter in an orchestra may not be experienced with children and may have a hard time relating to a teenager. Conversely, someone who hasn't played or taught at a high level likely won't be useful to a more advanced player. You want a teacher who can meet you where you are and take you to the next level.

✔ **Someone who can give you undivided attention:** Some teachers actually read the paper or enjoy a snack during lessons. You need someone who focuses 100 percent on you in your lesson — after all, that's what you're paying for. Teaching is an art, involving knowledge of the subject, communication skills, and a high degree of focused attention and careful thought. If a teacher doesn't pay any attention to you, you haven't found the right one.

Beyond these basics, you also want someone who can offer you the following:

✔ **Performance opportunities:** Playing a musical instrument is always a performance, even if you're alone in the basement playing scales. More generous performances, with people present, are a big part of musical life and add a lot to your study of the instrument. Ideally, your teacher will offer you the chance to perform in:

- **Recitals:** Many good teachers arrange to have concerts where all the students in the studio can play for each other, and for family and friends. This is a great chance to learn about performing, about stage fright, and about how other people are doing.

- **Small chamber groups:** Some teachers organize small chamber groups, even just reading sessions. These are wonderful for socializing with other like-minded people, and for possibly facilitating the formation of ongoing groups.

- **Master classes:** These are special meetings of students, the teacher, and possibly a guest clinician. You play etudes or solos for each other, rather than for an invited audience, and the teacher or guest offers comments and even teaches a mini-lesson in front of your peers.

✔ **Feedback on where you stand:** All students need a sense of their progress. You want a teacher who:

- **Has clearly articulated goals for you:** Many countries have conservatory grade levels or something like them, in which a syllabus of graded repertoire is published and students can play examinations to advance up the ladder. Even if such a formal system isn't used, you should have some sense of advancement in the music that you're assigned.

- **Gives you repertoire that challenges you but is within your reach:** This middle ground between playable and challenging repertoire is not always easy to achieve. If the music is too easy, you become bored; if it's too difficult, you get discouraged.

- **Has personal standards of excellence:** You want a teacher who expects that you'll play well and works with you to make that expectation come to fruition. A teacher who allows you to play less well than what you're capable of is giving up on you and taking the easy way out, which isn't what you need. On the other hand, someone who is never satisfied, who never acknowledges your efforts and achievements, is also not what you want.

✔ **Enrichment:** Part of a teacher's role is to inspire and guide by providing enrichment opportunities, such as the following:

- **Suggestions of concerts that you should attend:** Sometimes they'll even help you by giving you complimentary tickets or arranging for backstage passes. Okay, this isn't common, but it does happen, and generous teachers are a wonderful asset.

- **Recordings that will help your musical development:** Recordings can be tremendously valuable for the little trumpet in your head, and listening guided by your teacher is especially helpful.

- **Information on master classes taught by visiting artists:** Often, music stores, university music departments, or even high schools with very strong music programs host these classes. You can attend as a participant, preparing music to play for the guest clinician, or you can just audit the class, observing the performances and the interactions between the students and the clinician.

- **Information on private lessons taught by visiting trumpeters:** When a trumpeter is in your area for a performance, she may give private lessons for a limited number of trumpeters. Your teacher may encourage you to participate. A fresh pair of ears and new perspective can help a teaching and learning relationship.

Paying the price for lessons

Find out what your teacher's fee is, the way that he wants to be paid, and the cancellation policy. Some teachers charge for a certain number of lessons ahead, and attendance isn't negotiable. Other teachers are more flexible.

Be honest with your teacher if regular attendance is going to be difficult for valid reasons. If the teacher isn't flexible at all about schedules, you may have to find someone who is. If you're able to attend every week, find out what the teacher's policy is regarding his own conflicts. Mutual respect and consideration are required, and a genuine commitment by you to attend regularly will set the tone for a successful relationship. Be prepared to pay a reasonable fee for lessons with a good teacher. Cheap lessons are not necessarily a better deal!

I highly recommend that you ask for an introductory lesson before committing to any kind of relationship. Most teachers will want that opportunity to assess whether the teaching and learning partnership will be fruitful. If you both agree upfront that this is a trial, you can make your decision in an atmosphere of trust and respect.

Where to Find a Teacher

Finding the names of possible teachers requires some homework. Here are a few suggestions:

- ✔ **Your school music teacher:** A good place to start if you're still a student is your music teacher at school. If you're lucky, your teacher will be a practicing musician with some contacts in the community.

- ✔ **Your local music retailer:** If you aren't a student, your local music retailer is a good bet. Music stores promote good relationships with customers whom they hope will be good consumers for years to come, so you can expect some help from them.

- ✔ **Professional ensembles in your area:** Contact the business office of any orchestras in your area and ask about trumpet teachers. If there is a military base nearby, there will be trumpeters; the public relations officer is the first person to contact.

- ✔ **Universities and colleges:** You may get the name of a faculty member, either as a source of information or as a possible teacher.

- ✔ **University students:** College students often do some teaching on the side. If they themselves have good instructors, you'll get good information and at a cheaper price. Students aren't as experienced as professionals, but often they can relate very well to students.

✔ **Music conservatories:** There may be a conservatory of music or teaching studio in your area. The standard of teaching varies widely from place to place. Private studios aren't regulated in any way, so expertise in trumpet playing or teaching isn't guaranteed. Common sense plays a big role in your search, and you should trust your instincts.

✔ **Other trumpeters:** Word of mouth is the best way to find out about a teacher's style, ability, and personality.

How to Get the Most from Your Lessons

Even very fine teachers don't always succeed in turning out good students. The student has a huge impact on the success of the teaching relationship. It has to be a two-way street and your role is just as important as the teacher's, if not more.

Here are some things for you to keep in mind, if you want to be an excellent student:

✔ **Listen to what your teacher says, and try the ideas and techniques that she suggests.** You may feel a bit resistant to making changes, but give them a chance. If after a reasonable time the suggestions aren't helping, discuss it with your teacher. She may offer alternatives.

✔ **Arrive on time for every lesson.** You'd think that being on time would be obvious, but many students don't respect the teacher enough to adhere to the tenets of basic courtesy.

✔ **Warm up at home so that you're prepared to play well right away and you don't waste time.** There is some value in a teacher hearing your first notes of the day, but once is enough. Be prepared.

✔ **Bring your music, trumpet, and mouthpiece.** It's amazing how often students forget the music. I once went to a music camp without my trumpet, so I have sympathy for absent-minded types, but just make sure you have everything that you'll need.

✔ **Don't talk too much.** You can't listen if you're talking. Some students seem to want to have lessons so that they can tell the teacher all they know about the trumpet. But the teacher is the expert, and if you don't listen you won't learn anything new.

✔ **Don't be afraid to learn new things.** You're at the lesson to learn so be prepared to find out something you didn't know before.

✔ **Take notes.** Have a pad of paper or a notebook so that you can write down the week's assignments and any important insights or reminders. Some teachers like to write the assignment themselves, especially for younger students, but I think it's a good practice to keep notes. I used to sit outside the studio after my lesson and write down everything I could remember.

✔ **Ask the teacher if it's okay to record your lesson.** Even a basic recording can be a valuable reminder to you of what the lesson contained. Digital recorders are available now for a surprisingly low price, and the quality is very good.

✔ **If you have to cancel or change a lesson, give your teacher lots of notice.** Your teacher is busy. You won't be very popular if you have a casual attitude toward attending lessons and you change or cancel at a moment's notice and without a great reason. If you've established a good track record of attendance and good preparation, your teacher will tend to be more understanding of occasional lesson time changes.

✔ **Come with questions.** If you've had any problems throughout the week, ask your teacher about them. He'll be glad to give you guidance.

✔ **Practice!** Your teacher's plan for you is contingent on your doing your own preparation. Most teachers discuss the amount of practicing that they expect of you; some even give you a written set of expectations. You can inform your teacher of any limitations on your practice time. Together you can work out a reasonable schedule, and your teacher will assign practice materials accordingly.

Chapter 21

Getting in the Game

. . . .

In This Chapter
▶ Making music in ensembles

▶ Playing in groups of two, three, four, or more

▶ Networking with other musicians

. . . .

Making music with other people is one of life's great pleasures. Many aspects of ensemble participation contribute to making it the thrill and challenge that it is: There's the technical and musical challenge of sitting with other people, who you may not know so well at first, but who soon may be friends. There's the sheer joy and thrill of playing music in an ensemble — the harmonies, textures, and extended forms offer a whole new world, one that isn't available in solitary playing. The social and musical opportunities are so valuable that it's no surprise that community orchestras, choirs, and bands are springing up all around.

In this chapter, I fill you in on different playing opportunities and what they have to offer. I also share ways to connect with other trumpeters, as well as those poor people who play other instruments.

Playing in Community Bands and Orchestras

Community ensembles come in all sizes and at all levels of expertise, from beginner bands to groups of highly skilled part-time professionals and teachers, and everything in between. Here's a quick rundown on your two main options:

✔ **Orchestras:** In an orchestra, there are often only two trumpet players, occasionally three or four. Each player is responsible for his own part. Because orchestras use fewer trumpeters, your odds of playing in a band are greater.

The large contingent of stringed instruments in an orchestra has a big impact on the way the rehearsals proceed, and on the whole atmosphere in the group. The strings carry the bulk of the musical message in most orchestra works, and even if there are substantial wind, brass, or percussion parts, the work of teaching and coordinating the large string contingent takes up most of the rehearsal time.

The rest of the orchestra players tend to sit around a lot, and some people don't want to spend an evening listening to the strings practice — of course, others find the music and the soloistic style more suited to them and worth sitting around for. It's a wonderful opportunity to learn about the piece being rehearsed, especially if you have the full score.

Orchestras are more likely to play baroque, classical, or Romantic music from the 17th, 18th, and 19th centuries.

✔ **Bands:** There is a lot of *doubling* in a band, in which more than one trumpeter is playing the same part. Bands usually play music of the 20th and 21st centuries, often including new music by lesser-known but often excellent composers.

- **Brass bands:** Brass bands consist entirely of brass instruments, except for percussion. There are cornets, flugelhorns, alto horns, euphoniums, baritone horns, trombones, and tubas. Included in the cornets are a high E♭ sopranino cornet, which plays in the flute and piccolo range.

    For sheer hard work, the brass band is the best place for a trumpeter.

- **Wind bands:** The wind band has several forms, including the wind ensemble, the concert band, and the symphonic band. Wind ensembles tend to be smaller, with less doubling of parts, which means more individual responsibility. The music is often more advanced, and it's contemporary rather than classical or romantic. Concert bands play a wide variety of music, from overtures and transcriptions of orchestral music to show tunes. Some concert bands are very large; other community bands can have small trumpet sections. The symphonic band is a large ensemble with full sections, including many trumpeters, sometimes 15 or more.

- **Jazz bands:** There are four or five trumpet parts in most jazz-band arrangements, and with doubling there could be six trumpeters in the group, to go along with the four trombones, five saxophones, and rhythm section of piano, bass, sometimes guitar, and drums. Jazz bands are a lot of fun if you enjoy big-band repertoire, and like playing a lot of music.

Behaving yourself: Ensemble etiquette

When you join an ensemble, you'll want to observe a few simple rules, just to make your participation in the group a positive experience for everyone involved:

- ✔ **Don't be late.** If you're late, the whole ensemble suffers.

- ✔ **Bring your music, a music stand, your mutes, and a pencil.** If you bring several pencils to lend to all the slackers who didn't bother to bring one, you'll be even more popular.

- ✔ **Don't play or talk while the conductor is working with another section, or addressing the whole group.** There is always a flute player in the front row who will turn around and loudly say, "shush!" but that's just as annoying as the original infraction.

- ✔ **Listen to the lead player.** In every section, there is the player on the first part, and it's that person's responsibility to control the dynamics, intonation, and style of the section. If you're that lead player, take the responsibility seriously and lead by playing clearly, musically, and strongly. If you're a section player, follow the example of the leader and match all the musical elements as well as you can, never playing louder than the leader. Having said that, you must play strongly up to the level that is set. A section that works is one with a strong lead *and* a strong section playing.

- ✔ **Always play the articulations as written, so that the section can sound clear and accurate.** It's a wonderful sound and a great feeling to be part of when a section plays together well. Don't hold notes longer than the other players. If you feel you're right, discuss it at the break. Don't take anything up the octave to show off your high chops. If you miss, you sound incredibly dumb (take it from me), and besides, the composer didn't write it there so don't play it. And don't add little embellishments like trills or jazzy falls or scoops — just play what's written very well and you'll be in demand.

 You want to play in a good group, and one that not only plays well, but also is a happy bunch of people. You need a group with players who are around your level of expertise. And you should seek a good conductor, one with good musical and communication skills and with a sense of humor.

The most entertaining way to find out about a group is to go to one of their concerts. You'll get a sense of more than the skill level, especially if you sit close to the stage. Watch the body language and facial expressions of the players for a read on how much they're enjoying the music and how relaxed they are. Do they smile when a piece is over, and do they respond as the conductor gives them a bow? These are telltale signs of the relationship between the players and the conductor and between the players themselves.

Pay attention, too, to how well they play. You've been working on beautiful tone quality and good intonation, so you'll recognize it when you hear it. You can't expect a professional level, but a good community ensemble plays *as if* they're professionals in their attention, focus, and their pride in what they do. There's a big difference between players playing badly and being okay with that, and players playing not so well but trying to do better — it's discernible in the tone of the group and also in how they look and act.

After you've shopped around, attend a rehearsal. Most groups would be happy for you to sit in, but you could also just sit and listen from the back, observing the playing and the various interactions in the group. Staying for the social time after the rehearsal is a good idea, too.

How do you go about finding the various ensembles in your area? Look in your local newspaper, on bulletin boards at the library or supermarket, and on the Internet. Ask local school music teachers and music store employees. Talk to organists and choir directors at area churches — churches often have instrumental ensembles. And keep your ears open when you're talking to your fellow musicians. Word of mouth has always been the best way to find out about anything.

Doubling Your Pleasure

Playing duets is a valuable pastime for trumpeters. Not only is it a lot of fun, but you don't need a band room and you usually need only one music stand. But there are other benefits of playing duets:

- ✔ **They're demanding.** The first thing you notice about duet music is that there is almost no rest. With only two parts, the music demands almost constant playing from both partners. So, playing duets builds chops, and in a fairly painless way — you just play and enjoy the music, stopping when your lips insist, when somebody has to turn the page, or when refreshment is in order.

    Try to stop for a break before your chops are in crisis. If you notice a slight tingling in your lips, that's a signal to take a break.

- ✔ **They're excellent for sight-reading.** In an enjoyable musical and social atmosphere, you get valuable experience reading new music and trying to play it well the first time through, with all the articulation, dynamics, and expression. A healthy rivalry develops between you and your duet partner, and you both get better.

- ✔ **They give you someone to talk to about music.** You gain from the relationship with your duet partner. Not only do you play, but you discuss equipment, repertoire, teachers, concerts, recordings, mouthpieces, and all the other things that trumpeters love to talk about. It can be helpful to have another set of ears to try some new equipment, or a new piece. Plus, you can play an etude or a solo for your partner, to get the experience of playing it right through for an audience, even a very small one.

Of course, for all these good things to happen, you have to get along with each other, so finding the right partner is very important. Here's what to look for in a duet partner:

- ✔ **Someone you can get along with:** If you don't get along, your duets will become hostile fields of engagement instead of musical performances.

- ✔ **Someone of comparable ability and experience:** If your partner is a little better at some things than you are, you stand to improve in those areas, just by listening and responding. Avoid playing with someone whose playing standard is much below yours, especially his ability to play in tune. Playing with someone whose tuning is suspect has a bad effect on your own playing.

If you've found an ensemble to play with, talk to the other members of the trumpet section about duets. Your playing — and maybe even your social life — will benefit.

Finding repertoire is always a challenge. Many duet books are on the market, but not all of them are good music, and only some will be suitable for your level. If you have a teacher, she'll steer you in the right direction. Most music stores have a selection of material; if you're lucky, there will be a trumpeter on staff who can help you choose suitable music.

I recommend the following books for duets:

- ✔ *Selected Duets for Cornet or Trumpet, Volume I,* and *Selected Duets for Cornet or Trumpet, Volume II,* both compiled and edited by H. Voxman (Rubank Publications)

- ✔ *Miniature Classics for Two Trumpets* and *More Miniature Classics for Two Trumpets,* both by Sigmund Hering (Carl Fischer Music), and *Bach for Two Trumpets: 28 Short Works,* transcribed and edited by Sigmund Hering (Carl Fischer Music)

- ✔ *Arban's Complete Conservatory Method for Trumpet,* by Jean-Baptiste Arban (Carl Fischer Music)

Here are a few duets to get you started. I wrote these duets specifically for *Trumpet For Dummies.*

 TRACK 164

First Duet

This duet has a simple lower part, playable by a beginner, and a slightly more demanding upper part. Start with the lower part, which involves only whole notes and half notes and only two pitches, E and F. The lower part should be softer than the melody in the top part, as indicated by the printed dynamics. When you feel ready, play the top part. The top part is repeated on the CD, and you can play the lower part along with it. Finally, the lower part is performed, and you can play the top part in duet with it. So, there are three repetitions of the piece: one with both parts and one with each of the parts played separately. The whole performance is preceded by four clicks to give you the tempo and the starting place, and there are four clicks between each of the repeats.

Be sure to turn up the volume enough that you can hear the recording while you're playing.

 TRACK 165

Second Duet

This duet is slightly more advanced — play it when you feel ready. The CD track is in the same format as the first duet, with a full performance, then one with the upper part only, and then one with the lower part only. The range and rhythmic complexity is more advanced but still approachable. Listen to the recorded performance a few times to hear the style and the way the two trumpets sound together.

If this is your first try at playing with someone else, you may be distracted by the other part. But if you listen a few times and play your part alone until it's comfortable, you'll do well.

TRACK 166

Third Duet

The last duet is in a contrasting style. This time, the focus is on the two parts moving together in the same rhythms, in a flowing melody in three-four time. The CD includes a performance of the third duet, in the same format as the first two, with three versions, separated by three clicks (three clicks because the piece is in three beats to the bar). In this piece, the two parts move together an interval of a third apart most of the time. The feeling of three beats to the bar always seems to me to flow in a graceful way. Try to incorporate that easy motion into your performance.

Chamber Music: Trios, Quartets, and Quintets

Playing duets is fun, but it's a little self-indulgent: Not too many people want to listen to a duet session, except the two players. But adding a third voice creates a much richer harmonic palette and more diversity in tone color and dynamics. Adding a fourth increases the potential, and a fifth even more.

Getting a trumpet group together can be a challenge, kind of like herding cats. The best place to start is your band or orchestra, and the best tactic is to have some music ready to play. Good repertoire is the secret of success in any ensemble, and trumpet groups are no exception. In choosing music for your group, try to find the balance between playability and challenge. If it's too easy, you'll all get bored, but if it's too difficult you'll all get discouraged, and that's just as bad.

There are trumpet pieces written for three, four, or five trumpets, and even more. A good source of this material is Eighth Note Publications (www.enp-music.com); its publisher is a trumpet player.

Trumpet ensemble music is fun to play, but not really that great to listen to, even if played very well. The timbre, or tone quality, is too similar, even if varied by using flugelhorn and different mutes. But there are alternatives to trumpet-only chamber music:

- **Brass trios:** The standard brass trio consists of trumpet, French horn, and trombone. There is a substantial body of music for this combination, but most of it is quite difficult (in terms of technique and range requirements as well as endurance). To put it mildly, trios are chop-busters.

- **Brass quartets:** Adding one more player makes a big difference to a brass ensemble. There is more opportunity for rest (a major consideration), and the extra player adds that much more sound variety and harmonic richness. The standard brass quartet has two trumpets and two trombones, with an alternate French horn in place of one of the trombones. Much of the repertoire is from the Baroque Era, with German and Italian church music leading the way. Modern compositions have appeared over the last 50 years or so; they're usually technically difficult academic music. Quartets are challenging and fun to play, but the combination that has the widest popularity and the most repertoire is the brass quintet.

✔ **Brass quintets:** With five instruments, there is ample opportunity for resting the chops, and the two trumpets, French horn, trombone, and tuba (or bass trombone) enable composers and arrangers to write interesting and varied music. Brass quintets tour the world and record profusely. Some of the most popular quintets are the Canadian Brass, the American Brass, the Berlin Brass, and the Philip Jones Brass Ensemble. All these groups have spread the popularity of the brass quintet and have published large amounts of music, some of it original and some transcriptions.

Attending Concerts, Music Camps, and Workshops

A huge part of getting in the game is making connections with other like-minded people. If you're a university music student, you've got it easy: You're surrounded by fellow students and professors. But if you're not in school, you need to get involved with others who share your interest. The good news is that there are many such opportunities. That's what I cover in this section.

Going out on the town: Attending concerts

Attending concerts brings with it many benefits:

✔ The first and most important for you as a student of the trumpet is to fill your ears with great playing — to nurture the little trumpet in your head, the one that will guide you as you play.

✔ Concerts also give you the chance to hear other instruments or voices giving the kinds of performances that will further inspire your musical endeavors.

✔ When you attend concerts, you get a chance to talk to professionals, making contact at the stage door or at the nearby establishment where the players go to unwind after a concert. (There always is one.)

✔ A huge bonus of attending concerts, besides the sheer musical and social pleasure of it, is that you may meet other people like you who are studying the trumpet or another instrument and who may want to connect for music making.

In large metropolitan areas, there are too many concerts for anyone to be able to take them all in. I know a retiree who spends all day and night, every day of the week, attending free concerts. He looks online and finds the free ones, makes his list, and jumps on his bicycle. Even *he* can't get to all the concerts he'd like to attend.

In smaller towns, you may have to work a little harder to attend concerts, maybe even driving a few hours for the chance to hear world-class musicians. Touring groups do travel to far-flung places, though — you may be surprised to hear who is performing in your very own neighborhood.

Hello mudder, hello fadder: Going to camp

Ah, music camp! I've attended camp as a student, counselor, trumpet instructor, assistant camp director, and conductor since I was a teenager, and I've always had a wonderful time, made friends, learned lots, and played great music. The concentrated work — several hours of playing every day — and the close camaraderie with other enthusiastic people can make for an incredibly uplifting experience. In a short week or two, you can progress more than you would in a whole year in your regular routine.

The instrumental instructors at music camps are on a semi-holiday, so they tend to be relaxed and very approachable. Not only do you learn important concepts and repertoire, but you also get to know a professional player in a more personal setting than a school or studio. And you're surrounded by people who share your interest in music and in playing the trumpet.

All the ensembles that I mention earlier in this chapter are represented at a music camp. You engage in daily supervised warm-up sessions, where you learn new approaches to the basics; section rehearsals, where the music you're preparing for the concert at the end of the week is honed to a degree of polish that your regular group may never reach; and faculty concerts, where you can hear your teachers perform and get to know them in that important way while enjoying a great concert.

I'm a total fan of music camps, for all levels of players. If you're a middle school or high school trumpeter, talk to your music teacher about camps or search online for camps in your area. The summer music camps and festivals range from institutions such as Tanglewood (www.bu.edu/cfa/music/tanglewood), where the Boston Symphony musicians and visiting artists teach and perform, to the Aspen Music Festival (www.aspenmusicfestival.com), in Aspen, Colorado, where the splendor of the Rocky Mountains and the thrill of world-class music making unite, to local day camps run by area music teachers.

But don't think that you have to be an up-and-coming young trumpeter to attend a camp. Summer music camps for adult amateurs are very popular and include the entire gamut of musical and recreational activities found at camps for kids. Search online to find the names and locations of the summer camps in your area and beyond.

Often the same organizations that sponsor summer camps present workshops during the year. They're trying to attract new people for the summer camp, as well as to create positive educational experiences for amateur players. Look for announcements on bulletin boards at music stores, and keep searching the Internet. These one- or two-day workshops are a microcosm of the summer experience and can have the same galvanizing effect on your trumpet playing.

University music faculties also present music workshops. For three years, I was the director of the University of Toronto's weeklong trumpet symposium, which attracted trumpeters of all levels from all over North America, and included several players from Europe. Similar workshops are offered throughout Europe and North America. The level of expertise and teaching ability that you can find at such seminars is very high, with some of the greatest players in the world as the featured clinicians. Even if you just audit such sessions, you can benefit greatly, but the effects of full participation must be experienced to be believed.

The International Trumpet Guild

During the Renaissance and Baroque Era, trumpeters formed guilds, which were semisecret societies with strict membership rules and a hierarchical structure. They were, in some ways, the forerunner of the modern trade union, but they also foreshadowed a different organization and that is the International Trumpet Guild (ITG; www.trumpetguild.org). The ITG publishes a very interesting periodical on all matters to do with the trumpet and trumpeters. The magazine is a great way to find out about camps and workshops.

The ITG also holds a conference every year that features some of the greatest players worldwide and excellent teaching sessions, repertoire discussions, and ensemble playing. The conference also features a trade room where hundreds of instrument and mouthpiece makers, sheet music retailers, and other trumpet-related groups feature their products. You can spend more money than you thought possible, but it sure is fun. The ITG is a very useful organization for serious trumpeters of all ages and levels of playing.

Regular membership is $50 per year; students and seniors can join for $30 per year. For more information, visit the ITG Web site.

Part V
The Part of Tens

By Rich Tennant

"The problem with wine tastings is you're not supposed to swallow, and Clifford refuses to spit. Fortunately, he studied trumpet with Dizzy Gillespie."

In this part . . .

We're all inspired by greatness in other people, and for a trumpet player, nothing is more inspirational than the accomplishments of the great players. Chapter 22 tells you about ten great players who have changed the world of the trumpet.

Chapter 23 is a sad story of the ways in which we trumpeters sometimes go wrong. Happily, I offer advice on how to avoid ten common mistakes that trumpeters make.

Finally, in Chapter 24, I tell you ten ways to be the very best trumpet player you can be. That seemed like a pretty good way to wrap up this book, and I hope you agree!

Chapter 22

Ten Trumpet Kings and Queens

T he great trumpeters of the present are the inheritors of a long tradition of trumpet artistry. In this chapter, I introduce you to ten members of the "trumpet royalty": players who are the stars of the present and the future.

Note: Narrowing this down to just ten players was nearly impossible, but my editor swore to me that this was "The Part of Tens," not the "Part of Hundreds." So, read on, knowing that I've skipped over plenty of fantastic trumpet players to bring you these ten.

Soloists

The classical soloists who tour the world concertizing and recording are perhaps the most prominent trumpeters. They have an ample supply of charisma and individual style to go along with their technical prowess. Many great orchestral players also have had solo careers, but generally the job of playing orchestral parts with the clarity, accuracy, and beauty requires a different skill set from the equally skilled but more virtuosic soloist. Here are some of the most prominent soloists of our time.

Timofei Dokshizer

Timofei Dokshizer (1921–2005) became known as a leading trumpet virtuoso after he won the Prague Contest in 1947. In addition to performing as a soloist, Dokshizer performed as principal trumpet with the Bolshoi Ballet Orchestra. He's best known for his performances of the *Trumpet Concerto* by Alexander Arutunian, an alternately virtuosic and lyrical work recorded by Dokshizer on an album entitled *Trumpet Rhapsody*. Dokshizer was strongly influenced by singers, and his style is very operatic. He influenced trumpet soloists everywhere, with his emphasis on lyricism and personal expression. He also contributed to the practice of performing *transcriptions* (music that was not originally composed for trumpet, but adapted for us).

Maurice André

Maurice André (1933–) was a coal miner's son who became the first world-famous trumpet star. He was strongly influenced by the German virtuoso Adolf Scherbaum (1909–2000) in his performances of the concertos of Haydn and Hummel, as well as baroque masterpieces. André also is well known for his trumpet transcriptions of oboe or flute works and recorded albums of popular songs, paving the way for the kind of crossover career enjoyed by Wynton Marsalis.

I heard Maurice André play the trumpet concerto by Hummel, and my impression as he made his entrance was that of a genial and proud host welcoming us to a special meal. He couldn't wait to share his music with us, and when he played, that generosity of spirit came through in a very personal and direct way. It was an experience that I'll never forget, and I often advise my students to pretend that instead of fearfully and reluctantly bowing to a critical audience, they're eagerly welcoming people to their home for a feast. Andre's exuberance and generosity as a person shine through in his trumpet playing and he has had a profound influence on all the trumpeters who have followed him.

Håkan Hardenberger

Håkan Hardenberger was born in Mälmo, Sweden, in 1961. When he was only 8 years old, Hardenberger began studying the trumpet with Bo Nilsson in Mälmo. Hardenberger moved from studying with Nilsson in his hometown to studying with Pierre Thibaud at the Paris Conservatory and with Thomas Stevens of the Los Angeles Philharmonic after that. He's regarded by many as the top trumpet soloist in the world. His recordings range from baroque masters to composers of the 20th and 21st centuries.

Håkan Hardenberger visited the school where I teach a few years ago, and I had the pleasure of speaking to him and watching him work with my students. His approach was very musical — he talked about the music, sang excerpts, and demonstrated on his trumpet. When he played, his musical intention was clear — so obvious that even though he hadn't rehearsed with the accompanist, she was able to follow his nuances of tempo and phrasing perfectly. Although he was having an instrument designed for him, and spoke knowledgeably about the specifics of the model he was testing, when playing music, Hardenberger was concerned only with his own musical imagination, what Arnold Jacobs called the little trumpet in his head. It was a thrill to be with him for a few hours, and he remains an ongoing inspiration.

Sergei Nakariakov

Sergei Nakariakov is one of the "young lions," the trumpeters whose skill and artistry are shaping current styles. He was born in 1977 in the former Soviet Union. What's fascinating about this brilliant player is that he studied almost exclusively with his father. Clearly a prodigy, Nakariakov began playing the trumpet when he was 9 years old after starting on the piano the previous year, and was playing solos with orchestras in the Soviet Union after less than two years of playing! Sometimes parents and children have a difficult time with music lessons, but Nakariakov's daily lessons with his father must have been very productive, indeed.

Sergei Nakariakov's brilliant technique is balanced by a lovely lyrical tone quality. The title of one of his recordings is "No Limit," summing up his approach to the trumpet. His discography includes nearly every style of music, from baroque masterpieces to contemporary works, from trumpet concertos to works composed for the violin or cellos, from classical standards to Gershwin. There is a sense of risk-taking in Nakariakov's playing, as if he's daring himself to play faster and higher and more beautifully at every moment.

Jens Lindemann

Jens Lindemann is a Canadian soloist who became prominent with the Canadian Brass, one of the premier brass quintets of the past 30 years. Lindemann's style of playing fit perfectly with the quintet's eclectic and entertaining approach. As a soloist, he continues to enjoy performing in a wide variety of styles. His piccolo trumpet sound is one of the most beautiful timbres I've ever heard on a trumpet: full and rich, clear and sparkling, fluid and intense. Lindemann's personality is larger than life, and his style of entertaining an audience combines humor, artistry, and virtuosic technique.

Alison Balsom

One of the most prominent trumpeters today is Alison Balsom, whose musicality and technical prowess have propelled her to the top of her profession. She's able to perform on both the modern and the baroque trumpet, which is rare among trumpet players. Balsom's recording career is impressive in its variety and musical depth. She's more traditional in her repertoire choices than soloists such as Nakariakov and Lindemann, but her performances are fresh and personal. She's a wonderful example of the individual musician creating a new performance of even the most widely played works. Her Haydn and Hummel concertos are full of beautiful phrases and elegant, personal tone, coupled with impeccable technique.

Orchestral Players

The trumpeters who sit in the back row of a symphony orchestra are, for the most part, of a different breed from the soloists whose position is at the front of the stage. The task of playing the major orchestral compositions of the canon of Western music with accuracy and musicality, pleasing a series of conductors, and performing this feat on an almost daily basis requires the same discipline but a different mindset. Accuracy is vital — the slightest error can be regarded as ruining a performance.

Whereas a soloist expresses himself in repertoire choice and personal style, the orchestral trumpeter, particularly the principal player, must render the part as the composer intended, in the view of the conductor. Both soloists and orchestral players interpret the music they play, and express themselves through it, but the soloist's individuality is paramount, while accuracy is the most prized commodity in the orchestra. So, the trumpeters who manage to create an individual style and sound while in the orchestra are very special musicians.

Adolf Herseth

The Chicago Symphony Orchestra became known for its brass sound, anchored by the brilliant tuba virtuoso and equally renowned teacher Arnold Jacobs. Jacobs based his teaching on his observations of the trumpet artistry of Adolph Herseth. Herseth was the principal player of the Chicago orchestra from 1948 until he retired in 2001. This extraordinary feat is unparalleled in orchestral trumpeting. To perform at a consistently brilliant level for 53 years required brilliant musicianship and a total dedication to his art.

Adolph Herseth was born in 1921, in a small town in Minnesota. His father was a band director, and Herseth was encouraged and guided by a strong family influence. Herseth related in an interview that he vividly remembers his first concert, and what a thrill it was. That sense of excitement seems never to have left him — over 53 years, his performances were fresh and energized by his musical imagination.

Susan Slaughter

Susan Slaughter joined the St. Louis Symphony Orchestra in 1969 and became principal four years later, the first woman to be principal trumpet of a major symphony orchestra. Slaughter has continued her leadership beyond performing; she is the founder of the International Women's Brass Conference, which is dedicated to helping women advance and realize their full potential in music.

Susan Slaughter studied at Indiana University. With determination and talent, she advanced through her studies and became the principal trumpeter of the Toledo Symphony before advancing to her appointment in St. Louis, where she made history. As a principal trumpeter, pioneer, and mentor, Susan Slaughter has made an important contribution, and her influence is still seen as more and more women become professional trumpeters.

Jazz Artists

The jazz soloist is less likely to have "high chops" than other trumpeters, although there are exceptions to this rule. The emphasis is on personal expression. In improvising, there is much more scope for individuality than there is in a classical solo. In a jazz solo, the selection of notes, the actual on-the-spot composition, is in the creative palette of the performer, and the great jazz artists can be recognized instantly by their unique playing.

Ingrid Jensen

Ingrid Jensen is one of a small but growing group of women jazz trumpeters. She is from Nanaimo, Canada, one of many fine musicians from Canada's West Coast. She has worked with many of the top jazz musicians in New York, including Geoffrey Keezer, Billy Hart, and Clarke Terry (whose unique sound and articulation qualify him as one of the important voices in jazz). Jensen has a lyrical quality to her playing, and a sense of phrasing that is her own. When I hear Jensen solo, I think of the words of the great composer and leader Maria Schneider, who stated at a master class I attended that an artist has to just create what she wants to create, without asking if it's acceptable or allowable. Ingrid Jensen is working with that premise.

Wynton Marsalis

The amazing thing about Wynton Marsalis is his versatility. No other trumpeter is able to play convincingly, stylistically, and charismatically in baroque and classical music, early classic jazz, bebop, and contemporary jazz. His debut classical recording of the Leopold Mozart, Hummel, and Haydn concertos won a Grammy Award for best instrumental soloist with orchestra. In that same year, Marsalis won a Grammy for best jazz instrumentalist. This is a tremendous achievement, given the two poles of musical style and tradition represented by jazz and classical music. And even in the trumpet world, where versatility is well known, the ability to be a convincing, authentic voice in both genres at the highest level is unique to Wynton.

His influence has changed many minds about what is acceptable and possible for a trumpet player in terms of versatility. More players are likely to play in the jazz band during their classical studies or audition for the orchestra as a jazz major. The result can be a new level of musical ability. The self-generation of tempo is a skill that an experience in a jazz band can enhance.

Wynton Marsalis grew up in a musical atmosphere. His father, Ellis Marsalis, was a prominent jazz pianist in New Orleans. When Wynton was a young boy, he played traditional jazz with a legendary New Orleans musician, guitarist Danny Barker. So, he was influenced not just by his family, but also by his city, with its deep musical culture.

His career has not been without controversy: He's been accused of lacking musical depth in both classical and jazz performance. His deep interest in the early history of jazz has invited comments that he has turned jazz into classical music by taking away the creativity in his re-creations of Ellington and other early jazz pioneers. Another way of viewing the repertory approach of the award-winning Jazz at Lincoln Center performances is not as a mere echoing of the past but as instilling the older music with contemporary energy and respect.

Chapter 23

Ten Bad Habits to Avoid

As with most areas of life, there are many ways to get off the rails as a trumpeter. In this chapter, I point out ten common mistakes that trumpeters make, in the hopes that you'll avoid making them yourself. (*Hint:* I'm pretty familiar with a few of these mistakes myself.)

Not Listening to Great Music

Believe it or not, it's very easy for musicians to get so involved in the mechanics of playing their instruments that they forget they need to stay inspired. And the best way to stay inspired is to listen to great music! It doesn't all have to be trumpet music — in fact, listening to great singing feeds the all-important melodic part of your musical imagination, and I highly recommend it. Making a regular habit of nourishing your inner trumpet image with great models is very important.

Forgetting to Breathe

How can you forget to breathe? You breathe all day and all night, your entire life. But breathing for playing the trumpet is different — it's more focused, it's deeper, and it must be in the style and rhythm of the music you're playing. So, you can't just breathe — you have to *breathe*.

There's a deeper reason that trumpeters forget to breathe. Tension can become part of a trumpeter's approach to playing. The problem with this approach is that tension leads to immobility, and you need to be able to move freely if you want to get a deep, relaxed breath.

But why do some people get tense when they play the trumpet? Many trumpeters put a lot of pressure on themselves to get it right. So, even though playing the trumpet is something that they love to do, they still bring impossibly high standards to the activity, which leads to tension. Thinking too hard about playing the trumpet, instead of just playing, leads to tension and poor breathing.

High standards are very important, but standards that are impossible to attain only lead to frustration, tension, and forgetting to breathe.

Getting out of Shape

There are two kinds of getting out of shape for a trumpeter, and they're both mistakes. One is general: If you don't eat right and get enough sleep, and if you don't exercise your body regularly, you won't feel very well and you won't be in a very good state to play the trumpet.

The other way that trumpeters get out of shape has to do with the *embouchure* (the lips and muscles of the jaw and cheeks; see Chapter 5). Regular practice is essential for nourishing good playing habits. But regular practice also keeps the muscles of the embouchure, as well as the arms, hands, and tongue, in good shape. When you skip practice for a couple days, you experience less physical comfort and pleasure in playing, which, in turn, leads to even less practice — and so it goes, downhill.

Dodging the Warm-Up

Many trumpet players avoid warming up because they don't think they have time, or because they're just impatient. The problem is, playing too hard, too high, or too loud without a gradual warm-up can actually cause physical damage to the lips. Less dramatically, avoiding the warm-up leads to the development of some bad playing habits, without the regular nourishment of long tones, scales, and flexibilities.

Many people lead fast-paced lives. We rush our meals, speed on the way to work, and take very little time for ourselves. A warm-up can be a very relaxing time, just for yourself. The slow pace that's best for warming up can lead to a peaceful body and spirit. Just as important, the warm-up builds good habits of breathing, attack, and tone quality. The steady repetition of healthy exercises will keep you in good shape.

For more on warming up, including a thorough warm-up routine, turn to Chapter 9.

Playing Too Much, Too Hard

Sometimes playing the trumpet is so much fun that trumpet players keep the horn on their lips for too long. Resting as much as you play is a good rule to follow. The body needs recovery time after physical exercise.

Here are some telltale signs that your lips are tired:

- A tingling sensation.
- Trouble maintaining a tone. You might notice that your tone stops before you intended when trying to play a soft phrase.
- A pain in your lip, usually the upper lip. If this happens, stop right away and put the horn away until the next day.

When you experience any of these symptoms, stop playing for a while. Have some tea or coffee, listen to some great trumpet playing, or go for a walk around the block. If you're at a rehearsal, fake it! Unless you're the only trumpeter on the part, you can lie low for a few minutes when you need to rest. I'm not encouraging you to be a slacker — I just want you to pay attention to your chops and use common sense to avoid injury.

Practicing Only the Easy Parts

Many trumpeters practice only the easy parts of their repertoires, avoiding the more challenging areas. You can understand why: It's more fun to play what you can already handle. But you have to keep expanding your range, technique, fluency, and expression. And the way to do that is to challenge yourself with more difficult repertoire.

Avoid playing the more technical pieces and the higher parts all the time. As always, try to maintain a balance between what you can comfortably play and what you need to stretch to achieve. The easier pieces are helpful as warm-up material or as pleasurable opportunities for success. You can work on tone quality, phrasing, and articulation if the music isn't too technically demanding.

Neglecting the Care of Your Instrument

Serious problems can occur if you neglect your horn. Leaving the valves dry, without enough lubricating valve oil (see Chapter 18), can cause permanent damage and sticky valves. Putting your trumpet on a chair and leaving it there can result in someone accidentally knocking it to the floor, causing serious and expensive dents. Laying down your trumpet with the second valve slide resting on the ground can damage the slide and the valve casing. Banging the mouthpiece can cause it to become stuck, requiring a trip to the repair shop.

Keeping your trumpet lubricated with valve oil and slide grease and leaving it in a safe place when you set it down are very sensible precautions to take. They're worth the little bit of extra care.

Choosing the Wrong Equipment for You

Avoid buying a trumpet without advice from a reliable, knowledgeable trumpet source. Especially avoid trumpets that are not well-known brands.

Even good-quality instruments can be the wrong choice for a particular player. Different trumpets are designed for different kinds of players, and if you choose, for example, a large-bore trumpet with a heavy gold bell, you may not have the wind or the physical strength to play it.

Turn to Chapter 3 for my best advice on choosing a trumpet.

Missing Lessons, Rehearsals, and Concerts

When you're late or you skip lessons, rehearsals, and concerts, you're showing a lack of respect for what you're doing. Not taking care of your trumpet, not taking the time and effort to choose a good horn, being unreliable, getting out of shape, and avoiding the warm-up all are the modus operandi of a person who isn't serious about his trumpet playing and, perhaps, his life in general.

Forgetting to Have Fun

Playing the trumpet can be a pretty serious business. Tension can become a major detriment to playing. Forgetting to have fun can lead to not having any fun at all, and nothing good is likely to come from that.

Tension emerges as soon as you stop enjoying what you're doing, and poor posture, inadequate breathing, and a fearful approach to playing follow all too quickly from there.

How do you have fun? By practicing regularly, staying in good physical shape, warming up, maintaining your instrument, practicing a good balance of easy and challenging music, and meeting your obligations. Having fun isn't the only goal of a trumpeter, but it's a very important one.

Chapter 24

Ten Ways You Can Be Your Best

*P*eople are happiest when they're learning and growing, so in this chapter, I give you some ideas that will help you stay inspired and invigorated as you play.

The most important thing is sometimes the most difficult: Just do it. You have to play regularly, and for most people that means every day.

Garbage In, Garbage Out: Paying Attention to What You Eat

Eat well and watch your weight. If you eat too much and become overweight, breathing becomes problematic because your lungs don't have as much room to expand. If you don't eat enough, fatigue and concentration problems can make it much more difficult to focus on making music with your trumpet.

Getting Enough Sleep

We all know how hard it is to function when we don't get enough rest. Playing the trumpet in that state is a challenge, but then so is walking or brushing your teeth. Even *finding* your trumpet seems like a big deal. So, try to get seven or eight hours of sleep a night.

The difficulty in playing trumpet if you are fatigued is that your reflexes and muscle tone aren't in their normal state. You won't have the energy to breathe properly, your posture may be slumped or tight with the strain of staying focused, and you'll very likely begin to press too hard against your lips. Your ability to hear the music is enhanced by being rested and comfortable. If you're tired, you won't have as much access to your inner trumpet, and if you don't hear what you want to play, then the odds are that you won't perform very well.

Move It or Lose It: Staying in Shape

In case you haven't gotten the message so far in this chapter, here's a tip: Playing the trumpet is a physical activity, and you'll perform your best when you're in good physical condition.

Don't worry — you don't have to become Mr. or Ms. Universe to play the trumpet well. The best workouts for me involve a lot of emphasis on breathing. Yoga has helped me feel physically relaxed and supple, and increased my breathing capacity. Every posture in a yoga workout involves many deep breaths, and healthy respiration becomes habitual. (If you're new to yoga, check out *Yoga For Dummies,* 2nd Edition, by Georg Feuerstein, PhD, and Larry Payne, PhD [published by Wiley].)

Yoga isn't your only option, though. I know many trumpeters who jog, bike, or swim, and report beneficial effects on their playing. The key is to find an activity you enjoy, because if you enjoy it, you'll be more likely to do it regularly.

Getting Involved

Nothing is better for your playing than actually using your skills in battle. Not that trumpet playing is war, but the real thing makes different requirements on you than playing in your own room does. First, when is a conductor waiting to hear your part, or when your chamber-music colleagues are expecting some sound to keep the ship afloat, you can't stop and take a break when you feel like it. That extra sense of responsibility gives you the motivation to keep playing, thereby increasing your endurance.

Practicing Your People Skills

When you're making music with people, it helps if your relationships with them are smooth and conflict-free. Social and musical relationships are linked, and respect and friendship will make playing a lot more enjoyable and productive.

Here's how it works: You arrive on time with your music, music stand, mutes, valve oil, and a pencil or two. You don't kick over anybody's water glass, or step on a trombone slide, or tip over a music stand. Already you're very popular. You're friendly to everyone, without talking excessively about yourself or name-dropping shamelessly. You warm up quietly, without playing your highest note repeatedly directly behind someone's chair, and your stock goes up even more. You don't look at a fellow musician who plays a wrong note, and you don't look at another player if *you* play a wrong note. If you're sharing a ride, you pay for the gas when it's your turn. Finally, if you go out for refreshments after the rehearsal, you pay your share, without arguing about the bill.

Studying for Life

There are many ways to be a student — some formal and some informal. Study the trumpet with a teacher as long as you're enjoying it and benefiting from the experience. The goal is to keep learning; have the benefit of another set of very knowledgeable ears; and maintain the support of someone who can guide you, help you to avoid bad habits, and inspire you to keep practicing and making music.

If actively studying isn't possible or desirable, there are other ways to keep learning. Go to concerts and attend master classes and recitals at your local college or university. Read about the trumpet — this book is a great place to start, but check out other books and journals such as *Brass Bulletin* (www.brass-bulletin.com). Go online to sites like the International Trumpet Guild (www.trumpetguild.org) and Trumpet Herald (www.trumpetherald.com).

Playing New Music Every Day

There are good reasons for novelty in your repertoire. New music makes different demands on you as a musician and new challenges as a trumpeter. The most basic advantage of playing new music is that your sight-reading skills stay honed.

Play new music as a challenge for reading, a bit under tempo as common sense dictates. There's no advantage to hacking your way through a piece, stopping and starting, replaying passages, and swearing up a storm. You're better off setting a reasonable tempo and playing all the way through, letting the occasional error go by. When you've completed the piece, you can go back and practice the parts that caused problems.

Most public libraries have sheet music, so you don't have to buy everything that you play. You can also download music from the Internet.

Avoiding the Equipment Bug

The equipment bug is very easy to catch. Yes, new stuff is fun. Yes, it's fun to shop and try new things. But — and this is a big but — *nothing* should distract you from the most important thing about trumpet playing and that is a steady, regular diet of healthy, nourishing practice.

Performing, not Practicing

Of course, you practice. That's the daily playing that keeps you in good shape and helps you improve. But try calling it "performing" as often as you can. Have a performance mentality every time you play. Performing means playing the music as if it were part of a concert or recording, even if it's a scale study or a long tone.

Performing might mean slowing the tempo to where you can play the piece without any technical problems, even if it's supposed to be much faster. The speed will come, but unless the music is played well, beautifully, and accurately, then it will never be at a performance standard. So, start with a performance standard, maybe a slow performance or a lyrical version of a technical etude. As you continue to perform the music, always as beautifully as you possibly can, you can aim toward the tempo and style called for. You'll be ready to play it that way because you'll have established the sound, the phrasing, the connections between the notes, and the intonation at your early performance tempo.

Staying Inspired by Great Music

Scale studies, etudes, and flexibility exercises are wonderful, but none of those things is a great musical offering. Take advantage of the richness of all music to nourish your musical soul. Listen to African music, Asian music, folk music, European orchestral music, Dixieland jazz, Miles Davis, Glenn Gould, Joni Mitchell, Louis Armstrong, Maurice Ravel, Michael Jackson, the Beach Boys, and the Orchestra of the Age of Enlightenment.

There is so much to be learned by listening to music, so much that will directly and indirectly help you as a trumpeter, as a musician, and as a person. Take advantage of this wealth and let it work its way into your imagination. When you play a study, your performance will be informed by all that you've taken in. And when you play a lovely piece on your trumpet, it'll be all the more beautiful because of the nourishment you've given it. Take it all in, and let it all out! Enjoy your trumpet and let it make you a happier and more fulfilled person. You deserve it!

Appendix

About the CD

*W*hen writing this book, I tried to duplicate the immediacy of a private lesson by including numerous recorded tracks. Most of the tracks are complete performances of the musical examples; some are excerpts, to give you the idea. Hearing the sounds is the most direct way for you to learn how to play, so I hope you find this CD useful as you read *Trumpet For Dummies* and continue to play the trumpet.

System Requirements

Make sure that your computer meets the minimum system requirements shown in the following list. If your computer doesn't match up to most of these requirements, you may have problems using the software and files on the CD. For the latest and greatest information, please refer to the ReadMe file located at the root of the CD-ROM.

- ✔ A PC running Microsoft Windows
- ✔ A Macintosh running Apple OS X or later
- ✔ A CD-ROM drive
- ✔ A media player (such as RealPlayer or iTunes) to play MP3s

If you need more information on the basics, check out these books published by Wiley Publishing, Inc.: *PCs For Dummies,* 11th Edition, by Dan Gookin; *Macs For Dummies,* 10th Edition, by Edward C. Baig; *iMac For Dummies,* 6th Edition, by Mark L. Chambers; *Windows Vista For Dummies* or *Windows 7 For Dummies,* both by Andy Rathbone.

Using the CD

To listen to the MP3 tracks, follow these steps:

1. **Insert the CD into your computer's CD-ROM drive.**

   The license agreement appears.

   Note for Windows users: The interface won't launch if you have autorun disabled. In that case, choose Start⇨Run. (For Windows Vista and Windows 7, choose Start⇨All Programs⇨Accessories⇨Run.) In the dialog box that appears, type ***D:\Start.exe***. (Replace *D* with the proper letter if your CD drive uses a different letter. If you don't know the letter, see how your CD drive is listed under My Computer.) Click OK.

   Note for Mac users: When the CD icon appears on your desktop, double-click the icon to open the CD and double-click the Start icon. Also, note that the content menus may not function as expected in newer versions of Safari and Firefox; however, the documents are available by navigating to the Contents folder.

2. **Read through the license agreement and then click the Accept button if you want to use the CD.**

   The CD interface appears. The interface allows you to look at the MP3 tracks with just a click of a button (or two).

You also can access the MP3 files directly by clicking the Explore button, which opens a window that displays the different folders on the CD. This is handy if you want to transfer the MP3 files to your hard drive or a portable MP3 player.

What You'll Find on the CD

Here is a list of the MP3 files on the CD, along with the chapters and figure numbers (if any) that they correspond to in the book:

Track	Chapter	Figure Number	Song Title/Description
1	4	N/A	Two notes a tone apart, and two notes a semitone apart
2	4	N/A	Major scale played on a trumpet, up and down
3	4	Figure 4-24	"Yankee Doodle" in common time
4	4	Figure 4-25	"Yankee Doodle" in cut time

Track	Chapter	Figure Number	Song Title/Description
5	4	Figure 4-26	Theme from *Sleeping Beauty* by Tchaikovsky
6	4	Figure 4-27	"Beer Barrel Polka"
7	5	N/A	Two examples of breath
8	5	N/A	The sound of a good buzz
9	5, 6	N/A	The first mouthpiece note and the first trumpet note
10	5	N/A	The piano accompaniment
11	5	N/A	Imitating various sounds, such as a siren and a car revving
12	5	N/A	With the tongue and without the tongue
13	5	N/A	Articulation
14	5	N/A	"Twinkle, Twinkle, Little Star"
15	5	N/A	"Ode to Joy"
16	5	N/A	"Hot Cross Buns"
17	5	N/A	"Mexican Hat Dance"
18	6	N/A	How sharp and flat notes sound
19	6	Figure 6-13	Repeated notes
20	6	Figure 6-14	Playing low C
21	6	N/A	Buzzing on the mouthpiece alone, sliding down from G to C
22	6	Figure 6-15	Music for low C and G
23	7	N/A	Glissando from G up to C on the mouthpiece
24	7	Figure 7-1	Your first flexibility exercise
25	7	N/A	Mouthpiece glissando from G down to low C and back up to G
26	7	Figure 7-2	Another flexibility exercise
27	7	Figure 7-4	Practicing the valve positions
28	7	Figure 7-5	The chromatic scale
29	7	Figure 7-6	Chromatic flexibilities
30	7	Figure 7-7	The C scale, slurred
31	7	Figure 7-8	Scale study in C
32	7	Figure 7-9	Scale study in the key of F
33	7	Figure 7-10	Scale study in the key of G
34	7	N/A	"Oh, When the Saints Go Marching In"

(continued)

Track	Chapter	Figure Number	Song Title/Description
35	7	N/A	"Prince of Denmark's March"
36	7	N/A	"All through the Night"
37	8	Figure 8-1	Repeated note exercise
38	8	Figure 8-2	Changing notes and tonguing
39	8	Figure 8-3	A study for legato tonguing
40	8	Figure 8-4	Another study for legato tonguing
41	8	Figure 8-5	Marcato articulation
42	8	Figure 8-6	Staccato scale study
43	8	Figure 8-7	Study for slurring and tonguing
44	8	Figure 8-8	Songs and scales with slurring and tonguing combined
45	8	Figure 8-9	Scale in thirds
46	8	N/A	"Stepping Smoothly"
47	8	N/A	"Ceremonial March"
48	8	N/A	"Laughing, Singing"
49	9	N/A	Glissando
50	9	Figure 9-1	Breath-attack and tongue-attack routines
51	9	Figure 9-2	Warm-up flexibilities
52	9	Figure 9-3	Flow connectors
53	9	Figure 9-4	Chromatic range expander
54	9	Figure 9-5	Diminished seventh chords
55	9	Figure 9-6	Low-register setup
56	9	Figure 9-7	Scale-study tongue setup
57	9	Figure 9-8	Arpeggio tongue setup
58	9	Figure 9-9	Speeding up the tongue
59	9	Figure 9-10	Long tones with dynamics
60	9	Figure 9-11	Scales and arpeggios with dynamics
61	9	N/A	"Blowing with the Breeze"
62	9	N/A	"Lyrical Scale Tune"
63	10	Figure 10-1	Valve slurs in the middle register
64	10	Figure 10-2	Wind slurs in the middle and low registers
65	10	Figure 10-3	Valve slur scale study
66	10	Figure 10-4	Mouthpiece glissandi from the middle register to the low register and back

Track	Chapter	Figure Number	Song Title/Description
67	10	Figure 10-5	Establishing clear tonguing in the low register
68	10	N/A	A Variation of "Twinkle, Twinkle Little Star"
69	10	N/A	Several principale-style pieces
70	10	Figure 10-6	Exercises in the low register
71	10	Figure 10-7	Descending G major scale study
72	10	Figure 10-8	Long tones in the low register
73	10	Figure 10-9	Wind slurs in the low register
74	10	N/A	"Diving to the Deep End"
75	11	N/A	Higher songs on the mouthpiece
76	11	Figure 11-1	Using the overtone series to go higher
77	11	Figure 11-2	Scale studies for the C-to-D connection
78	11	Figure 11-3	Scales for the upper register
79	11	Figure 11-4	Leaping toward the upper register
80	11	Figure 11-5	Flexibilities for the upper register
81	11	Figure 11-6	Two fanfares in clarion style
82	11	N/A	"Flowing toward the Upper Register"
83	11	N/A	"Floating Up"
84	12	Figure 12-1	Arpeggio study
85	12	N/A	Flow studies in arpeggios
86	12	Figure 12-2	Lyrical study in scales and arpeggios
87	12	N/A	A warm-up
88	12	Figure 12-3	C diminished seventh arpeggio
89	12	Figure 12-4	Exercise on the C diminished seventh arpeggio
90	12	N/A	"Connecting the Dots"
91	13	Figure 13-1	Long tones and glissandi on the mouthpiece
92	13	Figure 13-2	Scale study for the fingers
93	13	Figure 13-3	Moving faster
94	13	Figure 13-4	Long tones for endurance
95	13	Figure 13-5	Wind slurs for endurance
96	13	N/A	"Etude in a Flowing Style"
97	13	N/A	"Etude in Staccato and Marcato Style"

(continued)

Track	Chapter	Figure Number	Song Title/Description
98	14	Figure 14-1	Setting up the basic legato
99	14	Figure 14-2	Speeding up the single tongue
100	14	Figure 14-3	Tonguing overtone connections
101	14	Figure 14-4	Tonguing valve connections
102	14	Figure 14-5	Etudes for speeding up the single tongue
103	14	Figure 14-7	A double-tonguing exercise on the mouthpiece
104	14	Figure 14-8	Double-tonguing on one note
105	14	Figure 14-9	Double-tonguing on overtone changes
106	14	Figure 14-10	Double-tonguing and the valves
107	14	Figure 14-11	Etudes in single and double tonguing
108	14	N/A	The exercises from Figure 14-13, done on the mouthpiece
109	14	Figure 14-14	Triple-tonguing exercises on the trumpet
110	14	Figure 14-15	Changing notes while triple-tonguing
111	14	Figure 14-17	Exercises in the slur and double tongue
112	14	N/A	"Tongue-Twister Etude"
113	14	N/A	"Triple-Threat Chromatic Etude"
114	15	N/A	"The Last Rose of Summer"
115	15	N/A	"Lyrical Etude #1"
116	15	N/A	"Lyrical Etude #2"
117	15	Figure 15-1	Exercises in marcato tonguing
118	15	N/A	"Leonore #3"
119	15	N/A	"Trumpet Tune"
120	15	N/A	"Capriccio Italien"
121	15	N/A	"Etude in March Style"
122	16	N/A	"Flowing Along"
123	16	Figure 16-1	Major scale pattern in all keys
124	16	Figure 16-2	Scale and articulation studies
125	16	N/A	"Etude in the Major Scales"
126	16	N/A	"November Dusk"
127	16	Figure 16-3	D harmonic minor study
128	16	Figure 16-4	Melodic minor study

Track	Chapter	Figure Number	Song Title/Description
129	16	Figure 16-5	Minor scales in A minor, E minor, and G minor
130	16	Figure 16-6	Major arpeggios
131	16	Figure 16-7	Minor arpeggios
132	16	Figure 16-8	Exercises in legato style
133	16	Figure 16-9	Jolly staccato exercises
134	16	Figure 16-10	The illusion of staccato in F major
135	16	N/A	"Etude in Staccato Style"
136	16	Figure 16-11	Scale study for tonguing speed and coordination
137	16	Figure 16-12	Scale study for double tonguing
138	16	Figure 16-13	Tripling your fun
139	16	Figure 16-14	Combining slurring and tonguing
140	16	Figure 16-15	An exercise combining the low and middle registers
141	16	Figure 16-16	Wind slurs for the upper register
142	16	Figure 16-17	Upward scale exercise
143	16	Figure 16-18	Arpeggios for range development
144	16	Figure 16-19	Pedal relaxer
145	16	N/A	"Etude in the Low and Middle Registers"
146	16	N/A	"Etude in the Middle and Upper Registers"
147	16	N/A	"Prince of Denmark's March"
148	17	N/A	"Basin Street Blues"
149	17	Figure 17-1	Three common ornaments
150	17	Figure 17-2	Excerpt from "Prince of Denmark's March" with trills
151	17	Figure 17-3	Exercise for trills in F
152	17	Figure 17-4	Plumbing the depths of the doo-wah effect
153	17	Figure 17-6	Trumpet solo from *An American in Paris* by George Gershwin
154	17	Figure 17-7	Making strange sounds on the trumpet
155	17	Figure 17-8	Wind vibrato
156	17	Figure 17-9	Hand vibrato
157	17	Figure 17-10	Lip or jaw vibrato

(continued)

Track	Chapter	Figure Number	Song Title/Description
158	17	N/A	"Etude for Vibrato"
159	17	Figure 17-11	Practice with concert pitch
160	17	N/A	"Sight-Reading Etude"
161	19	N/A	"Straight Mute Etude"
162	19	N/A	"Cup Mute Etude"
163	19	N/A	"Etude for the Harmon Mute"
164	21	N/A	"First Duet"
165	21	N/A	"Second Duet"
166	21	N/A	"Third Duet"

Customer Care

If you have trouble with the CD, please call Wiley Product Technical Support at 800-762-2974. Outside the United States, call 317-572-3993. You also can contact Wiley Product Technical Support at http://support.wiley.com. John Wiley & Sons will provide technical support only for installation and other general quality-control items. For technical support on the applications that play the MP3 files, consult the program's vendor or author.

To place additional orders or to request information about other Wiley products, please call 877-762-2974.

Index

● *C* ●

• G •

• H •

• N •

• O •

John Wiley & Sons Canada, Ltd., End-User License Agreement